▲ ▲ ▲

MARY AUSTIN

Mary Austin

▲▲▲▲▲▲▲▲▲▲▲▲▲▲▲▲▲▲▲▲▲▲▲▲▲▲▲▲▲

SONG OF A MAVERICK

ESTHER F. LANIGAN

The University of Arizona Press   Tucson

First University of Arizona Press edition 1997
© 1989 by Yale University Press
All rights reserved
♾ This book is printed on acid-free, archival-quality paper.
Manufactured in the United States of America
02 01 00 99 98 97   6 5 4 3 2 1

Library of Congress Cataloging-in-Publication Data
Lanigan, Esther F.
    Mary Austin : song of a maverick / Esther F. Lanigan.
        p.   cm.
    Originally published: New Haven : Yale University Press, c1989.
    Includes bibliographical references and index.
    ISBN 0-8165-1714-2
    1. Austin, Mary Hunter, 1868–1934.   2. Women authors,
American—20th century—Biography.   3. Western stories—History
and criticism.   4. West (U.S.) in literature.   1. Title.
    PS3501.U8Z88   1997
    818′.5209—dc20   96-42224
    [B]   CIP

British Library Cataloguing-in-Publication Data
A catalogue record for this book is available from the British Library.

Quotations from the letters of Ansel Adams and from *Ansel Adams:
An Autobiography* appear here courtesy of the trustees of the Ansel
Adams Publishing Rights Trust. All rights reserved.

Frontispiece: Louis Betts's portrait of Mary Austin, painted in 1929
and used for the frontispiece of the writer's autobiography, *Earth
Horizon*. (Reproduced, by permission, from a photograph in the
collection of the Huntington Library, San Marino, California)

CONTENTS

ILLUSTRATIONS

ACKNOWLEDGMENTS

I owe my acquaintance with Mary Austin's life and work to Prof. Howard Lamar of Yale, who suggested I read her autobiography when I showed an interest in intellectual women of the West. Since then, he has remained a staunch supporter of my work and has offered encouragement and perceptive suggestions. I have greatly benefited from discussing the problems of writing a literary life with R. W. B. Lewis, whose Pulitzer Prize–winning *Edith Wharton* is a model of grace and eloquence. Nancy Cott's work in American women's history has also inspired me; I appreciate her thoughtful comments on one version of the manuscript. I am grateful to Patricia Nelson Limerick for helpful criticism of chapter 6.

Mary Hunter Wolf, Austin's niece, has kindly assisted me in better understanding her aunt during our conversations in her New Haven home, by telephone, and through correspondence. I am indeed grateful to be able to take her perspective into account. Virginia Best Adams (Mrs. Ansel Adams) has granted me permission to use her husband's letters and has shared her recollections of Austin with me.

A Woodrow Wilson Fellowship for Women's Studies Research assisted me in the substantial task of tracing primary sources on Austin. I have been fortunate to do most of my work in two of this country's major research libraries: the Huntington Library in San Marino, California, and the Beinecke Rare Book and Manuscript Library at Yale. No scholar could ask for more generous staff or for more congenial facilities than those provided by the Huntington and the Beinecke. At the Huntington I would like to acknowledge the guidance of Sara S. Hodson, associate curator of literary manuscripts, and of Brita Mack, photo archivist.

I have been fortunate to have the assistance of Patricia Lanigan Franco, whose admirable editorial skills and knowledge about the 1930s have improved my manuscript. Ruth Wild's dexterity on the word processor and her first-rate editorial abilities have saved me from several embarrassing errors. Richard Leggett is responsible for the original artwork in the map and genealogy. I appreciate Charles Grench's faith in the book, and I am grateful for the editorial expertise of Harry Haskell at Yale University Press. Finally, Charles Hinkle, my spouse, knows that without his encouragement and affectionate assistance in countless ways this biography of Mary Austin would not have been possible.

1868   Born Sept. 9 in Carlinville, Ill., to George and Susanna Hunter.

1878   Austin's father and sister die.

1884   Enrolls in Blackburn College.

1885   Transfers to State Normal School in Bloomington, Ill. Has first breakdown and returns to Carlinville to recover.

1887   James Hunter travels to California.

1888   Austin graduates from Blackburn College. Joins James in California with mother and younger brother; family establishes homestead in Tejon district.

1889   "One Hundred Miles on Horseback" published in *The Blackburnian*. Boards with Pyle family, teaches school, and meets General Edward Fitzgerald Beale.

1890   Becomes engaged to Stafford Wallace Austin.

1891   Marries Austin. Travels to San Francisco and meets Ina Coolbrith. Wallace's irrigation project in Owens Valley fails.

1892   Austins move to Lone Pine; daughter Ruth born. Mary's first story, "The Mother of Felipe," published in the *Overland Monthly*. Austins move to Inyo district.

1895   Mary moves to Bishop to teach, taking Ruth with her.

1896   Susanna Hunter dies. Wallace becomes teacher in Lone Pine.

1897   Mary joins him in Lone Pine to teach.

1898   Wallace promoted to county superintendent of schools;
        Mary fills out his term teaching. Visits Oakland, where
        she meets William James.

1899   Wallace appointed registrar of Land Office in
        Independence. Mary moves to Los Angeles with Ruth,
        meets Charles Lummis, and teaches at Normal School.

1900   Mary returns to Independence and begins writing seriously.

1903   *The Land of Little Rain* published by Houghton Mifflin.

1904   Visits Carmel and San Francisco; meets George Sterling
        and other literary figures. *The Basket Woman* published.

1905   *Isidro* published. Ruth formally committed to institution for
        the retarded in Santa Clara.

1906   Mary witnesses San Francisco earthquake and fire. Buys
        land in Carmel and joins artists' colony there.

1907   Breast cancer diagnosed. Visits New York and Europe.
        Wallace charges Mary with desertion.

1908   Tours Italy and France on first trip abroad. *Santa Lucia*
        published.

1909   *Lost Borders* published while Austin is in England.

1910   Moves to New York. *Outland* published under pseudonym
        in England.

1911   Her play *The Arrow Maker* produced in New York. Returns
        to Carmel to write and lecture.

1912   *A Woman of Genius* published. Austin becomes involved
        with women's movement in New York.

1913   Spends year in California. *The Lovely Lady, The Green
        Bough*, and *Love and the Soul Maker* published.

1914   Divorced from Wallace. Divides time between New York
        and California. *California: Land of the Sun* published in U.S.
        and England.

1915   *The Man Jesus* published by Harper and Brothers.

1917   *The Ford* published by Houghton Mifflin. James Hunter dies.

1918   Visits Santa Fe to study Indian poetry. Ruth dies in flu epidemic.

1920   *No. 26 Jayne Street* published.

1921   Travels to England.

1922–   National Arts Club dinner in her honor on Jan. 8, 1922.
1923   Makes several trips to Santa Fe and Southwest; has breakdown during summer of 1923. *The American Rhythm* published.

1924   *The Land of Journeys' Ending* published. Decides to move to Santa Fe.

1925   Builds Casa Querida (Beloved House) in Santa Fe; initiates reform work on behalf of Indians.

1927   Organizes Spanish Colonial Arts Society with Frank Applegate. Experiences health problems. Ansel Adams and Albert Bender visit Santa Fe.

1929   Collaborates with Adams on Taos Pueblo project and begins research for autobiography.

1930   *Taos Pueblo* published.

1931   *Starry Adventure* and *Experiences Facing Death* published.

1932   *Earth Horizon* published by Houghton Mifflin. Coronary disease diagnosed.

1933   Suffers heart attack. Brother George murdered by patient in Los Angeles.

1934   *One Smoke Stories* published by Houghton Mifflin. Dies Aug. 13, 1934, in Santa Fe after lingering illness and heart attack.

ABBREVIATIONS

The titles of works by Mary Austin are abbreviated in the text as follows. Full citations for all of her books are given in the bibliography.

EH	*Earth Horizon: An Autobiography* (1932)
JS	*No. 26 Jayne Street* (1920)
LB	*Lost Borders* (1909)
LOJE	*The Land of Journeys' Ending* (1924)
LOLR	*The Land of Little Rain* (1903)
OHM	"One Hundred Miles on Horseback" (1889)
SA	*Starry Adventure* (1931)
SL	*Santa Lucia* (1908)
TP	*Taos Pueblo* (1930)
WOG	*A Woman of Genius* (1912)

INTRODUCTION

Mary Hunter Austin's voice is one of the most unusual, gifted, eccentric, exasperating, tragic, enigmatic, elitist, and idiosyncratic in American literature. A Midwesterner by birth, Austin (1868–1934) emigrated with her family from a tightly knit Methodist community in Illinois to forge a new life in the rapidly changing, postboom California of the late 1880s. Her literary career began at the turn of the century with the publication of her best-known naturist work, *The Land of Little Rain* (1903), and proceeded along a haphazard course through the Progressive Era into the early 1930s. During these thirty years Austin embraced many extraliterary causes: women's and Indians' rights, the preservation of indigenous arts and crafts, ecological awareness, and collective actions of all sorts, especially the war effort in the teens.

Austin's oeuvre comprises a prodigious quantity of books, plays, poetry, and journalism, in addition to notes, manuscripts, and correspondence. Yet despite the acclaim she earned in her lifetime, many scholars of American literature remain unfamiliar with her work, perhaps because much of it centers on the American West. Apart from fourteen years when she was based in New York, she spent all of her adult life in California and New Mexico. It was a large and a rich life, and I have been able to present only a montage of it. My energies have been directed toward exploring a few relationships that illuminate Austin's problematic career. I have not attempted to catalog the many people and events in her busy life. Rather, I have focused on specific moments in it, moments that I believe suggest the complexity of Austin and her writings and that other biographers have not fully appreciated. Similarly, I have chosen to discuss some works in greater depth than others, leaving out analysis of her poetry altogether except for brief mentions.

Several personal misfortunes that marked Austin's life receive the attention they deserve in this book. Daughterhood, marriage, and motherhood each held a separate tragedy for her. At the same time, they infused her work with a power and depth that are altogether original, if not always artistically successful. Hence, my biocritical study is not the triumphant saga of a woman for whom renown came easily. Austin's remarkable nature writing made clear the direction in which she was moving as an artist, a feminist, an environmentalist, a mystic. *The Land of Little Rain*, praised for its humanistic eloquence and "analytical" balance, and her autobiographical *Earth Horizon* (1932) were largely responsible for establishing her literary reputation. Yet this legacy would have disappointed the writer who finally yearned for an enduring reputation as a social novelist.[1]

Although she greatly admired beauty, Austin did not possess it herself. Her appearance never ceased to amaze those who met her for the first time. Behind the demeanor of "a seemingly plain housewife," Louis Adamic wrote, she made "herself—with her bold, original mind —into one of the most interesting American women of her time and a force in the awakening culture of the West."[2] Indeed, Austin's personality was so strong that it tended, at times, to overpower people's recollection of her work. It lent itself to myth. The stories about her are legion, and many have been incorporated into biographical accounts; some are surely apocryphal. Since she wrote much of her own publicity for her thirty books and hundreds of lectures, she is the source of several of the more hyperbolic accounts of her career. Other myths originated in her autobiography. Carl Van Doren remembered her as a woman whose "greatness" impressed all who met her. Another friend and literary admirer called her "a tragic and heroic woman" whose "unhappiness, almost indescribable, was with her all her life."[3]

Austin understood from the beginning that a writer's career was contingent upon selling work to a public. She took every opportunity to tell her publishers about the peculiar conditions of the West, and was exasperated when they ignored her advice about how to exploit that market. Not unlike Virginia Woolf, who in *Granite and Rainbow* observed that a writer's work is "frivolous if unpaid for," or the unfortunate protagonist of Jack London's autobiographical novel *Martin Eden*, a man literally driven to the brink by the marketing process that would confer legitimacy on him as a professional writer, Austin took the idea of payment for her work very seriously.[4] Payment raised a writer from the rank of amateur to that of professional. Yet her publishers barely covered costs on many of her books, and she was forced to supplement her meager income by lecturing.[5]

Early in her career Austin faulted Houghton Mifflin in Boston for failing to adapt their marketing strategies to the "hundreds of thousands of people in the west who never see a bookstore." Her pragmatic judgment owed more than she knew to her entrepreneurial relatives in Illinois. "You can't sell books to people unless you get at them where they live, and you have to tell them what is in a book before they will buy it without seeing." Austin was frustrated by her publisher's insensitivity to the concerns of the western writer. "I am quite willing to bear my share of the experiment, but it will require a man [marketing person] who knows the west well enough to know that *The Land of Little Rain* is not about Southern California and that miners and sheepmen do not frequent book stores," she continued in the same letter.[6]

Like other women writers of her period, Austin was caught up in social definitions of "femininity" even as she criticized "feminine" values that disempowered women. She agitated against the male-dominated hierarchy wherever she found it, publicly in her lectures and writing, privately in her letters. Her career testifies to her indomitable will and her commitment to interpret the world in a way that affirmed her unique, woman's voice, a voice that she claimed was never "meant to chirrup nor twitter."[7]

It is impossible to read Austin's work without concluding that she was ahead of her time. Her ideas were considered controversial and not readily accepted. One of her major themes is the disempowerment of women by men; even her naturist works subvert male-defined values and power relationships. In examining this theme, I have found it useful to view her life and career against those of other women writers of her period—Gertrude Atherton, Willa Cather, Edith Wharton, and Kate Chopin. Unlike them, Austin was preoccupied with matters of class, race, and gender, focusing on American Indian and Hispanic folkways in her short fiction and essays. Interestingly, although she embraced the theory underpinning the cause of women's rights, she preferred to identify intellectually with men.

Place was important to Austin, in both its environmental and its geographical and geopolitical aspects. She insisted, with almost evangelical fervor, that indigenous America should take its rightful place in the world of American ideas and literature. She sought a sense of participation in a literary community that extended from New York to Los Angeles, San Francisco, Carmel, Santa Fe, and even the remote Owens Valley of California. This last location inspired some of her most original and beautifully wrought material, especially when it dealt with the people who lived there: Anglos, Indians and Hispanics, shepherds, ranchers, craftspeople, and miners.

Austin's fame as a public figure and her paradoxical neglect as a writer are not an uncommon phenomenon in the history of women's literature. The glaring omissions of women writers from the American canon has sparked lively debate among scholars for several years.[8] Annette Kolodny is persuaded that "males ignorant of women's 'values' or conceptions of the world will, necessarily, be poor readers of works that in any sense recapitulate their codes."[9] Kolodny's thesis may be extended to the reading of works that in any way deviate from the prescribed canon. Yet why Austin has been dismissed by many literary historians is not altogether clear. Until quite recently, literary histories of the United States, reference books, and anthologies of American literature failed to include her name and work even when updated to embrace short works by New England women writers and other regionalists.[10] Only in the last decade or so have Wharton and Cather, the one a New Yorker ensconced in France, the latter a Middle Westerner transplanted to New York, been included on university syllabi. People read and remember writers whose works are readily available. Austin's work has generally been inaccessible, although recently a few of her books have been reprinted.

As a result, a new audience has begun to discover not only Austin's distinctive and eloquent prose style but also the radical critique of marriage and the social arrangements between men and women in her writings, which went virtually unnoticed for more than half a century. Austin wrote with great perception about women, and she was especially compelled to write the stories of people who lived on the margins of society, perhaps because as a woman and an artist she considered herself different and apart from others. She never doubted her own genius and could not understand how others could miss it. Her convictions, always passionately felt and sometimes fractiously expressed, endeared her to some while often jeopardizing her career. I have tried to attend to these concerns in Austin's writing.

Although the chronological details of Austin's life have been admirably addressed by biographers, friends, and scholars, much work remains to be done.[11] Her autobiography, *Earth Horizon*, is as eloquent and revelatory in its omissions as in its disclosures. My task—to position Austin in the history of American letters—is both biographical and critical. Austin insisted upon her own distinctive voice, the voice of "I-Mary."[12] If we consider her a representative writer, she was representative in having overcome the obstacles encountered by a western woman writer in establishing a serious literary reputation. Although Austin can be said to have taken on representative issues—the critique of modern marriage, feminism, the rights of Indians, and the recovery of an indigenous American tradition—her interpretations are the expressions of an exceptional, not a representative, voice: the utterances of the "I-Mary" aspect of her ego that she discovered and nurtured deep within herself from her youth into her adult life.

I have found it useful to draw upon contemporary biographical theory and, as the critic David Bromwich writes, "to confuse as much as possible the boundaries between criticism and biography." I have also kept in mind the "elusive mystery of personality" to which Ralph Barton Perry refers in his study of William James. According to Perry, "there is an ultimate flavor, a spiritual physiognomy, that remains after the analysis has been made, and after every tributary influence has been traced and named."[13] Any analysis of Austin must consider her personality in its formidable and inescapable aspects, some of which are not altogether pleasant.

Several questions emerge from such an analysis. What literary and extraliterary strategies did Austin employ to become a literary presence? Why did she situate her career in the West, thus making it difficult to forge literary connections that might have made her more visible? How did the great inconvenience, stress, and expense involved in commuting color her New York period? How did she support herself as a writer? What are the central themes in Austin's oeuvre and how did they grow out of her life? How did these thematic ideas jibe or conflict with the society in which she lived and the market for which she wrote? How did she interact with the literary communities in the East and the West? My exploration of these questions will, I hope, bring Austin's career into sharper relief, particularly in light of the new scholarship on women.

1

▲ ▲ ▲

BEGINNINGS

All these things come back with the shattered brilliance of light through stained glass. I remember the orchard with great clumps of frail spring-beauties coming up through the sod; the smell of budding sassafras on the winds of March, and the sheets of blue violets about rotting tree-trunks in the woodlot.

—Earth Horizon

Carlinville, Illinois, where Mary Austin grew up during the 1870s and 1880s, resembled a thousand other small towns of its time on the "middle border." With its churches and schools, dry-goods stores and livery stables, social organizations, newspaper, and handful of professional offices, it presented a typical picture of late nineteenth-century village life, a life that Lewis Atherton characterized as "rootless, new and raw, booming and optimistic."[1] As Austin recalls her youth in *Earth Horizon*, her principal memory is of Carlinville's commonplaceness—a theme that recurs in her novels and other writings. To Austin, the Carlinville of the late nineteenth century (like the Taylorville of her 1912 novel *A Woman of Genius*) represented a bastion of conformity and anti-intellectualism that impeded her own creative potential.

Although Austin's small-town, middle-class background differed greatly from Edith Wharton's upper-class New York upbringing, both felt stifled by what they perceived as provincialism. Almost exact contemporaries, both writers escaped the confines of their youth—Wharton to Europe, Austin to California, New Mexico, and New York—and described their negative encounters with anti-intellectualism in their fictions. Austin's recollection of childhood was dominated by "pretensions to culture" that she observed around her. "The status of being cultivated was something like the preciousness of women: nothing you could cash in upon, but a shame to do without. . . . The pioneer stress was over, prosperity had come upon the Middlewest and leisure into the lives of women. The day of large families, families of from a dozen to fifteen, was over" (*EH* 100–101).

Mary Hunter was born to George and Susanna Savilla Graham Hunter in Carlinville on September 9, 1868 (see genealogy). Jarrot and Polly McAdams Dugger, Mary's maternal great-grandparents, had been among the earliest settlers in the area; Jarrot Dugger bought Carlinville's first Methodist church site in 1834.[2] The surname Dugger probably was an Americanization of Daguerre, and the family claimed to be related to Louis Daguerre, the French scene painter and physicist who invented the daguerreotype and the diorama (*EH* 12 and 370, n. 8).

The Methodist Graham family, also early Carlinville pioneers and town planners, were descended from Janot Graham, a Scottish schoolteacher, violinist, and amateur poet who emigrated to Connecticut as a young man and settled in Nelsonville, Ohio, in the 1830s. Graham "had decided views on many questions but never argued, was averse to infant baptism and would never contribute to the Foreign Missions."[3] His wife, Theda Case Graham, an Irish Protestant, was remembered by family chroniclers as "one of the most placid and lovable women of her time."[4] Central to Austin's later feminism was the emphasis she placed on the legacy of her pioneering female relatives. "I can never recall a single incident that was told me about my revolutionary and pioneering ancestry, that did not revolve about my great and greater grandmothers," she wrote.[5]

Austin recounted stories about her strong-willed female forebears in her autobiography. In particular, she relished the anecdote of her maternal grandmother Hannah Dugger Graham's first confrontation with the Methodist church when she came to Carlinville as a bride (a prefiguration of Austin's own doctrinal differences with the church). Hannah was disciplined for "vanity" on account of a daguerreotype that she and her husband, Milo, had sat for in St. Louis. Milo, who had been a tailor, fashioned Hannah's traveling outfit from a "fine length of broadcloth" for their wedding trip to Carlinville. In the excitement of the journey, the newlyweds forgot the Methodist sanction against being photographed and showed their daguerreotype to friends and relatives (*EH* 20). "What I liked best about the story," Austin recalled, "was that on the day of the reproving sermon, grandmother sailed down the aisle to hear it *dressed in her tailored gown*" (*EH* 434). Hannah Graham had twelve brothers and sisters, two of whom died in infancy.

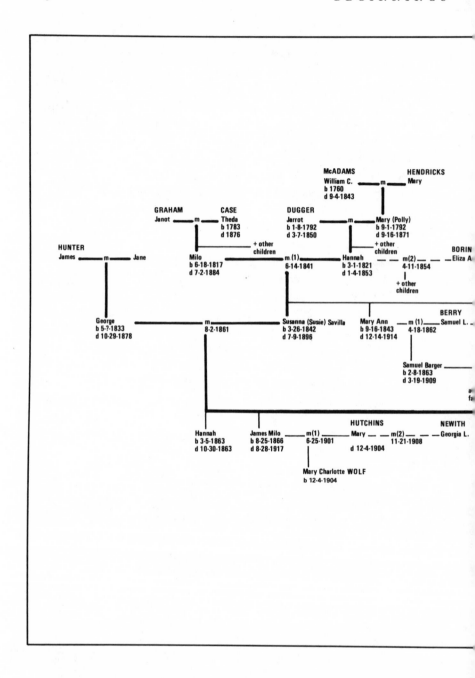

Genealogy of Mary Austin's family.

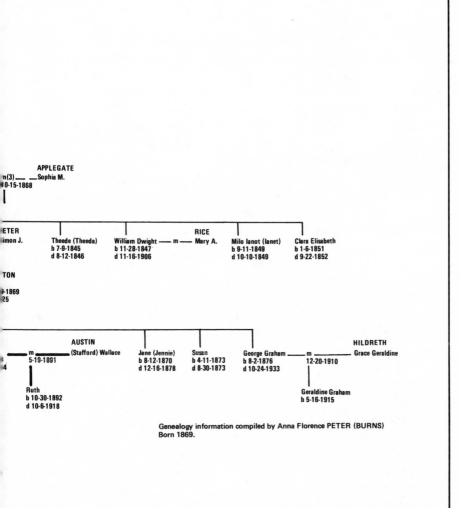

APPLEGATE
m(3) ___ ___Sophia M.
10-15-1868

ETER
Simon J.

			RICE		
Theede (Theeda)	William Dwight —— m —— Mary A.		Milo Ianot (Ianet)	Clara Elisabeth
b 7-9-1845	b 11-28-1847		b 9-11-1849	b 1-6-1851
d 8-12-1846	d 11-16-1906		d 10-10-1849	d 9-22-1852

TON

-1869
25

AUSTIN   HILDRETH
___ m ___ (Stafford) Wallace   Jane (Jennie)   Susan   George Graham ___ m ___ Grace Geraldine
  5-19-1891   b 8-12-1870   b 4-11-1873   b 8-2-1876   12-20-1910
4   d 12-16-1878   d 8-30-1873   d 10-24-1933

Ruth
b 10-30-1892
d 10-6-1918

Geraldine Graham
b 5-16-1915

Genealogy information compiled by Anna Florence PETER (BURNS)
Born 1869.

She herself bore six children—Mary's mother was one of three who survived infancy—before dying in her early thirties. Milo Graham, a vigorous and many-talented man, married twice more and outlived two of his wives, a not uncommon pattern at a time when many women died in childbirth.

Of Mary's father, George Hunter, less is known. Born in England in 1833, he emigrated in 1851 with his older brother, William, who had previously established himself with cousins in Alton, Illinois. Austin gives a romantic account of their trip "from New Orleans to St. Louis on a Mississippi packet" (*EH* 3–9). George clerked in a boot dealer's shop for a couple of years before returning to England to fetch their sister, who eventually married and settled in British America. An intellectual man, George was more interested in education than in merchandising. When he returned to Alton, he worked as a clerk to support his law studies at nearby Shurtleff College.[6] He soon became one of Carlinville's most prominent citizens, immersing himself in civic life and establishing a law practice before the "guns of treason fired on Fort Sumter."[7]

Austin and her brothers and sister came to regard the Civil War as "a wholly romantic war . . . fought by Father, General Grant, and Cousin Bill Dugger, although of course there were others from the town who helped along" (*EH* 26). Lieutenant George Hunter had rallied to President Lincoln's call for seventy-five thousand men when Company K of the Seventh Illinois Regiment was mustered into service in April 1861. Carlinville citizens swelled with patriotism, knowing that they were providing the first Union regiment from Illinois, and they were particularly proud of their three commissioned officers, who made "a fine appearance in their new uniforms."[8] When Susanna Savilla Graham married Lieutenant Hunter that August, she pushed her teaching ambitions aside to accommodate the demanding duties of being a wife and mother. They had eight children, of whom four survived: Mary; her older brother, James Milo, born in 1866; her younger sister Jennie, born in 1870; and George, Jr., born in 1876. Thus, Susanna Hunter was either pregnant or caring for a toddler from the earliest days of her marriage until her husband's death in 1878.

When Lieutenant Hunter took Susanna to Cairo, Illinois, where his regiment was stationed during his second enlistment, the new Mrs. Hunter was the envy of her friends as the town's first war bride. George was elected a captain in Company K when his regiment was summoned to Corinth, Mississippi, in 1863.[9] Susanna returned to Carlinville to wait for the war to end, having borne a baby daughter who died at a remote, mosquito-infested military outpost in Corinth (*EH* 29).[10] Although George was never wounded in combat, he was plagued by malarial fever, the result of his war years in the swamp. These bouts continued to enervate him even after he was mustered out of the service at the end of his three-year appointment in June 1864. "He was never again to enjoy the finely strung good health and spirits which he had taken into the war," Austin wrote (*EH* 30).

George returned from the war a local hero by virtue of his rank and literary abilities. The people of Carlinville regarded him as "a man of intelligence, of noble manly bearing, not loquacious by any means but with a pleasant gift of conversation."[11] During the war his health had made him unfit for field service, but his legal training suited him admirably for court-martial duty and gave him the leisure to file war reports for the *Carlinville Democrat*. Captain Hunter's accounts from the front were written in a style that his daughter was later to characterize as "virile, direct, cool, and somehow graceful, lacking the Byronic note which characterizes too many contemporary writings . . . English rather than American but without any touch of self-consciousness" (*EH* 30).

George's "virile" style became a model for his daughter's own writing. In her novel *Starry Adventure*, published in 1931, Austin evokes her father, an invalid with literary tastes, in the person of the narrator. This character's son, Gard, reveals himself to be an avid reader. "He [Gard] seems to have inherited my literary taste. Who knows . . . I really ought to have written. I have a gift—don't you think, Marian?" the narrator asks his wife (*SA* 27). A dispatch in the form of a hurriedly sketched letter illustrates George's skill at reportage. "Tell Messrs. Chesnut, Rinaker, and Halderman we are sorry they did not get up to Nashville; to see if nothing more how the mighty have fallen; and with what craven cowardice and wanton malignity the rebel army through its generals, has acted, in the treatment of persons and property, both public and private. . . . It is a matter of great satisfaction that our army by its behavior in the field and in camp, in comparison with that of the rebels, is commanding perforce the respect of the most uncompromising secessionists, and contributes in no small degree to mitigate their chagrin, while it strengthens the conviction that the cause of rebellion, in such hands is hopeless."[12] When George returned to Carlinville, now bustling with entrepreneurial activity, he promptly had business cards printed to inform the public of his law office over the Grahams' drug store.[13]

Carlinville in the 1870s was experiencing the growing pains of a town teetering on the brink of modernity; old and new coexisted in awkward harmony. The Graham drug emporium, newly opened by Susanna Hunter's family, stocked wallpapers and carpets for its middle-class clientele. Austin's Dugger relatives were in business as well. The year of her birth saw the improvement of the Dugger Building in Carlinville; the newspaper remarked that the Duggers "always presented a good front." The Grahams and the Duggers deferred to George Hunter's intellectual prowess, although they considered themselves his superior in business. "He was," they agreed, "a gentleman of fine intellectual attainments, possessed of rare conversational powers, and a remarkably retentive memory—a man to whom it was a pleasure to listen." [14]

By 1867 Hunter began to specialize in army claims and pensions. In 1870 he was elected police magistrate, even though he lived outside the city limits. However, the fact that he was not listed in income tax records as earning more than a thousand dollars a year, coupled with his frequent illnesses, suggests that the Hunter family struggled along in genteel poverty. Nevertheless, Hunter publicly supported Horace Greeley in the presidential election of 1872, acted as secretary for the Commission on Relief for the victims of the 1871 Chicago fire, wrote occasional articles for the *Democrat*, and performed in Carlinville's amateur theatricals. (Several of Mary Austin's relatives played significant roles in the fetes and high jinks of the 1860s and 1870s.) [15]

Death in the Family

Hunter's untimely death in 1878 marked the end of an era of stability in the Hunter household and, for Mary, the passing of her literary mentor. As a law clerk her father had bought "first American editions of Keats and Shelley, Mrs. Browning and Ruskin" and strove "to keep pace with the writers of genuine distinction in the United States; with Herman Melville, Hawthorne, Poe, and Longfellow, particularly with Emerson" (*EH* 34). Emerson was to remain a model for Mary's own work. Hunter's literary interests contrasted with those of his fellow townsfolk, who were partial to the stories of Bret Harte and Harriet Beecher Stowe that were serialized in the local newspaper.

Carlinville citizens eagerly followed the shocking autobiographical account *The Mormon Wife* and found much to enjoy in Twain's *Innocents Abroad*, soothing as it was to their own embarrassed uncertainties about art and culture. Mary recalled that her mother's literary background derived chiefly from *Godey's Lady's Book*, where she read the writings of Lydia Marie Child, Maria Cummins, and Augusta Evans (*EH* 23). Romanticized in Mary's imagination, Hunter represented the halcyon days of her girlhood, when he nurtured her abiding interest in nature and the intellectual life. "The appalling thing that had happened to Mary by the loss of her father was that she was also deprived of most of the items that, out of the place where you stay, make home," Austin wrote in her third-person autobiography (*EH* 91). For Mary, Hunter's death meant the dispossession not only of her childhood home, but also of "the wide circle of activities tangent to it, the community of interest, family ritual, the dramatic climax of Father's daily return, the praise, the blame, evenings around the lamp" (*EH* 91).

Austin reserves some of the more lyrical, even purple, prose in *Earth Horizon* for describing her relationship with him. "I remember the tree toads musically trilling, the katydids in the hickory tree by the pump and a raw Yorkshire lad who had come to work for father not being able to sleep because of them. . . . I more than recall the hot honeyscent of red clover, and the heavy, low flying bumble-bees; long walks in winter over the snow with Father, and the discovery of green fronds of fern and leafy wild blackberry vines under the edge of February thaws" (*EH* 48). Much like Wharton, who was removed from the Hunters' world by strata of privilege and position, Mary saw her father as an almost luminous presence, supportive and guiding, proud of her intellectual accomplishments, encouraging her to read *Alice in Wonderland* while he read *The Pilgrim's Progress* and other classics aloud to her in the evenings. She read the Bible, too, but only when her grandfather Graham offered a prize of five dollars to the grandchild who first read it through. In the winter between her ninth and tenth birthdays, she "bored everybody in the family to death, keeping up with the condition that somebody should be able to vouch for her reading" (*EH* 67–68) —an incident recast in her last novel, *Starry Adventure*. Her father was the patient tutor of Mary's intellect, bringing home *St. Nicholas* magazine and allowing her to browse among the complete works on his shelves.[16]

Hunter's death, probably the result of "a tumor on one of his hips," though not unexpected, left a void in Mary's life that was deepened by Jennie's death of diphtheria in December of the same year. The guilt that Mary experienced after her sister died profoundly affected her life and work. Her mother had not summoned the doctor for Jennie because Mary had initially shown symptoms of a sore throat and then recovered. Moreover, Mary knew that Jennie was a favorite child and always believed her mother held her responsible for Jennie's death. "The loss of her is never cold in me, tears start freshly at the mere mention of her name. . . . She was the only one who ever unselfishly loved me. She is the only one who stays," she wrote more than fifty years later (*EH* 87). The memory of Jennie's burial haunted her and shredded any emotional bond between Mary and her mother. She recorded their rift in her autobiography and alluded to it again and again in novels such as *A Woman of Genius*. When she sought to comfort and be comforted, Mary wrote that her mother rejected her, "thrusting me away [from Father's grave] to throw herself upon it" (*EH* 86).

Significant changes disrupted the family's life after Hunter's death. Mrs. Hunter, once the envy of every young woman in Carlinville, now found herself in straitened circumstances with several young children to manage, the oldest being twelve. On her widow's pension she could no longer afford to maintain the attractive semirural Plum Street house, so the Hunters moved back to town, first to temporary quarters and then to a new house built with proceeds from the sale of the farm. Mary hated the new place for its ugliness and its proportions that were "all neat and hard and squared up with a purely objective domesticity" (*EH* 108).

Mary paints a grim picture of this period in her autobiography. Perceiving herself to have been ensnared in her mother's widowhood, she recollects that in Carlinville "the wife's economic dependence on her husband [was] a kind of sanctity which was violated by his death; dependence that made widowhood . . . little less than improbity," for "the Wife became the poor Widow, the object of family bounty, not infrequently grudged, the grateful recipient of left-overs, the half-menial helper in the households of women whose husbands had simply not died" (*EH* 91–92). Even though Mrs. Hunter's sister, widowed during the Civil War, had remarried and borne eleven children, she apparently resisted the idea of a second marriage, or perhaps believed that this alternative did not exist for her. Yet after the initial period of mourning, she realized that a new world was opening up to her—the world of work, of associations with other women, especially through local study groups and the Woman's Christian Temperance Union (WCTU). With George no longer in the civic limelight, Susanna could venture into the world without feeling that she was stepping outside her assigned sphere.

Constrained by an ideology of domesticity, which held that woman's place was in the home where she held moral sway over her husband and children, Mrs. Hunter found few avenues of respectable work open to her. She turned to nursing to augment her widow's pension, as it merely extended her natural domestic function into the world.[17] During her frequent absences, she depended on Mary to manage the household, prepare meals, and tend her baby brothers. George was Mary's charge before and after school, "and if anything went wrong, [she would] be held responsible" (*EH* 92). Austin's later writings suggest that she deeply resented George and her mother for heaping these domestic cares upon her merely because she was the elder daughter (*EH* 127).

The loss of Mary's father also meant a loss of family prestige. It was he who had received attention for reading essays on flowers and shrubbery to the Horticultural Club, he who had been cited in the paper for his prize Berkshire hogs at the county fair, he who had represented the county at the transportation convention in Chicago. The notes that Mary compiled for her autobiography offer a number of clues to the life that was being taken away from her and the life that lay ahead. A newspaper notice protested the custom of fathers "giving away the bride," implicitly questioning whether this signified that daughters were their fathers' slaves. In 1878 Bret Harte was reported to have fled abroad just as the "rush for the coast" gained momentum. The most macabre headlines of this tragic year for the Hunter family hailed the advent of cremation and corpse preservative. George Hunter's death meant that Mary would not be given away at her wedding, but she could not have foreseen that in the next few years her family would join the thousands heading west by rail. Charles Nordhoff's *California for Health, Pleasure, and Residence* (1875) was gaining prominence as a guide for travelers and settlers. It is likely that the Hunters knew about this book even before George's death, as some Graham relatives had already settled in the Pasadena area.

The WCTU *and Chautauqua*

In its heyday in the 1880s, the Woman's Christian Temperance Union provided the impetus for afternoon meetings, teas, picnics, lectures, and a host of other social activities. Typically, members of local chapters "not only agitated against liquor and tobacco, but also urged social reforms—visited the sick, and donated food and money to the destitute." Associated with the WCTU were the "purity" groups for men and women, in which discussions ranged over such controversial topics as prostitution, the prescribed treatment of syphilis for men (bichloride

of gold), and narcotics addiction.[18] Carlinville probably had little reason to worry about drugs, but it was ripe for the WCTU in the late
1870s. Frequent stories appeared in the *Democrat* about "the most respectable ladies" distributing pamphlets for their cause "in business
houses and saloons notifying all the morally decrepit and infirm of
temperance meetings."[19]

Mrs. Hunter became president of the local WCTU in 1882 and invited
Frances Willard to speak at the ninth annual convention in Carlinville.[20]
Mary attended the convention and became infatuated with Willard,
then at the height of her fame. It may have been her highly polished
oratorical style that influenced Mary to become a member of the newly
organized temperance society for girls, the "Broom Brigade."[21] Mary's
mother gave the welcoming address on the first night of the confer-
ence, and later that year Mary herself delivered a temperance speech
entitled "Little Causes, Big Results."[22] As popular as temperance was
among the women and many of the men, especially Methodists, its
advocates were unsuccessful in introducing temperance textbooks into
Carlinville's schools. But for Mary the ideas gleaned from the WCTU
"about marriage and politics, about the place of women in the scheme
of things," were radical and enduring.[23]

During the late 1870s Carlinville's citizens became acutely "anxious
about the state of their culture, where formerly they had been chiefly
concerned about their souls." The issue of religious salvation was preempted by "a general consensus of opinion . . . that you did have to
read to maintain your pretensions to culture" (*EH* 100). In addition
to the temperance meetings at Pentecost Hill and the lyceum series,
adult education was furthered by the Chautauqua movement, which
sought to present stimulating public speakers who would hold forth
on matters of general interest and religious uplift. During the summer,
crowds gathered to listen to speakers and entertainers in carnival-like
settings under tents or pavilions. The visiting lecturer was an integral
part of small-town life before the turn of the century.[24] It appears that
the Hunters attended some Chautauqua events, but given a choice,
the circus was the more compelling recreation for James, Mary, and
George.

Book-learning in Carlinville (as in many small towns) was distinguished from the applied knowledge that accounted for "pioneer types
of success" (*EH* 102).[25] Mary's mother belonged to the Chautauqua
Library and Scientific Circle, which met at a neighbor's house to discuss the readings outlined in the Chautauqua literature course. These
included selections from Longfellow's *Evangeline* and *Tales of a Way-*

side Inn, works that substantially influenced Mary's literary tastes. Her favorite author was Milton, who mesmerized her with "the magic of verse—like watching a thunder-storm at sunset" (*EH* 105).

In later years Mary made fun of the pretentiousness of the Chautauqua Library and Scientific Circle and of those who read Milton because of the handsome Doré illustrations—"Biblical, grandiose, and with no reference to reality" (*EH* 105). In Santa Fe, she spearheaded a movement to prevent a women's organization from establishing a summer Chautauqua, which she believed would jeopardize the environment of the elite artists' colony there.[26]

Methodism and Mysticism

Mary's girlhood years were strongly colored by Methodism. Her older brother, Jim, accepted the doctrine of sin, repentance, and reconciliation. Mary, however, interpreted grace as a natural condition, "inward" and "not achieved"; she considered herself a "pragmatist" and admired the philosophy of William James when she heard him lecture in California in the early 1900s. Meeting James made her realize that she had been born with a bias against emotional treatment of what might be called "moral" problems, and she remembered the Methodism of her adolescence as menacing.

Although she joined the church officially when she was about fifteen, Austin looked back on her conversion as a blind response to the sense of community that had been kindled during the revivalist meeting when she stepped forward and that drew her as an adult to Indian rituals.[27] The inhabitants of her fictional town of Taylorville, she wrote, were "caught up in one of those acute crises called Revival where the citizenry liked [evangelism] with a deeper more soul-stretching enjoyment than the operas, theatres, social adventure of the cities" (*WOG* 52–53). As a matter of fact, she "personally always loathed the mouthy public praying of Methodists" (*EH* 116–17). What she was searching for was the Methodism of her grandmother Graham's day: the excitement of immersions, picnics, camp meetings, watch meetings, sitting up with the dead—in short, a Methodism that furnished myriad excuses for socializing and possibly romance (*EH* 22).[28]

Mary Hunter's rebellious attitude toward Methodism reflected a growing unrest among all classes opposed to domination of any sort in late nineteenth-century America. A precocious child, Mary simply did not wish to submit to the authority inherent in organized religion.[29]

Perhaps, like many converts to Methodism, Mary failed to accept intellectually the doctrine of Salvation, never feeling "lost—simply out of touch." To her the "appallingly terrible thing was that you lived your religious life in the judgment of the congregation," an environment of communal gossiping that she found intolerable even as a child. Not without satisfaction, she records being "finally read out of the Methodist Church for organizing a community theatre movement and failing to maintain that Moses wrote the Pentateuch" (*EH* 119).

Mary experienced her first mystical communion with nature at the age of six, when she became aware of her capacity for perceiving the world with heightened consciousness. This experience occurred one morning when an enormous walnut tree near the Hunter home captured her attention. She describes it in *Experiences Facing Death* (1931) as an "ineffable moment" of ecstatic knowledge that all living things are interconnected—"I in them and they in me and all of us enclosed in a warm lucent bubble of livingness." She remembers trying to locate "the source of this happy wonder" and recounts that "at last she questioned —'God?'—because it was the only awesome word she knew. Deep inside, like the murmurous swing of a bell, she heard the answer, 'God, God.'" From this moment on, Mary believed that she was in touch with "a force, a source of energy."[30] In her autobiography she writes simply, "God happened to Mary under the walnut tree" (*EH* 51).

Liberation would come to her in a more profound and personal way when she observed her first California springtime in the Tejon country. Admiring the white borage and blue lupine, the blue nemophila and flame-colored poppies peeking through the sandy soil, "released" her from the "long spiritual drought that was coincident with her commitment to organized religion" (*EH* 198). Still later she experienced mysticism in the desert, where "for all the toll the desert takes of a man it gives compensations, deep breaths, deep sleep, and the communion of the stars" (*LOLR* 8).

Head of the Household

Perhaps more onerous than Methodism, however, during her adolescent years was her mother's elevation of her older brother, Jim, to head of the household when he was fifteen. A photograph from this period shows Mary standing tall and clear-eyed in a Victorian dress. Mrs. Hunter is seated, weighted down by her heavy black dress, her expression severe, looking much like the middle-aged Mary Austin.

The Hunter family in Carlinville, Illinois, 1880.
From left: *James, Mary, Susanna, and George.*

She holds the hand of her youngest child, George. Jim, with mud on his boots, occupies the authority position in the image.[31] His special position brought home to Mary why "women of high intelligence and education [in the first wave of feminism's version of consciousness-raising sessions] went white and sick telling how, in their own families, the mere whim of the dominant male member, even in the fields which should have been exempt from his interference, had been allowed to assume the weight of moral significance" (*EH* 128). In a brief life story, published anonymously in a 1926 number of the *Nation*, Mary accused her mother of disliking her and claiming for Jim honors in forensics and writing that she herself had earned. "For life played an ironic trick on my mother. The pretty and darling daughters were taken away, and only the unwished-for ugly duckling left, between the oldest and youngest sons. As if this were not enough, by the time the elder son was ripe for college there began to be signs that the daughter not the son was the clever one."[32]

Mary openly resented Jim's privileged status, and her mother's reliance upon his judgment and bragging about his achievements. *Earth Horizon* is one of many works in which (using the third-person pronoun) she chronicles her mother's affronts; yet the manner in which she sums up her resistance speaks of the tragic loneliness of her life as well as of her determination to become impervious to the "danger of giving away her gift to brother, husband, or lover. She had, for one thing, too much inherent drive; she had for another the good luck never to meet, until she had trademarked it to herself, with a man clever enough to take the measure of what she had to give" (*EH* 136).

Early on Austin recognized that her life could never be lived as an insider. As a mystic, she positioned herself at the margins of daily life in her relations with others and in her writing. The liminal status she consciously chose, which kept her aloof even from those closest to her, was the vantage point of truth. She used this perspective to infuse her stories with oracular clarity of vision. Nowhere does this emerge so clearly as in *Lost Borders*, a collection in which the narrator's voice (I am persuaded that the stories represent Austin's own utterances) speaks to the reader as from the shadows.

The venom she stored up about her place in the family poured forth in later years in letters to George. Her family's insensitivity to her genius left her querulously resigned. "My family has always taken the attitude of inferior minds toward what they did not understand, and assumed that I am always wrong because I did not agree with them. From my childhood on I have been accustomed to be treated as if I were morally and intellectually inferior to the rest of the family. *And I have not only believed it, I have known that this attitude is* something for my family to be ashamed of, and I have been ashamed for them."[33]

It is fair to say that Austin grew up skeptical of, if not antagonistic to, the traditional view of family. The summer after her father's death, the Hunters had been guests of her aunt Mary in Boston. It was a memorable summer, not least because it made Mary "dimly aware of the extent to which her mother was reshaping the family and her own affectional life around her eldest son, shaping him to that part it was so widely agreed was suitable to be played, and 'sweet' to observe him playing, as the widow's son" (*EH* 127). In a remarkably parallel autobiographical passage in *A Woman of Genius*, the central character reflects on the code of deference to men that she observed and absorbed in adolescence. "At times when I felt this going on in our house, there rose up like a wisp of fog between me and the glittering promise of the future, a kind of horror of the destiny of women." The narrator, Olivia, denounces the requirement of true womanhood "to defer and adjust, to maintain the attitude of acquiescence toward opinions and capabilities that had nothing more to recommend them than merely that they were a man's!" (*WOG* 75). Austin's adult rage against the irrational differentiation of women from men owed much to the lively debate about androcentrism in contemporary American and British social sciences.

As a young woman, Austin's views reflected those of the "new" social scientists who were advancing theories positing the basis of gender inequality. Lester Ward (with whose work she was familiar), Thorstein Veblen, and Charlotte Perkins Gilman argued that women's subordinate status perpetuated an unjust social scheme based on gender. Due to an evolutionary mistake, according to this reasoning, women who had once been superior in a gynocentric society had lost their position by choosing male consorts who eventually dominated them.

Ward, Veblen, and Gilman agreed that women's ornamental position in society was due not to natural inferiority, but rather to an imposed inferiority. Ward's liberal evolutionary theory granted women a natural endowment of intuition that, tempered with education, would fit them to be congenial companions for men. In rebutting the natural inferiority of women, Ward argued that "in spite of Mr. Grant Allen [a prominent evolutionist] and the chivalrous band who stand with him around this little pen to keep [women] in, a considerable number of the precious creatures have already got out, and others are daily escaping."[34]

Daughter of the Household

After her father's death, Mary perceived her family outside of the normative view of "family" life in Carlinville. She judged Jim unexceptional in every way, certainly unworthy to assume the position of head of the household. His monopoly on their mother's scant resources of love and affection grew increasingly intolerable to her. The festering antipathy toward her mother and brothers evolved into a canker that is impossible to overlook in considering her development as a writer and intellectual figure. "The attitude of my family was crushing," she asserts in describing their mockery of her literary ambitions.

Reflecting upon her achievements in the autobiographical piece in the *Nation*, she tried to distance the bitterness by assuming the role of a cultural historian. "For the greater part of the nineteenth century . . . it was not only usual but proper for parents openly to deplore that the sons had not inherited talents inconveniently bestowed upon the daughters." Austin called her readers' attention to "current if out-moded novels of that period, such, for example as the novels of Madame Sarah Grand or May Sinclair's 'Mary Olivier'" to support her analysis. "Looking back on the idea of a literary career which prevailed in the Middle West of that period, it was probably as well for me that nobody knew" about her literary talent, she declared.[35]

But while she understood the etiology of her family's insensitivity, Mary could never forgive them for real and imagined slights.[36] One of these slights had to do with her education as she compared it to Jim's. Both attended Blackburn College in Illinois, but because of health problems, Mary was sent to the State Normal School in Bloomington in 1885–86. She scorned the education she received there for its "regimentation of method, of pedagogical sleights, of tricks and devices . . . to accomplish the great American desideratum of getting everybody, no matter of what type or degree of capacity through the eight grades of the public school system" (*EH* 155).

Twice during her college years she suffered what could be termed nervous breakdowns. The first, in 1885, she attributed to the "cruel and incessant" pace of the State Normal School, where she drove herself to conform to a stultifying curriculum devoid of creativity (*EH* 152). Mary further ascribed her ill health to the conditions of the school, the lack of outdoor exercise, and the absence of fresh vegetables in her diet. The same malady recurred later in California, owing, in Mary's view, to the canned food upon which the homesteaders subsisted in their barren environment. The doctor's decision to send her home from college for a rest, however, was consistent with received medical knowledge in the late nineteenth century about women's physical incapacity for sustained intellectual endeavor. Women's brains, it was generally acknowledged, were ill suited for such work. Even doctors in small midwestern towns were conversant with the theoretical connection between a woman's uterus and her nervous system.

Institutions of higher education had begun to formulate policy based on the reasoning of the medical establishment. An 1877 statement of the University of Wisconsin regents summarized widely held views about university education for women. "Education is greatly to be desired, but it is better that the future matrons of our state should be without a University training than that it should be produced at the expense of ruined health; better that the future mothers of the state should be robust, hearty, healthy women, than by over study, they entail upon their descendants the germs of disease." [37]

But Mary was not about to be denied her college education because of the prevailing medical opinion about female mental overexertion. In fact, during "the interval of her convalescence . . . she began to realize that the breakdown represented for her the need of a quicker intellectual tempo, a more expansive and varied rhythm" (*EH* 156–57). In her conclusion, one is reminded of Alice James, the intellectually stifled sister of Henry and William James, whose neurasthenia abated to a degree when she was free of the Boston family environment. Touring Europe in 1882 renewed her with "energy and elasticity [that] astounded her family." [38]

Neurasthenia, the "national disease," struck across class lines. While victims like Alice James, Charlotte Perkins Gilman, Jane Addams, and Edith Wharton received therapy away from home at the hands of S. Weir Mitchell and his disciples, Mary was treated at home in Carlinville by her family physician. She probably followed the standard regimen of a carefully managed diet, bed rest, and abstinence from reading or other mental work. Dr. Mitchell asserted that isolation from family was essential, but the Hunters would not have been able to afford such expensive therapies as private nurses or a rest cure at a clinic.

Returning to Blackburn College furnished Mary with a new environment that sustained her health. She enjoyed the atmosphere of the Presbyterian school near Carlinville and found science a stimulating major at a time when modern scientific methodology was just entering the classroom (*EH* 167). The study of science, particularly biology, was opening up the debate about gender differences and challenging entrenched biological doctrines of women's passivity and emotional lability as opposed to men's supposed rationality and assertiveness. [39] Austin developed a lifelong interest in the objectivity claimed by science with regard to women's biological capabilities as distinct from those that resulted from cultural conditioning. In electing her major she anticipated a trend in American universities that elevated science to new heights, following the model of German universities. Even literary studies were undertaken with "scientific ardor" and "the whole realm of academic culture" was "suddenly magnetized by the methods and the prestige of science."[40] As an established writer, Austin participated in the public discussions of the issue, often reaching idiosyncratic conclusions that were at odds with much contemporary feminist theory. In the main, however, she agreed with those who believed that women were acculturated to their roles in society.[41]

Nevertheless, during her college years, Mary tried to justify the curriculum she had chosen to her mother, who criticized her "instability of purpose." Mary had stated so adamantly her desire to write; wouldn't an English major be more suitable? Mary persistently argued that she could teach herself English, but "for science I have to have laboratories and a teacher" (*EH* 167). Later she would contend in print that "a new type of writer will have to be evolved, writers whose approach is purely literary but who are capable of immersing themselves in the data of science to the point of saturation," a task that "may easily prove superior to the average literary career."[42] Although she bristled against male dominance as she saw it enacted in the Hunter household, it apparently never occurred to her in college to take issue with the male-dominated discourse of the scientific curriculum.

Mary's college career became a hard-fought contest against her family. "I won a college degree by dint of insisting on it, and by crowding its four years into two and a half while my brother had the full four years," she wrote. And she believed that she came away with the education she fought for only because "with a college education I could teach, and teaching was regarded then a profession, eminently suited to women." Since she considered herself physically unattractive in her family's eyes, she interpreted her education as the family's "concession to the necessity of my earning a living."[43]

In her struggle to gain a college education, Mary was not unlike other "modern women." Even in wealthy families parents fretted over their daughters' "extradomestic ambitions," as in the case of anthropologist Elsie Clewes Parsons, who settled for her father's "grudging permission to enroll at Barnard," according to Rosalind Rosenberg's study of intellectual women at the turn of the century.[44] Blackburn introduced Mary to the world of ideas and permitted her to test her intellectual powers in writing and discussion. She sarcastically maintained that college did nothing more for Jim than to put him "at a higher level of reading interest than would otherwise have been the case" (*EH* 169). In her autobiographical account of Hunter family history, Blackburn merely provided her brother with the credentials to "join the University Club of Los Angeles, among men whom he would have greatly missed if he had been excluded" (*EH* 169).

At Blackburn Mary discovered that as "profoundly as she was stirred by higher mathematics in a strange aching way," she was not a gifted mathematician. She dabbled in "something called political economy . . . and psychology. . . . Then there was the flying trapeze of logic, and something called theology, proving that, since there can be no watch without a Watchmaker, so there can be no Universe without a Creator" (*EH* 168). Mary characterized her formal education as a succession of "smatterings" and "dabs," but forty years later she recalled that her Blackburn days were "happy and important seeming" (*EH* 175).

The Lure of the West

Family responsibilities collared Jim as soon as he graduated from Blackburn in 1886. He showed an interest in medicine (which his mother frowned upon) and taught school during his first year out of college. Casting about for a life of his own, he responded hopefully to the news of southern California's growth and development from his cousin George Dugger, who had emigrated there. Jim had little agricultural experience, but he was under considerable pressure to fulfill his mother's expectations and make his own way in the world; California may have represented an escape from his responsibilities as much as an opportunity. When he departed for the coast, preceding the rest of the family and leaving his sweetheart behind, he sought out other relatives, including the George Dugger clan.

During the 1880s California boom, publicity about free and cheap public lands and emigrants' guides extolling the area's possibilities and the ease and comfort of travel westward were readily available from the railroads, whose promotional literature ballyhooed the extensive tracts of land they had purchased to facilitate development. To attract settlers in the post-pioneer period, the railroads publicized the West as everyone's dream—a land of sunshine where fortunes could easily be made not by picking gold from the ground, as in the 1840s, but by picking fruit from the trees and grapes from the vines. "The possessor of a few acres in orange trees is lifted above the ordinary drudgery of farm labor. . . . Reliable authorities say that an acre of orange trees twelve years old will surely yield $1,000 per year," declared the Atchison, Topeka, and

Santa Fe literature. As for grapes, the work of harvesting "is so light and pleasant that the labor of women and children can be employed."[45]

Jim Hunter could hardly be blamed for succumbing to the tales of the extraordinary cultivation of fruits, especially citrus, or the hyperbolic anecdotes of great oil deposits and cheap electric power. This western paradise did exist, especially around Los Angeles; but Los Angeles, securely in the hands of the development interests, was decidedly not where the free land was. Nor could Jim know that he would arrive at the beginning of the post-boom decline, given the optimistic news he had received from his relatives in California.

The come-on to new settlers portrayed California as a lush, Edenic environment with cheap land prices and, in some sections, land free for the taking. As Charles Dudley Warner wrote a few years later, "California is our commercial Mediterranean. The time is not distant when this corner of the United States will produce in abundance, and year after year without failure, all the fruits and nuts which for a thousand years the civilized world of Europe has looked to the Mediterranean to supply." He included in that list of California comestibles "raisins, English walnuts, almonds, figs, olives, prunes, oranges, lemons, limes, and a variety of other things."[46] By the time the Hunter family reached California the most fertile public lands were gone, but like many settlers they were undaunted because they had heard that "the government and railroad lands [were] the cheapest, and possibly the best, in the State."[47] Only one barrier stood between the settler and wealth: water.

Irrigation in Southern California was, the experts agreed, "far cheaper than manure on an Eastern farm" and often could be achieved cooperatively "by means of windmills, which pump water into small tanks." Charles Nordhoff optimistically stated that even the sparsely settled, cheap land at the foot of the Sierra Nevada could support profitable wine making ventures as well as raisin growing. "Men do here more easily what they used to do in Illinois and Indiana—buy a farm, and with their first crop clear all their expenses and the price of the land." However, Nordhoff admonished strongly against settling in the most arid areas. "Water is not scarce in California, but there are tracts of land which have it not, and these it is best to avoid. It is astonishing how small a stream answers every purpose; and to an Eastern man few things are more surprising than the ease, skill, and cheapness with which a small stream is tapped by half a dozen California farmers according to a plan matured at a 'ditch meeting,' led into a reservoir, and made available for irrigation."[48]

Water remained a passionate interest for Austin, even a metaphor for her life: lack of it doomed her family's land venture in the late 1880s and early 1890s, while, paradoxically, the drought-plagued area of Inyo near the Mojave Desert, the subject of her first book and early stories, provided a creative wellspring.

From Carlinville to California

Jim's journey to Pasadena in 1888 caused his family extreme emotional distress. Mary recalled the "anxious inquiry for letters, the waiting, walking the floor, the weeping in the night; the arrival of the letter and the relief of reading it over and over to anybody who would listen, the happy hour of answering it, the waiting again" (*EH* 176). Mrs. Hunter, left behind with Mary and George in Carlinville, had entered into something like a second period of widowhood.

Others from Carlinville had relocated to California and, in Mrs. Hunter's judgment, the proper place for the rest of the family was with Jim. She planned to cross the plains by rail after Mary's graduation in the spring of 1888. Although Mary insisted that Jim deserved a life of his own, she empathized with her mother's sense of loss. Ambivalence about this situation continued to disturb her. She later wrote in *A Woman of Genius*, "I do not yet know how to deal with sufficient tenderness and without exasperation with the disposition of widowed women, bred to dependence, to build out of their sons the shape of a man proper to be leaned on" (p. 73).

Mary's writings indicate that she was initially unenthusiastic about the trip, fearing that she would simply end up being trapped in another Carlinville. Pasadena in the late 1880s contained so many Midwesterners that it was known as "the Indiana colony." By 1888 Illinois emigrants represented a sizable population in Los Angeles, with 859 registered voters, the fifth largest group in the city after native Californians, New Yorkers, Ohioans, and Pennsylvanians.[49] Despite its rapidly growing population of twelve thousand, Mary described Pasadena as "a city of residences, beautiful as the dream of a poet, but quite staid and sedate, and proud of its quietness."[50]

"Before the Pacific Coast filled up with Mid Westerners it was a gorgeous, an exciting place to be," Austin reminisced in her 1926 *Nation* article. She must have been speaking of California before she and her family found its "natural beauty slavered over with the impudicity of purely material culture." So self-conscious was the West Coast about this image among eastern visitors that it unashamedly boasted how like their home it was. Pasadena's hotels in 1889, for example, were described as "well appointed, and better kept, and . . . of such sort that the traveler, were it not for the fact that he is one of a crowd, would easily imagine himself at his own home surrounded by its comforts."[51]

Despite Mary's reluctance, the idea of moving westward no doubt opened up many possibilities to her imagination. Her only previous travel had been a family trip to her aunt Mary's house in Boston after her father's death, where they visited literary shrines and relatives (*EH* 96–97).[52] In response to her plan to teach and write, her mother observed that California might serve as well as any other place. Like many who emigrated, Mary had gleaned a scant knowledge of California from the literature of Bret Harte and Helen Hunt Jackson, whose writing she admired, although she shared her father's predilection for the English poets and novelists.

Regarding their move to the coast as something of an excursion, the Hunters stopped over for almost a week in Denver to visit Carlinville friends. Mary's colorful sketch of the coach journey on the Union Pacific conveys the flavor of such an expedition in the 1880s:

> We traveled "tourist," a special provision for the flocks of home-seekers which, in spite of the recent collapse of the California "boom," crowded westward with their families and as much of their goods as the passenger traffic allowed. As "tourist" you were permitted to carry your own food, with arrangements for making tea and warming up the baby's milk, and otherwise full Pullman accommodations minus the green plush and obsequiousness of porters. Also you had to listen to an intolerable amount of repetitious comment; people reading railroad guides aloud to each other; men travelers counting the family wash hung out at farmhouses, to guess, from the reduplication of feminine wearing apparel, whether it was or wasn't a polygamous household. (*EH* 181)

Before they set off for their homesteading land in the southernmost area of the San Joaquin Valley, an area in the hills of Kern County called the Tejon, Mrs. Hunter, Mary, and George lingered to see the sights of San Francisco, where Aunt Mary and Uncle Charlie Lane operated a boardinghouse (a common means of getting started in business on the coast). The Hunters toured the city with their fellow boarders, stopping to see the Chinese quarter and other attractions. From there they proceeded south to the newly sprouted suburb of Monrovia, where Jim had a job in a drugstore. After a short visit, the family traveled to Los Angeles in late summer of 1888 to stay with George Dugger. Los

Angelinos were self-consciously proud of their position as the second largest city in the state. The population of ninety thousand grew to a hundred thousand by the end of the century. The atmosphere of the city was tense; "it was the end of the first land boom, [and] everybody [was] busted," Mary wrote.[53] But to the Hunters, Los Angeles, with the old John Charles Frémont house and adobes, its heterogeneous population including the Spanish and the "Chinese merchants in native dress, carrying fans" in Chinatown, must have seemed fascinating and exotic, a fulfillment of the wonders promised in the guidebooks.

Mary took in the unfamiliar contours of the land; its rich colors stayed with her always. Almost effortlessly, words came to her to describe the scene. Within her welled up a western aesthetic based upon California's irresistible physical beauty, one that "affronted the puritan temperament with its too abundant charm; gold it was, and blue and amber, over miles and miles of up-flung foot-hill slopes and indolent mesa. Beyond that it melted, between green and blueness, to peaks of opalescent white. It was a country of which one of the wittiest of its writers said, 'You couldn't tell the truth about it without lying,' and got into the blood of the Iowans and New Englanders within a generation. It charged not only their hopes, but their speech; made it rich in figures, full of warmth and amplitude."[54]

"One Hundred Miles on Horseback"

Accompanied by friends, the Hunters set off in late 1888 for the Tejon, hoping to farm in an area quite unlike their native Illinois. Mrs. Hunter, Jim, and George traveled in a wagon, Mary on horseback. If they had known that only parched, unirrigated land free for the filing awaited them, in every way a contrast to the "rich and very easily cultivated" soil Nordhoff had described in his guide, doubtless spirits would not have run so high during the journey. Yet it was well known that the region had many desert-like patches that were scarcely suitable for any agricultural undertaking.

With only his younger brother to help, and responsibility for the family resting on his shoulders, Jim's situation must have appeared grim. He had little experience to draw on or equipment to use in building shelter and harvesting a food crop. For twenty-one-year-old Mary, however, the journey to the extreme southern tip of the San Joaquin Valley (see map) was an epiphanic experience that moved her to write "One Hundred Miles on Horseback." She sent her account

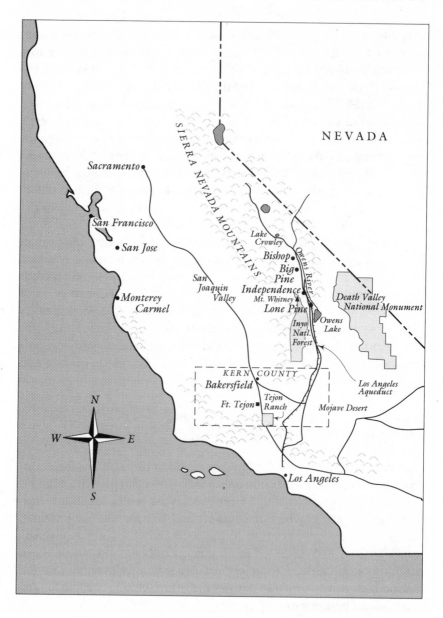

Map of southern California, showing places where Mary Austin lived.

to the *Blackburnian* at Blackburn College, where it was published in 1889.[55] A writer seldom hits full stride with her first work, but Mary Hunter's rhapsodic account of her introductory encounter with the land, a varied landscape of valleys, canyons, deserts, and mountains, proved a tour de force of descriptive writing that more mature American nature writers have failed to achieve until late into their careers. Sarah Orne Jewett, for example, took "twenty-five years not only of experimenting with words, but of charging them with a richness of an unfolding and ripening nature, before she [could] write a description that would not merely record the facts, but would enmesh the light and shadow, the shifting clouds and restless air," according to her biographer, F. O. Matthiessen.[56]

At first the autumnal California landscape "made us homesick for the glory of the October hills of Illinois," Mary recounted (*OHM* 3). But as she rode on horseback into the San Joaquin Valley, the land gradually freed her imagination. She wrote of the "indescribably awesome" experience of "traveling thus in the fast deepening twilight through these narrow gorges where the mountains close in upon us so silently and mysteriously that one unfamiliar with such scenes would declare there is no outlet in either direction" (p. 14).

The language of exhilaration so brilliantly deployed by this writer has caused more than one critic to locate her genius in the western nature essay. Franklin Walker described Austin as a woman with "a keen ability at perception and recording impressions, and an appreciation of transcendental thought as expressed by Emerson, Thoreau, and John Muir." The credo of transcendentalism—that nature heals, teaches, and enraptures and "is permeated with the spirit of God"— gave her "a theme and form on which rests her major claim to literary fame."[57] Hence, "One Hundred Miles on Horseback" limns a journey of liberation encompassing body and spirit. "On previous nights the petticoated members of our party had camped in the wagon, but to-night, wrapped in our blankets, Indian fashion, we lay peacefully down under the bright stars of California in the shadow of the majestic mountains—and snored." Such details resonate with the concerns familiar to diarists of overland journeys of the 1840s and 1850s. "The next day being Sunday we rested a part of the day," Mary continued in her account of the week-long trek from Pasadena to the Tejon, "but owing to the difficulty of finding suitable camping places, were obliged to break camp about three o'clock in the afternoon" (pp. 14-15).

Yet, her narrative of this first momentous encounter with the land transcends the routine details of daily life and crystalizes in exquisite

language the writer's perception of grandeur, adventure, and sacred-
ness in "the landscape line" of the West. Although Kern County, their
destination, was considered "the poorest in natural resources in Southern California," containing "great tracts" that could "never be available
for any practicable purpose," Mary was oblivious to its disadvantages,
so intense was her pleasure in the aesthetic experience it offered.[58] The
Tejon's lush vegetation prompted her to declare: "Never have I seen
such magnificent trees as the live oaks that crowded each other in the
canyon and on the hills. Festoons of grapevines hung from the willows
across the noisy stream, and heavy garlands of mistletoe dropped from
the branches of oak and sycamore" (*OHM* 17). But as the Hunters
moved farther east, where the oranges were "getting ripe and yellow
and the olives purpling under the December sun," and closer to the
parched parcel that they were to inhabit, the land became increasingly
stark. At journey's end Mary wrote that "the tarantulas sun themselves
on our roof at night, and gray coyotes come trotting up under our very
windows" (pp. 18-19).

Mary found California's variousness immensely seductive. Unlike
male writers who described the frontier in terms of brutal ravishment,
she experienced the land as neither its ravisher nor its victim. Annette
Kolodny employs a gendered interpretation of the land in her examination of the generation of women diarists and writers before Austin.
From close readings of frontier diaries, she argues that women saw
nature as a garden to be cultivated rather than a virgin to be despoiled;
she makes a persuasive case that women characteristically came to terms
with the land by domesticating it. "Avoiding for a time male assertions
of rediscovered Eden," Kolodny writes, "women claimed the frontiers
as a potential sanctuary for idealized domesticity. . . . They dreamed
. . . of locating a home and a familial human community within a cultivated garden."[59] Austin, however, was not moved to domesticate the
land she first encountered in California; in fact, she seemed content to
celebrate its proud unavailability for garden plots and agriculture.

The eerie beauty that Austin perceived proved a nightmare for the
settlers who depended on agriculture for a living. When the Hunters
arrived in the Tejon Valley, the housing situation was bleak: simple
shanties had been hastily erected to fulfill the conditions of land claims.
The family endured these rough surroundings until spring, when
Edward Fitzgerald Beale, the often-absentee owner of the prosperous
Tejon Ranch, offered Mary and her mother lodging at Rose Station,
an unoccupied stage hostelry. In return the two women cooked meals,
while George and Jim cared for livestock to earn their keep.[60]

The culinary skills that Mary had acquired in pie-baking contests and cooking for the family in Carlinville served her well in these early California days; however, her college training and intellectual interests pushed her toward teaching to earn a living. While she prepared for the teacher's examination, her restless mind reveled in experiencing the land and talking with its inhabitants. Drawing away from her fellow settlers and gravitating toward the Indians and others who would share the land's mysteries with her, she became an oddity among her own, even a subject of gossip.[61]

The acquaintance that the Hunters struck up with General Beale proved key to Mary's literary career. Beale was an early settler who had played a seminal role in California's development. As a young lieutenant he had been dispatched to Washington with the official evidence of the discovery of gold, and he had been California's first superintendent of Indian affairs. Mary found him an immensely interesting man, a bibliophile and a mine of folkloric information about the Tejon area, where descendants of the surviving California tribes still lived. He enthusiastically shared with her geological and botanical surveys, and government documents on agriculture and military expeditions, much of which she incorporated into *The Land of Little Rain* (1903), *The Flock* (1906), and the tales later collected in *One Smoke Stories* (1934).

Beale, then in his late sixties, had known "Kit" Carson, whom he remembered as "a man pure, not lustful, calm, serious, sweet, [of] moderate stature, broad front, head of remarkable size, by no means robust but of immense endurance, [and] nerves of steel."[62] Mary thrilled to the story of how Beale had saved the day for General Stephen Kearney and his men in 1846, when "Kearney's entire command became surrounded on a barren hilltop by the superbly mounted California lancers who planned to starve the Americans into surrender." He amused her with anecdotes, such as one about his stint as surveyor of the wagon road between Fort Defiance in New Mexico and the Colorado River when he was appointed commander of the first U.S. Camel Corps. In California Beale had united several racial groups in making a success of his vast Tejon Ranch, a truly remarkable feat that had eluded owners of the great Spanish ranchos before him.[63]

Next to her father, Mary had never met a man so enchanting. Beale expected nothing more than interest, and she was freed from self-consciousness with him because she knew he valued her intellect. While her fellow settlers considered Mary somewhat odd, he accepted her for what she was—an intense young woman with an unquenchable appetite for the country that lay before her. As he patiently described what he knew of the area and the people who lived there, Mary made detailed notes, a habit she retained throughout her literary life. In 1917 she came across some of "these chips of my earlier workshop" and appended a typed memorandum that illuminates her creative process:

> There were such quantities of the words, facts, fortunate phrases jotted down on any scrap of paper that came to hand. It was a relief to the poignancy with which every thing in nature affected me. I was too much alive to these things, almost a part of the[m], I suffered. Nobody around me cared in the least.
>
> I wrote them down and after I had written a book I used to go through my notes and destroy everything I had used in the book. Even with that precaution I used to repeat. . . . It took me years to let the thing go out of my mind, the picture[,] the poignant perception. It was always necessary to my happiness to do something with these gleanings of the wild. After I had found just the right use for a descriptive phrase, the final absolute use of it would leave me. I kept too much, was always indanger [*sic*] of using too much, putting too many good phrases into my book, not because they were good phrase[s] but because they were living perceptions that tormented me. I had to get my house in order. I am crowded, stiffled [*sic*] always with pictures. I know too much and not well enough. Fortunately those phrases of the Wild have been snowed under by later phrases of sophistication. These are merely reminders[;] drift of a flood. As such they may interest somebody.[64]

General Beale's vast knowledge of the West nourished her during a physical breakdown—probably from malnutrition—in her first months of homesteading on the dry Tejon in 1889. As she rode with him around the countryside and compiled notes, Mary began to see the Tejon almost from the perspective of an ethnographer. Beale's friendship and attentions healed her mentally, as the fresh air did physically. While recuperating, she took a position tutoring the children of the Pyle family and teaching in the school that Darius Pyle, manager of Mountain View Dairy, maintained for the children in the vicinity. Boarding with the Pyles after this period of "something like a complete collapse," away from the strains of her family, restored the health she had lost because of "undernourishment . . . to which nobody paid any attention" (*EH* 192–93).

That first winter the Hunters subsisted mainly on canned food, which Mary detested and rejected. Whether she suffered from what modern medicine terms anorexia—an eating disorder that afflicts women who perceive themselves to be starved for familial love—can only be a conjecture. Mary states that she cured herself by discovering wild grapes in a Tejon canyon. In truth, the more friendships she developed outside her family, the better she felt. Separation from family, often cited as a modern therapy for anorexics, led to her recovery.[65]

California required teachers in the state system to take a particularly rigorous examination. Mary failed it twice, but she continued to teach at the dairy, a congenial position that offered some social opportunities. The Pyle children encircled her with the love and caring that she missed in her own family. That spring was a time of keen observation. Years later she recalled how in May and June the herders "would go peering along the edge of the down-pouring rivers for the floating yellow scum, pollen drift from the forests hundreds of miles away on the uplifted flanks of the Sierras. By the date of the first appearance of the floating pollen, and the quantity, they judged whether the summer feed would be full or scanty, and on indications as slight as these they bargained with the dealers who came out from San Francisco for their spring lambs." Perhaps referring to her own development as a poet, Mary writes, "Intimacies such as these between land and the people breed poets faster, and much better ones, than do universities."[66] She would write further of the shepherds' habits in *Isidro* (1905) and *The Flock*, first in the district of the Tejon and then in the Owens Valley.

In 1891, however, Mary was developing another kind of intimacy. The previous summer she had met Stafford Wallace Austin at the May Ranch and agreed to marry him. Wallace, a graduate of the University of California and a member of a transplanted New England family, had spent his youth in Hawaii. He and his brother Frank were speculating in the Inyo area with the idea of establishing vineyards there. Having lost all of his belongings in the Bakersfield fire of 1889, Wallace had bought a twenty-acre property near the city, where he would eventually build a house for himself and Mary. Their wedding took place in May 1891.

2

▲ ▲ ▲

THE EARLY CALIFORNIA YEARS

She would be looking at something that all the world could see, had seen,

without being stirred by it, and suddenly, from deep down, there would come a

fountain jet of recognition.

—Earth Horizon

Mary had physically separated from her mother and brothers when she began teaching privately in 1890. Her status as an unmarried woman employed as a teacher at the Mountain View Dairy underscored her modest independence. Mary liked teaching her few pupils. In 1897, after twice failing the county teacher's examination, she finally became eligible for a position in the public school system. Wallace may have helped her obtain this qualification through his position as school superintendent.

Methodism had given her the opportunity to develop certain pedagogical skills when she taught Sunday school in Carlinville as a teenager. As a result of her early success, she accounted herself a "naturally good teacher; never at a loss for a word, a cross-reference, a memorable illustration" (*EH* 208), and she was remembered favorably by her students.[1] (Her talent to hold people's attention would later serve her well on the lecture platform.) She used her skills of observation to enrich students' awareness of natural beauty and the rhythms of the land, sometimes by making poetry. In the preface to *The Children Sing in the Far West*, Austin explains that it contained "songs that children could have for their own. Partly because I was teaching school and felt obliged to have something for my pupils about the land they lived in, and partly because I loved the land so much I couldn't bear not having grown up in it, I made most of the poems in this collection with the help of the children in my school."[2] Through her work, new friendships, and independent living situation, Mary was seeking her own path.

General Beale continued to help her meet older men whose interest was comradely rather than romantic. She was fascinated by the powerful Anglos who owned the large, post-frontier California ranches—men whom Frank Norris would celebrate in his novels of "the primitive and brutal," especially *The Octopus* (1901), set in the San Joaquin Valley where Mary lived.[3] She herself would come to terms with such men in her novel *The Ford*, a vivid portrait of the period of American acquisition of the Mexican land-grant ranchos. Beale introduced her to indigenous inhabitants, workers, and others who knew the lore of the Tejon country intimately, providing sources for the stories she would interpret in her writing. Although Beale left no written record of the relationship with his protégée, he apparently found in her important qualities worth his time and trouble.[4] Among those Mary met through him were José Jesus Lopez, a member of one of the distinguished old Hispanic families, and former sheeprancher James Vineyard Rosemeyre, manager of the Tejon Ranch store.

Beale probably introduced her to Henry Miller, a powerful, German-born rancher whose "decisions were Jovian in effect" (*EH* 204). Unlike Wallace Austin, Miller had the "capacity to arrive directly without noticeable fumbling at the structural features of any situation, and to maintain with the main structures and immense amount of detail," a quality Mary admired immensely. His "essentially Nordic" manner of handling the land was equally attractive to her (*EH* 205). In Beale Mary had encountered a man of extraordinary sophistication and administrative abilities who, by the combination of power, money, sensitivity, and knowledge, had realized the dream of the old Hispanic patriarchal ranchos in a way that traditional ranchers had never achieved.[5] He and other powerful men came to represent, if subliminally, father/hero figures with whom Austin longed to claim affiliation. To compensate for the devastating loss of her father and the failure of her brothers to measure up to her ideal of maleness, she fit men like Beale and Miller into a mythology of strength and virility. In her imagination they assumed the stature of "Jovian" beings who knew her for the exceptional person she considered herself to be. In 1889 and 1890 she absorbed, spongelike, the personal histories and adventures of such men. Later she would transform them into books—notably *The Flock*,

Isidro, and *The Ford*—and short fiction. From the silence and solitude of the parched, sun-baked land, she created a flourishing inscape that prepared her to write *The Land of Little Rain*.[6]

In repudiating her midwestern background, Austin found a community of friends among "the shy hairy shepherds, taciturn, given to seeing visions, who might have been David's brethren on the ancient plains" and who, according to her friend Van Wyck Brooks, returned her admiration. Brooks imagines her sitting under the stars among these desert people, sharing their garlic-spiked venison and acquiring a mysticism that resulted from "a kind of concentration that narcotized the outer man and evoked both hallucinations and genuine powers." In Brooks's assessment, the mysticism revealed in Austin's writings was both a curse and a blessing. Through her association with the Indians she absorbed what was authentic of their experience, and Brooks greatly admired her vast knowledge of Indian ritual and lore. But he also believed that her "adoration of the Indians" lay behind her failure to "establish a real relation with the world beyond the desert." Like many critics then and now, Brooks found her writing "always abortive when she left this world," as she did in her less successful novels and critical writing.[7] Austin has been likened to the visual artist Maynard Dixon, her California contemporary, who associated the world of the Indians with "an older, better way of knowledge and behavior."[8]

Writing from the "Wild Zone"

Because Brooks, like most male critics of this period, was not prepared to examine the gender-related cultural ideals that shaped his view of literature, he was unable to see that Austin was writing from what feminist theorist Elaine Showalter terms "the wild zone" when she situated her work in the desert or in the area she called "lost borders." Almost from the first, Austin set some of her best work outside of patriarchal strictures and structures.[9] Other women writers who have taken the land and its indigenous inhabitants as their subjects have been faulted when they stray from what is perceived to be their territory. For example, Isak Dinesen, the Danish author best remembered for her collection *Out of Africa*, was thought most successful when she wrote about the Kikuyo people among whom she lived and least successful when she made connection with a more recognizable European world.[10]

In contrast to Austin, the California writer Gertrude Atherton betrays the racism of the privileged class toward native Americans. She describes the Digger Indians of California as "brainless, little higher in the scale of life than the wild beast of their plains and forests." Atherton's attitude was in tune with the commonly held views of Anglo racial superiority in her period, bolstered by arguments that Indians were naturally backward. She spoke for many of her generation when she asserted that the Indian "is far below any white standard, and there is no evidence of modern or any sort of civilization in his villages."[11] Austin, on the other hand, found spiritual liberation from the restraints of Methodism through the Indian way of life. Historian Richard Drinnon has acknowledged her sincerity in praising Austin's connection with the Paiutes, Yokuts, Washoes, Utes, Shoshones, and other American Indians. "Unlike the historian [Frederick Jackson Turner] and his pioneers, Mary Austin took the trouble to enter Indian lives, found therein the reverse of 'primitive' simplicity, gave way to their rhythmic utterances, and thereby experienced a true rebirth in the spirit of the land."[12] If we judge authentic the writer's earliest mystical encounters with nature—the shock of recognition when she realized that her deepest self communed with what Emerson called the "Over-Soul"—then Drinnon's assessment suggests an important aspect of her character.

Nonetheless, Austin never escaped the charges of inferiority leveled at women writers as a group. Late in her career, she expressed her opinion on the subject in a letter to Henry Seidel Canby, a literary friend, professor of English at Yale, and editor of the *Saturday Review of Literature*. "If you will observe the meannesses which women feel at liberty to uncover in men, they are chiefly meanness [*sic*] of sex behavior, which are always debatable, weakness of ignorance, of manners, of temperament, of provocation. Women do not . . . they cannot, in the very nature of their constitution, face the weakness which men seem to see as inherent in human kind. Deep within themselves, women can not speak the final contemptuous word of the species preceding out of their bodies." In this crucial statement Austin summarizes her deeply held conviction about why women were not reckoned "great in the way men reckon greatness" in drama, satire, or poetry.[13] What she seems to be saying is that since women writers are often mothers, they are constrained by this intimate bond from honestly observing, critiquing, and writing about men in the same free way that men observe, critique, and write about both men and women.

Although there is no evidence that Austin knew the work of Virginia Woolf, she and Woolf held remarkably similar views about the central problem of the woman novelist: telling the truth about a patriarchal society. "For if she begins to tell the truth," Woolf wrote, "the figure in the looking-glass shrinks; his fitness for life is diminished. How is he to go on giving judgment, civilizing natives, making laws, writing books, dressing up and speechifying at banquets, unless he can see himself at breakfast and at dinner twice the size he really is?"[14]

In this regard, it is interesting to examine Austin's effort to achieve a gender-neutral, mystical voice in many of her western stories, and her use of a male narrator's voice throughout the narrative of her last major novel, *Starry Adventure*. A convincing argument can be made that her conscious cultivation of this empowered voice, whether male or mystically gender-neutral, was instrumental in dislocating what had been thought to be women's perception of wilderness, as evidenced in the writings of the first generation of western women writers, mainly diarists.[15] It is tempting to speculate that by writing about the land, Indians, and others who lived on the fringes of Anglo society, Austin avoided the criticisms she faced in her later social novels, which sometimes suffer from the very constitutional weakness she outlined to Canby. When Austin allowed herself the luxury of speaking contemptuously of men in her most realistic fictions—*No. 26 Jayne Street*, for instance—she laid herself open to the most severe criticism.

Marriage

Such literary issues had only begun to gel in her mind when she met Wallace Austin. Mary's awakening to her vocation as a writer shunted her approaching marriage into the background. American women's marital expectations were shifting, especially in California, where new settlers had escaped the traditional social boundaries that had governed their intimate relationships in the small midwestern towns from which they had emigrated. Many young women looked forward vaguely to achieving a sense of fulfillment and an increased measure of personal autonomy in their relationships with men. Unfortunately for Wallace, he inadvertently strayed at the wrong time into Mary's life, and consequently into the private preserve of her imagination. This terrain was incomprehensible to him and even at times to Mary herself, as she discovered her identity as a writer. During their courtship, Wallace had seemed a sensitive lover. He read poetry aloud very well and appeared to possess refined literary tastes. However, Austin later confessed that this was only pretense, "the reading of poetry being a fairly familiar custom in courtships of the time."[16] Mary, the poet, creative worker, and "woman of genius," found Wallace, the engineer, painfully ordinary as they struggled toward the awesome intimacy of marriage.

During the couple's engagement, Jim and Mrs. Hunter soon faced up to the fiasco of the family's homesteading venture. They had learned the hard way the frustrations of owning land in an area plagued by drought that killed the cattle and rendered agriculture a futile enterprise. Full of hope, they had arrived in the San Joaquin Valley in the early nineties at the "peak of desolation," when "pocket gophers and kangaroo rats walked in the powder-dry furrows" stealing the seed sowed by the pessimistic settlers. When the cattle died, Mary wrote, the loam "was all black with buzzards and the horrid announcing croak of them" (*EH* 192).

In 1890, while Jim struggled to fulfill the five-year residence requirement on the land in order to claim ownership, Mrs. Hunter used funds realized from sale of the Carlinville house to purchase a small ranch close to well-irrigated Bakersfield, considerably to the southwest of the homestead. In claiming unowned public land, the Hunters unwittingly found themselves in what historians William Harland and Rodman Paul have called a "middle border"—an area removed from the area of cattle raising, requiring vast outlays of capital for irrigation to farm successfully, and lagging behind other areas in mining. Kern County for years had been marginal to many important commercial, mining, and agricultural activities, but never at the center.[17] Typical of those who had come from the black, moist "little Egypt" area of Illinois, the Hunters lacked the agricultural experience necessary to work land that was unsuitable for the crops they envisioned.

Their first homestead was so desolate that Mary never understood how Jim could have selected it when more desirable land was still available. Perhaps, like many of the newly arrived settlers, he was taken in by the irrigation schemes that were much talked about by developers but often came to naught.[18] These first years taught Mary a respect for water that was to mark her nature writing. "To underestimate one's thirst," she meditates, writing of the Mojave area, "to pass a given landmark to the right or left, to find a dry spring where one looked for running water—there is no help for any of these things" (*LOLR* 6). The Hunters learned quickly that there was no help for the farmer who failed to consider the water situation with due caution. Morally, because she advocated temperance, Mrs. Hunter could not abide the one crop they might have raised—grapes. At the Bakersfield property she acquired, the grapevines were torn out "root and branch . . . and nobody thought of counting the cost" (*EH* 219). Even the frequently

Mary and Wallace Austin's wedding portrait, 1891.

invoked rationalization of wine as a temperance beverage did not move her.

Hard times in the Hunter family, and the realization that men her own age failed to attract her interest and vice versa, may have caused Mary to engage herself to Wallace so quickly. Their simple wedding ceremony in May 1891 at Mrs. Hunter's Bakersfield home was remarkable for its lack of celebration. Mrs. Hunter remained notably reserved about her daughter's marriage (*EH* 22) and the two women scarcely discussed the matter before the wedding. Mary thought the important questions had been asked, while her mother dared not voice her objections to the match, for "there was always the consideration that a daughter married was a problem settled, a responsibility ridded." Mrs.

Hunter's reaction seems peculiar. According to Mary, her mother believed that Wallace did not measure up to the Hunter standard. Mrs. Hunter did not speak out against the marriage, however, and allowed her daughter " 'to meet her fate.' " [19]

In fact, Wallace's family was superior to Mary's as measured by wealth, education, and social class. When Mary's father was a shoe clerk in Carlinville, Wallace's father, Stafford Lapham Austin, was serving as a high-ranking governmental secretary in Hawaii. In 1856 he married Caroline Hannah Clark, the daughter of missionaries and a descendant of Revolutionary War hero Edward Clark. Wallace and his brother Frank grew up on the island of Hilo, where their father owned a sugar plantation. When the family lost their fortune, Mr. Austin brought his sons to California to attend high school in Oakland. Wallace received his degree from the University of California at Berkeley.[20]

With regard to the sexual aspect of marriage, Mary's experience was much like that of Edith Wharton, whose mother responded negatively to her questions on the subject before her wedding day.[21] For both writers, sexuality expressed in marriage appears to have been disastrous from the first. If Edith Newbold Jones did the "inconceivable thing" (as Henry James termed it) in joining her life to Teddy Wharton's, a man oblivious of her real needs and interests, Mary Hunter's union with Wallace Austin was equally inconceivable. The similarities between the two women are striking: Both had widowed mothers whose limited vision for their daughters and lack of nurturant qualities made their relationships troubled and strained. Both rejected their mothers while cherishing the influence of their dead fathers. Both entered into unfortunate marriages, disastrously timed and stunting to their creative growth. And both did so for the same reason: marriage was expected of them.[22]

If Mary was drawn to Wallace because she trusted him to nurture her and her talent as General Beale had done, she was wrong. Although he was seven years older than she and had a superior education, Wallace's insecurities and failures before and during their marriage, and above all his lack of genuine empathy for Mary's creative work, ensured that the match would be riven by mutual misunderstanding.[23] Wallace's wedding gift to Mary—a pearl-handled pen—suggested that he approved of her plan to write. However, his actions proved that he did not fully understand how his wife's writing would affect their marriage. Mary knew no literary people at the time. If she had, she wrote in 1926, she might have learned before her marriage that domesticity and a literary career were incompatible for a woman in her circumstances.[24]

Spencer and James

When they married, Wallace probably had no inkling of his wife's bent toward "radicalism" as she defined it. Her idiosyncratic social and political philosophy was a selective blending of her reading of Darwin, Spencer, and Engels with the social theory that she later discussed with Jack London and others in Carmel and New York.[25] "I saw the beginning of institutionalized marriage out of natural monogamous mating as the species mark: the rise of capital, not out of greed and oppression as my urban contemporaries would have it, but out of the inescapable tendency of goods to accumulate around dominant personalities," Austin wrote in 1929, sculpting Marx to suit her argument. Instead of espousing Marxism, however, she articulated her own version of Spencerian social theory: "I watched man's primitive struggle with this tendency, which . . . since it happened before wage labor was invented, he found clogging. I watched the development of the city-state, and the inevitable evolution of republicanism into communism, and saw communism die of its own inhibitions."[26]

Austin, like London, was a disciple of Herbert Spencer, the English agnostic who popularized Darwinism, especially in the United States. She believed in the interrelatedness of all things and in the redistribution of matter and motion operating through the Darwinian principles of evolution.[27] However, Austin differed from Spencer on several key points, finding William James's pragmatism more to her taste. Indeed, like Gertrude Stein, Austin may have consciously incorporated a Jamesian philosophical and psychological view into her creative work. In discussing her own writing process, she frequently alluded to her extensive contact with the Indians, from whom she had learned many relaxation techniques used ritualistically by the tribes. She believed, along with James, that one could employ such knowledge consciously to unlock the inhibited sources of true creativity dormant in the unconscious.[28] In fact, she credited a "long talk" with James for convincing her that "there is no such thing as fatigue of the Mind, there is only fatigue of the instrument that Mind uses, and there are various planes of Mind which seem to be able to function at the same time in different keys," a phenomenon Austin likened to "receiving several messages over the same wire."[29] The conversation with William James probably took place in the winter of 1898, when he delivered a lecture in Oakland titled "The Power of Repose," based on Annie Payson Call's *Power through Repose*.

Austin claimed that such a method could be tapped to write an epic if she chose to do so. At the very least, her facility in moving from genre to genre in her own work was attributable to her ability to stand back from herself as a recipient of the messages that coursed through her. Even Jesus's mysticism could be reduced to his finely attuned aspect of genius. In a 1924 article, Austin called Jesus "the best exemplar of a man working harmoniously with his destiny, refusing nothing, repenting nothing, losing no ground."[30] Of her own work she stated rather simply, "There are . . . times when the intelligence is likely to interfere seriously with the working of the spontaneous knowingness of the individual."[31]

Early San Francisco Literary Connections

In the spring of 1891, the Austin brothers' enterprise appeared to be on a solid footing, but their attempt to establish successful vineyards hinged upon finding capital in San Francisco to irrigate the Owens Valley. Frank handled the financial details in the partnership, while Wallace studied viticulture. Unfortunately, Wallace was perhaps unduly influenced by the optimistic predictions of Charles Nordhoff, who wrote that in California he had "seen vines—such as grow only in hot-houses with us at home—which bore and matured clusters of grapes the same year in which the cuttings were planted."[32] The brothers' entry into the complex field of viticulture coincided with a recession in the industry, and their scheme soon failed.

Mary stayed resolutely at her writing desk, convinced "that her husband had no natural qualifications for the calling of the vineyardist" (*EH* 227). While Wallace's every venture floundered, she grew increasingly assured of her vocation. Her subjects—the land around her and the people she had encountered in California—were more compelling than anything she had ever experienced. At the same time she learned how uncomfortable Wallace was when she discussed her work. When he was called to San Francisco by his brother to work on a more ambitious irrigation project, she found her opportunity to give herself over completely to her writing. By the time Mary joined Wallace in the spring of 1892, she had finished two fine stories, "The Mother of Felipe" and "The Conversion of Ah Lew Sing," both simple, unsentimental tales written in a spare prose that was to give her work a distinctive style. "Only in the hearts of mothers lives unconsolable regret," she wrote about the burdens of maternity in "The Mother of Felipe." (Mary was pregnant at the time with their daughter Ruth.) In

"The Conversion of Ah Lew Sing," she tells a humorous story of sexual politics in the Chinese community with a sharp moral twist.[33] From the first Austin wanted to sell her work, and she looked toward the San Francisco market, targeting the *Overland Monthly* for her first stories. The magazine paid her twelve dollars for "The Mother of Felipe."

Austin entered the literary scene in San Francisco just as a new generation of talent was emerging. Jack London, former oyster pirate, cannery worker, and "sailor before the mast" (as he referred to himself), was on the threshold not only of a successful literary career—he was one of the first American writers to earn over one million dollars—but also of a life of radicalism and celebrity. Frank Norris's star would soon be in the ascendant, as well. Like London, he took as his subject the theme of strength, particularly of Anglo-Saxon dominance. His characters revelled in the heroic, even the primitive. Van Wyck Brooks wrote that Norris's fiction marked "the beginning of the 'cave-man' tendency in American writing that reappeared in Hemingway and John Steinbeck a generation later, and Jack London's exaltation of the 'primitive brutality' in the Anglo-Saxon was anticipated by Norris's description of the 'Anglo-Saxon's birthright.'"[34] Both Norris's and London's writing promised to infuse the San Francisco literary scene with unprecedented —and manifestly virile—energy.

Such fictions—whether their setting was a ranch, the Arctic, or Alaska—were simply unavailable to Austin because of the culturally inscribed gender restrictions that severely limited her access to "adventure" in the masculinist sense. Nina Baym argues in a pathbreaking critical essay about American fiction that "the [male] myth narrates a confrontation of the American individual, the pure American self divorced from specific social circumstances, with the promise offered by the idea of America." The only way this isolation can occur is to situate the main character in the wilderness "on which he may inscribe, unhindered, his own destiny and his own nature."[35]

Kevin Starr's critical assessment of Norris as the writer who "helped Californians in their quest for an imaginative relationship to the land," and the one who "came the closest in his generation's attempt to put the ranch era into significant fiction," must be understood as a positive response to the androcentric world created by Norris, a fictional representation of male codes and ideology.[36] In a letter to London, Austin wrote: "Yes I have a grouch against you. . . . Not against you so much as against all men writers for missing the essential feminine note of the day." She faulted him for failing to represent "the note of feminine power which is quite as powerful in its way as the power of men. . . . I notice in your work—thank heaven that you haven't pretended at any time to know much about women,—but I notice that though they show an increasing naturalness, your women are never really great women." She referred him to reformists Charlotte Perkins Gilman, Jane Addams, and Emmeline Pankhurst as examples of superior women upon whom he might model future heroines.[37]

In her novel *The Ford*, Austin created a prototype of her "new woman" in the form of Anne Brent, a savvy rancher who holds her own against the most notorious of rancho capitalists (modeled on Henry Miller, the millionaire rancher whom General Beale had introduced to her). Significantly, Brent achieves success on her own terms and chooses freely to relinquish romance and marriage in favor of female friendship and a life she has built for herself.

Later in their careers London, who liked to think of himself as a revolutionary (but never a reformist), criticized Austin for her feminism. And Austin, who knew London's limitations in fictively representing women, chided him in terms that foreshadowed later feminist criticism of American literature: "Like most males, you have no capacity for knowing superior women."[38]

Austin's advisor was Ina Coolbrith, the reigning matriarch of San Francisco literati. A generation older than Austin, Coolbrith herself had emigrated from Illinois in a Mormon wagon train; in fact, she was a niece of the Mormon prophet Joseph Smith. With Bret Harte and Charles Warren Stoddard (they were known as the "Golden Gate Trinity"), she edited the *Overland Monthly* and benignly presided over a group of writers that included Mark Twain and Joaquin Miller. Many of them drifted elsewhere over the years, but Coolbrith remained at her post in the Oakland Public Library, lending staunch support to the orphaned, the elderly, and the sick.[39] The literary friendship between Austin and Coolbrith was warm, especially on the older poet's part. Coolbrith's encouragement of the young writer during her sojourn in San Francisco filled a need at a time when Austin had no literary friends and when her own family remained cool and aloof toward her work; she relied on Coolbrith's guidance in preparing manuscripts and placing them for publication.[40] Coolbrith instilled in Austin a confidence about writing that proved inestimably important. Though Austin later dismissed the older woman as a "minor poet" and the *Overland Monthly* as "an unimportant publication," she had learned in San Francisco "how the trick was done" and asserted that now "she would fly higher" than Coolbrith (*EH* 232). Nevertheless, Coolbrith would later show an empathy that the young writer found wanting in other quarters.

The Move to the Owens Valley

After the productive spring of 1892, when Austin's time was taken up chiefly with the details of launching her literary career, she and Wallace moved to Inyo "into that region which is still largely known by the name she gave it, 'The Land of Little Rain'" (*EH* 232). The Indian name *Inyo* signified "dwelling place of a great spirit" (*LOLR* 117). While Wallace continued with his brother's promotion company, Mary awaited the birth of their child and drank in the stark, dry beauty of the Owens Valley. Its spectacular location, between the majestic mountains of the Sierra Nevada and the desolate splendor of Death Valley, ignited the writer's imagination. She regarded this place as no less than "delectable." In the preface to *The Land of Little Rain*, she wrote in anthropomorphic terms of a place that yielded up its beauties only to the patient beholder:

> The country where you may have sight and touch of that which is written lies between the high Sierras south from Yosemite—east and south over a very great assemblage of broken ranges beyond Death Valley, and on illimitably into the Mojave Desert. You may come into the borders of it from the south by a stage journey that has the effect of involving a great lapse of time, or from the north by rail, dropping out of the overland route at Reno. The best of all ways is over the Sierra passes by pack and trail, seeing and believing. But the real heart and core of the country are not to be come at in a month's vacation. One must summer and winter with the land and wait its occasions. Pine woods that take two and three seasons to the ripening of cones, roots that lie by in the sand seven years awaiting a growing rain, first that grow fifty years before flowering,—these do not scrape acquaintance. (*LOLR* xvi)

Mary's relationship with this barren place differed from Wallace's. While Mary wrote of being in mystical harmony with the land, Wallace fought an impossible political battle as an engineer for the Owens Valley irrigation project, which employed technology to change, even to exploit, the land for the convenience of settlers. The forces of development in Los Angeles were girding themselves to do battle against residents of the valley who sought to preserve their water rights. In the early 1900s unscrupulous speculators moved into the valley for the sole purpose of buying up land along the Owens River. They tricked the local population into believing that the land was to be reclaimed by irrigation, all the while planning to divert water to Los Angeles in one of the most massive—and scandalous—aqueduct projects in American history. When the valley residents learned of the plot, they dynamited the aqueduct several times to no avail.

Although the Owens River controversy did not come to a head until 1907, long after Wallace and his brother had gone broke in the mid-nineties, the ill-fated project Wallace supervised when he and Mary moved to Inyo probably accentuated the stress in their marriage. From the onset, it appears, their relationship was faltering. The failure of the irrigation project, which Mary considered yet another of Wallace's disasters, impelled her to strike out on her own as a writer. Perhaps the dryness of Inyo and the perceived aridity in her marriage inspired some of her most poignant lines of poetry. "The Song of the Maverick" begins: "I am too arid for tears, and for laughter / Too sere with unslaked desires."[41] Everything Mary wrote about those first years suggests that she and her husband were moving in different directions. "What society fails to understand or dishonesty fails to admit, is that marriage as an act is not invariably the stroke that ushers in the experience of being married," pontificates her narrator in A Woman of Genius (p. 136).

Mary's conclusion that Wallace lacked the "natural qualifications for the calling of vineyardist" may have been bitter and unfair considering the widespread agricultural debacle in which many California farmers, including her own family, participated. Mary's nascent feminism developed against the backdrop of the small-town family ideology of Carlinville, where the role of provider was assigned to the husband. She might just as well have excoriated Wallace for his deficiency as husband and father for her child. Wallace did, in fact, have teaching qualifications. He had begun teaching as early as 1885 to help out when his father's coconut plantation failed, but soon gave it up in favor of ill-fated land reclamation projects. Mary was galled by her husband's refusal to acknowledge financial defeat; she never forgave him for turning down a remunerative teaching job in the early days of their marriage when she was pregnant. Instead, the couple depended on her small income from tutoring private pupils, which drained the energy she needed to devote to "her own business of writing" (EH 227).

As their financial situation became desperate in the 1890s, Wallace supported the family by returning to teaching, an occupation that he disliked and for which he was temperamentally ill suited. Despite his distaste for the classroom, he was appointed county superintendent of schools at Lone Pine, where Mary eventually secured a teaching job, while struggling to care for Ruth at home and to write. The two salaries relieved the couple of "the worst of their obligations," Mary recalled (*EH* 281). Later Mary would filter her unhappy experiences as a young wife and mother through fictional characters. Serena, the protagonist of *Santa Lucia*, for whom "marriage was a doorway into which she had stepped in a day of rough weather" (p. 76), emblematized what Mary had discovered about the collision of personal ambition and the demands of marriage.

Ruth's Birth

Leaving Inyo late in the fall of 1892, Mary had journeyed southwest to her mother's house in Bakersfield to deliver her baby in more comfortable circumstances. She did not return to Wallace until the summer of 1893 (*EH* 238). The young couple's adjustment to each other, their separations, and Wallace's business failures had been difficult enough; now they were faced with the fact that their daughter Ruth was profoundly retarded from birth. This tragedy crushed Mary, who had hoped for a healthy and brilliant child.

"When I realized that I was pregnant, I promised myself that I would give birth to the smartest child that was ever born," she confessed. During her pregnancy she worked compulsively, hardly stopping to eat or sleep; it appears that she never considered this might have had something to do with her daughter's retardation.[42] Until Ruth died in her twenties, Mary held Wallace responsible for her condition, suggesting that his family had a history of mental retardation.[43] The story of Ruth's handicap is one of concealment and shame, mainly on Mary's part. It gradually became apparent to Mary and Wallace, but for some time no one on the Hunter side realized the extent of Ruth's disabilities—or perhaps they denied the obvious as too painful to face. Mary and her mother seemingly needed a scapegoat: Mrs. Hunter blamed her daughter, Mary her husband.

Mary wrote that Ruth's birth left her "a tortured wreck" and blamed her condition on "improper medical treatment." She added: "My memory of the first seven or eight years of marriage is like some poor martyr's memory of the wheel and the rack, all the best things of mar-

Ruth Austin before she entered the sanatarium in Santa Clara.

riage obscured by the fog of drudgery impossible to be met and by recurrent physical anguish. . . . Brought up as I was, in the possession of eugenic knowledge, it never occurred to me that the man I married would be less frank about his own inheritance than I had been about mine." In a passage both cryptic and less than frank, Austin reports in this account that Ruth was born "a child with tainted blood."[44] To a good friend she reflected upon the injustice done her: "Mr. Austin had been so sedulously brought up in the idea that these things must not be told, that it never occurred to him that I had the right to such information, and I finally discovered it only by accident. In part . . . separation from him was a protest against that indignity. For though my marriage was not satisfying in any particular, I am too thoroughly a democrat to have left him without his full consent unless there had been something like this."[45]

While the Austin family remained tight-lipped about Ruth's condition, Mrs. Hunter had an almost biblical confrontation with Mary while the child was small. "I don't know what you have done, daughter, to have such a judgment upon you," she exclaimed.[46] Susanna Hunter's condemnation effectively ruptured the relationship between the two women. Mary avoided visiting her mother again. That Mary used the pseudonym "Savilla Graham"—her mother's maiden name—poignantly attests to her anguish and conflict.[47] Mrs. Hunter died in 1896, before she and Mary could reconcile their differences. In her autobiography Mary expresses grief for the loss of her mother, a grief more profound than she felt for Ruth or her broken marriage. "There is an element of incalculable ravening in the loss of your mother; deep under the shock of broken habit and the ache of present grief, there is the psychic wound, the severed root of being; such loss as makes itself felt as the companion of immortality. For how should the branch suffer, torn from the dead tree? It is only when the tree is green that the cut bough bleeds" (*EH* 273).

A remarkable number of Austin's stories contain the characters of a widowed mother and her son. Typically, the son is jealous of his mother being courted by another man. Austin's fictional boys intimate what life might have been like had she been a beloved son to her mother, a George or Jim, rather than the woman she was. Perhaps, like young Jack in her story "The Truscott Luck," through the act of writing fiction Mary figuratively "went out and walked in the meadow . . . for though I wished my mother to be happy, it came hard to realize that anyone should take my place with her."[48]

Twice discarded by her mother—first as the cause of Jennie's death, later as the cause of her own child's disability—Mary sought to transcend the pain and alienation through what she recognized in herself as genius. She manipulated the concept by merging her own public persona with the characters she created. "This is the story of the struggle between a Genius for Tragic Acting and the daughter of a County

Clerk," her narrator announces in *A Woman of Genius* (p. 5). Seeking a public identity to circulate in the market through her writing, she consciously buried her personal tragedies in a literary life that absorbed her as no private life could. Many close friends never knew about her marriage or about Ruth, but they could not miss the signs of genius. "Everybody who talked with Mary Austin knew there was greatness in her," Carl Van Doren recalled after her death. "What she may have been like in the days of her early struggles and ambitions I could never quite make out."[49]

In several sources Austin claims that Ruth's retardation provided the financial impetus for her writing. "Caring for a hopelessly invalid child is expensive business. I had to write to make money."[50] Elsewhere she characterized her motive for writing as "the need of . . . the reality of the writing experience; getting it onto paper, into print, the reality of the job" (*EH* 290). Whether she needed the money to care for Ruth is not really at issue; other serious writers had discovered that writing and child care were incompatible. Of Austin's contemporaries, Willa Cather, Ellen Glasgow, and Gertrude Stein were single. Edith Wharton was childless. Charlotte Perkins Gilman left her one daughter to the care of her husband, who later remarried. Gertrude Atherton left her daughter with her mother-in-law after her husband's death. Helen Hunt Jackson, a prodigious writer and lecturer about the West, married late and remained childless. Contrastively, Kate Chopin was the widowed mother of a brood of children, and her literary productivity was slender.

Writing and establishing a literary identity obsessed Mary increasingly as she saw the hopelessness of her marriage. Wallace was seemingly a kind man but, from Mary's viewpoint, unsuccessful in his every undertaking. In her autobiography he emerges as a buffoon and an incompetent, tainted in some unspeakable way that allowed her to contemplate excising him from her life as she disentangled herself from her daughter's. Mary's niece remembered her uncle Wallace, who visited frequently even after the divorce in 1914, as a "rather shy and quiet man . . . but kind and thoughtful."[51] From 1895 to 1897 he and Mary lived apart while she taught art, music, and English at Bishop, about sixty miles north of Lone Pine. At the end of that time she received a Grammar Grade County Certificate for Inyo County, on the strength of which she obtained a position in Lone Pine and moved back permanently with Wallace. Though there is no way to know for certain whether he was any better than Mary in managing Ruth, matters could hardly have been worse than when Mary was alone. Dr. Helen Mac-

Knight Doyle, Mary's physician in Bishop, recalled that Mary often left Ruth unattended while she was teaching. People gossiped about her irresponsibility and cruelty to the child, who soiled herself, went hungry, and was often screaming when Mary returned, exhausted, to their cramped quarters at the end of the school day.[52]

When the young doctor was first called upon to attend Ruth, she was shocked by Mary's seeming coldness toward her retarded daughter. Ultimately, however, she came to a more sympathetic understanding of the situation and endorsed the distraught mother's decision to leave Ruth in the care of a patient, childless couple who could better cope with the difficult child. Doyle became a friend to Mary while she wrote *The Land of Little Rain*; in the evenings, "Dr. Nellie" would listen to Mary work through the ideas that she would later cast into literary form.[53]

Mary placed Ruth in an institution in Santa Clara for a year of evaluation in 1904, following the successful publication of *The Land of Little Rain*. After deciding to permanently commit her daughter in 1905, she frequently used the expression "we have lost her" when referring to Ruth.[54] As a girl, Mary Hunter Wolf heard her aunt say that Ruth "was lost" and concluded that her cousin was dead. Mary Austin reportedly did not visit her daughter and believed that her family thought she had abandoned Ruth. When her niece was orphaned in 1917, the writer concluded that the Hunter family was making a moral judgment in denying her custody of thirteen-year-old Mary Hunter. Ruth remained institutionalized until her death of pneumonia in 1918.[55]

Afterwards Mary confided to Charles Lummis, the noted California folklorist, poet, and cultural preservationist, that "there were so few people who ever had the courage to know about my Ruth, even my own family found it easier to speak of her as lost. But you like me, have eaten the bread of sorrow on which the gods feed those they specially endow." (Lummis's young son Amado had died when Ruth was still quite small.) Mary shared with Lummis her conviction "that the trouble was hereditary on her father's side, and the facts were suppressed out of that strange vanity called Family Pride."[56] Displacing the blame onto Wallace somehow made the fact of Ruth's disability more bearable for Mary. It even gave her a rationale for rejecting Wallace and, in turn, protected her against social opprobrium.

Although the Austins were to remain married until 1914, the ultimate dissolution of their marriage supports Robert Griswold's conclusion that divorce statistics during the latter half of the nineteenth century paralleled "rising marital expectations."[57] In *The Ford*, a novel set in the Owens Valley, Austin focuses not merely on issues of power and water in the fictional valley of Tierra Longa, but also on the struggle of women to retain power outside of traditional domestic arrangements. Anne Brent, the independent young businesswoman who wins a water rights battle against ruthless development interests, speaks for many Austin characters when she rejects marriage because she is unwilling "to tie up my life so close to anybody that any-thing he can do will make me want to die rather than live."[58]

Austin was heavily influenced by Ellen Key's *Love and Marriage*, a book she recommended and referred to frequently.[59] Key, an influential social theorist, enjoyed considerable success as an author and lecturer after the turn of the century and advocated a "new morality," one that would countenance sexual love without marriage as well as greater acceptance of divorce. Key was misunderstood by many readers as promoting immorality, a misreading that she tried to correct in *Love and Ethics*. Arguing from the perspective of eugenics, she wrote: "In 'Love and Marriage' I pointed out that those who insist on monogamy, that is, a lifelong love relation, as the only moral relationship between the sexes disregard the inevitable consequence of such an ethical standard, namely, the waste of a large amount of splendid life energy which if utilized would produce fine offspring and so aid in the improvement of the race; while the worst elements of society would not be deterred by any ethical principle from propagating their kind."[60]

In 1891, however, marriage was a logical step for a woman of Mary's financial situation and background. The companionate view of marriage, which Carl Degler and other social historians define as a marriage based on mutual affection, was predicated on the domestic ideal of the family and the sacred and protected place of women within it. But, as Griswold demonstrates, with the advent of a female population "more self-confident, more sure of their own importance and the legitimacy of their own desires, more women began to question the assumptions of domesticity itself."[61]

In the 1890s Austin's views on marriage were largely colored by observation and by her girlhood exposure to temperance literature. In addition to the sobriety of husbands, it called for a reevaluation of married women's contribution to the household, compensation for the work they performed, and the right to control pregnancy by refusing sex.[62] Historians suggest that the temperance movement radicalized women and changed the American family in much more profound ways than have been explored until recently. Many women who considered themselves feminists, as Austin did, began to revise their perceptions of the ideal marriage decades before the turn of the century. Austin admired Ellen Key's essentialist views of womanhood and the primacy of motherhood—within or outside of marriage. Unlike Charlotte Perkins Gilman, who advocated what Nancy Cott has called "human feminism," Austin and Key paid homage to the innate superiority of womanhood. Both condemned the double standard inherent in applying a male-defined morality to women.[63]

Austin did not encounter Key's writing, however, until she had undergone the painful vicissitudes of several more years of marital unhappiness, accompanied by the deeply scarring experience of an unfulfilling motherhood. Mary and Wallace married at precisely the time when women and men alike were demanding relationships of increasing emotional complexity. As Griswold writes, "By the late nineteenth century, wives complained to the courts about cold, aloof husbands, of husbands who did not spend enough time at home, who failed to check their sexual desires, or who ignored women's emotional needs." Predictably, men complained "of unloving, peevish, quarrelsome wives, of wives who were poor housekeepers or insensitive mothers."[64]

By 1912, before Ruth's death but after she had separated from her husband, Austin articulated the pain in a story titled "Frustrate." Though it is unwise to read fiction as a direct transcription of life, Austin's story contains a poignant commentary on an unhappy "writer woman" whom men respect, "though they never took her to walk or to see the moon rise, or the boats come in. They spent all that on the pretty women, young and empty-headed."[65] Dealing with a woman who is childless and whose husband is uncommunicative, "Frustrate" doubtlessly expresses Mary's own feelings about rejection and her loveless marriage: "I know that I am a disappointed woman and that nobody cares at all about it, not even Henry; and if anybody thought of it, it would only be to think it ridiculous. It is ridiculous, too, with my waist, and not knowing how to do my hair or anything. I look at Henry sometimes of evenings, when he has his feet on the fender, and wonder if he has the least idea how disappointed I am. I even have days of wondering if Henry isn't disappointed, too. He might be disappointed in himself, which would be even more dreadful; but I don't suppose we shall ever find out about each other. It is part of my disappointment that Henry never seemed to want to find out."[66]

3

▲ ▲ ▲

A WRITER'S DEBUT

My family thought I was doing well to marry Henry. He had no bad habits,

and his people were well-to-do; and then I wasn't particularly pretty or rich.

. . . I suppose it is difficult for some folks to understand how you can be excited

by the way a shadow falls, or a bird singing on a wet bough; and somehow

young men get the idea that the excitement had something to do with them.

—*"Frustrate"*

In Mary's eyes Wallace appeared to be an inadequate husband and provider, yet he managed to land a variety of supervisory positions commensurate with his educational background. After serving as superintendent of schools in Lone Pine, he became registrar of the Desert Land Office at Independence, California. Mary finished his term at Lone Pine in the spring of 1898 after he went on to Independence. Reluctantly, she planned to join him after the school term ended, but again she suffered a breakdown. Leaving Ruth with a family friend, she traveled to Oakland for medical treatment. The breakdown, if we infer it to have been caused by hysteria, could have been a passive aggressive strategy, perhaps unconscious.[1]

The exact nature of her illness remains obscure mainly because although Mary could write exceptionally clear prose, she chose not to when referring to her health. We know that she was annoyed by her husband's new job, which required "residence in a smaller town, with, from Mary's point of view, no single alleviating circumstance" (*EH* 281). Wallace had not consulted with her about his change in jobs or the attendant move. Instead, he had proceeded in "secrecy" to settle the matter so crucial to their future.

The monthly salary of a public school teacher in California in the late 1890s hovered between eighty and one hundred dollars, depending on the district; that of a superintendent was somewhat higher. Their earnings put the Austins roughly at the level of skilled workers —masons, carpenters, bricklayers, tinners, machinists, and jewelers— and distinctly above the income level of day laborers. Having passed the difficult examination for the teacher's certificate, Mary at last felt a measure of financial security in Lone Pine with both of them employed. She was biding her time in Inyo, hoping that they could earn enough money to enable them to relocate to an environment more suitable to the literary life. Perhaps Wallace might realize one of his business schemes at long last, given a change and a chance.[2] However, Mary failed to take the measure of her husband's attachment to the remote surroundings of the Inyo district, or to reconcile herself to his determination to stay in the area. Nor did she face up to his adamant aversion to teaching and city life. Moreover, Mary had given Wallace credit for an egalitarian view toward their marriage that he did not possess and for which his upbringing had not prepared him. For him, the surroundings of Inyo compensated for their lack of financial security. To be fair, Wallace never stopped hatching schemes for irrigation that could improve the lot of people in the area. But his plans never came to fruition, and communication between the couple soon broke down.

From Lone Pine to Independence

Founded in 1861, Independence, like many California towns, began as a trading post. With gold discoveries in the Inyo Mountains during the 1860s, the "town" emerged as the focus of the mining operations. Nearby Bell's Mill, one of the oldest flour mills in the Owens Valley, was perhaps the most vital enterprise to this sprawling territory and its few inhabitants in the early days. After platting was completed in 1866, Independence became the county seat by the process of natural selection. Eventually it became the headquarters for the massive Owens Valley Aqueduct. When the Austins moved there, however, Independence was considered remote, accessible only by stagecoach. Cactus, chapparal, mesquite, and sagebrush met the eye at every turn, providing a hospitable home for rabbits, coyotes, rattlesnakes, tarantulas, and horned toads. The town's amenities included a hotel, three stores, and a saloon. A *campoodie* (or *campody*, the Indian word for encampment) contained the Indians and an Indian school trained the children. The three hundred inhabitants lived "in unattractive houses which petered out into the desert by dusty windbreaks and that ever constant fringe of tin cans that edges a desert town."[3]

Without hard evidence, the reason behind Wallace's decision to move to Independence is open to speculation. Ruth was becoming increasingly unmanageable; perhaps Wallace hoped that Independence would be less critical of the child and her mother, whom neighbors in Lone Pine tended to judge harshly. Then, too, he could not have been unaware of Mary's reputation for bizarre behavior and a routine anything but housewifely. Even early in their marriage, friends praised her skill as a cook but noted her complete disregard of dirty dishes. When engrossed in her writing she often let them pile up for days until a sympathetic neighbor "came to the rescue."[4] Wallace may have felt that his control over the family would be assured in Independence. He may also have become weary of Mary's trips to San Francisco and Los Angeles, and hopeful that the difficulties of the journey from Independence would keep her close to home.

Mary predicted that the move would result only in another financial setback. Barely grinding out a livelihood with their combined salaries in Lone Pine, the couple had managed—with Mary's careful stewardship—to climb out from under the debt that had threatened to bury them following Wallace's several business failures in the first eight years of their marriage. Lone Pine looked askance at the married woman's employment as a teacher, but accepted it because of Wallace's position; many citizens considered him very liberal to allow his wife to work outside the home. Employment as a teacher, it was thought, allowed a wife to think of herself as independent and diverted her from her true calling. Even after the turn of the century, male social scientists warned that "the vast horde of female teachers in the United States" was undermining "both the school and family."[5]

Mary, crushed by Wallace's announcement, raged against the impending move to Independence. She responded with her own strategy for coping with his "obliviousness" to her "claim on [his] consideration," and resolved firmly "to do something about it" (*EH* 281). Dr. Doyle recalled that neighbors "would see her with her hair down pacing the floor at night and railing at Wallace. Sometimes Mary was able to rouse him from his smug satisfaction. Then Wallace would seem to comprehend that she was not just talking—that she was really distressed over the hopelessness of their ever being able to make anything of their life together, and she was going to do something about it.

Sometimes he would be roused to the possibility that she really would do something and be provoked to remind her of the pattern." Mary balked at "the pattern," the traditional code of conduct between married people, which defined the husband's position as the head of the family. In Victorian times, her response would have been classified as hysterical. According to Doyle, she longed for an "environment . . . more suited to her activities," which probably meant a literary world such as she had glimpsed briefly in San Francisco during the early 1890s or the "Arroyo Seco" community of writers and artists in Los Angeles, led by Charles Lummis.[6]

William James

During the summer of 1898 Mary fled from her overwhelming domestic problems. "On this occasion she went off to San Francisco to the hospital, and met William James," she wrote simply (*EH* 281–82). The medical care she received in San Francisco must have left her free to attend lectures and do pretty much as she wished. It was at a lecture in Oakland on the topic of relaxation that she made her momentous encounter with James. Mary interpreted his talk as a personal message. "What he recommended to all intellectuals was the relaxation of the rather strained surface tensions which was the preferred intellectual mode of the time, in order that the whole personality might be flooded by the deep life that welled up from below the threshold of selfness, to make the augmented unity of I-Mary," she remembered later (*EH* 282). In other words, accumulated knowledge and the weight of tradition more often than not impeded spontaneous creativity. Mary had already observed Indians using forms of meditation. The Swiss psychologist Carl Jung, whom Mary may have met during the 1920s, was impressed with the Indians when he visited the chief of the Taos Pueblo in 1925 to observe their holistic way of life and, in particular, their symbol system in art. Jung noted the recurrence of the mandala in the Navajo sand paintings, an impressive instance of the representation of the holistic Self.[7]

Long before Jung encountered American Indians, however, Mary had argued that spontaneously produced art—similar to that created by Indians after powerful dreams—could be facilitated by exploring one's own unconscious. She herself meditated before writing to perfect an automatic technique, utilizing repetitive prayers—mantras and the rosary—to drain her surface consciousness of superficial considerations and to facilitate connection with her deeper Self, the aspect of her being she called "I-Mary."

Early in her artistic career, Mary was struck by James's readiness to accept her ideas about the creativity inherent in "the Paiute technique of Prayer" (*EH* 282). She recounted the interview with James many times in minutest detail, repeating verbatim the views they had shared in Oakland. Mary was hungry for legitimation of her ideas about creativity, and James's response was all that she could wish for. "I am firm in my conviction that he validated my own experience of the swinging door, the door that opens out of consciousness with the same effect of . . . an icy shiver as when an actual door behind you shudders on the latch and lets in a draught of coolness. When you are sitting with the elders of the tribe, when the sayings of the Ancient Men are passing, and suddenly at a word dropped, an incident related, whole areas of human evolution let blow upon you, a wind out of your own past" (*EH* 283).

So memorable was their meeting that "for the first time" in her life Mary came away "assured . . . that the true Middle of my search was in myself" (*EH* 283). No philosopher could compare with James, she thought; no other had the breadth of vision to accept with interest what she had to teach about the Indian way of prayer. Through him she linked what she had learned from the Paiutes about consciousness to the philosophy of the premier theorist of consciousness in the twentieth century. "What I got out of William James and the Medicine-Man was a continuing experience of wholeness, a power to expand the least premonitory shiver along the edge of primitive apprehension to the full diapason of spiritual sophistication, which I have never lost" (*EH* 281).

Mary Austin sought fulfillment through interactions with intellectual figures; she had tracked James down to his Oakland hotel to converse with him, and was gratified—and incredulous—when he received her. Not long after this buoying experience she returned to Independence and her stultifying marriage. It would have been difficult for most men to measure up intellectually to James; Wallace's disadvantage appears immediately obvious. In the winter of 1899 Mary packed her bags again, this time taking Ruth to Los Angeles, ostensibly to obtain a medical consultation on the child's disability.

Although Mary was not yet prepared to divorce Wallace, she was unwilling to follow him obediently to Independence. Her first excursion to San Francisco for what Wallace termed "hospital treatment" suggests that she took the only socially acceptable route for a woman

Charles Lummis, author, editor, and scholar of the Southwest,
ca. 1900. He introduced Austin to his literary circle in California.

to leave home in the late nineteenth century. Charlotte Perkins Gilman
had initiated her own separation, and finally divorce, in this way several years earlier.[8] Austin first met Gilman at Charles Lummis's home
in Los Angeles. Later she recalled that "all Los Angeles and Pasadena
were upset" by Gilman's decision to leave her young daughter with
her former husband and his new wife (Gilman's best friend, Grace
Ellery Channing).[9] Austin must have read Gilman's story "An Unnatural Mother," about a woman who abandons her child during a flood to
alert others to the danger. When she drowns, the child is left to the care
of the town gossips.[10] In this transparent and somewhat clumsy fiction,
Gilman thinly disguises the painful act of leaving her own daughter in
order to save other women by participating visibly in the feminist cru-
sade. In many ways Charlotte's divorce provided a blueprint for Mary's
—Mary mentions it in her autobiography (*EH* 281)—though the Austins' separation and divorce were characterized not by impetuousness
but by foot-dragging on both sides.

Charles Lummis

Lummis, host to Austin, Gilman, and many other scholars, writers,
and reformers, was by all accounts an eccentric. A Harvard alumnus,
he had once crossed the country on foot for the pleasure of the experience. By the time Austin met him in 1899 he had already been city
editor of the *Los Angeles Times* (1885) and had served as the paper's
correspondent when Geronimo was captured by the army in 1887.
With his friend Adolph Bandelier, he had organized a scientific expedition to Bolivia and Peru. He built his home, El Alisal (then on
the outskirts of Los Angeles, on the west bank of the Arroyo Seco),
with his own hands and crammed into it the Indian and Spanish objects he had collected. Lummis devoted his life to scholarly research
into Indian folklore and the Spanish arts. He established the Southwest
Museum in his house and founded and edited *Land of Sunshine* (later
Out West magazine), all the while writing his own books and con-
ducting archaeological and ethnographic expeditions to Central and
South America. He considered himself the savior of the California missions. In 1895, with funds raised from the Landmarks Club (another
of his projects), he began reroofing southern California missions and
preserving other historical landmarks.[11]

Lummis welcomed the thirty-one-year-old Austin to his home, just
as he welcomed all artists and those seriously interested in California to

meet and partake of his hospitality. He had no patience for those who had not immersed themselves in the subject of the American Indian as thoroughly as he. Having spent five years living among the Indians of Pueblo Ysleta in New Mexico, mastering Indian languages and lore, he expected no less from anyone else entering the field. He was also deeply involved with Indian advocacy.[12]

Austin was quite taken with "Don Carlos" Lummis, as his friends dubbed him; how could she not be impressed by such immense learning and wit? Wearing his adopted Hispanic costume, "an old sombrero, the corduroy trousers, the lace-drawn shirt and the red serape," he seemed to encapsulate all that she was looking for in a western literary mentor.[13] He advised Austin during her nascent career, turning testy when she failed to measure up to his standard. Once he reprimanded her about her cavalier disregard of Spanish etymologies in a manuscript she had given him to read. "If you are 'not in the least ashamed of Spanish derivations' then you ought to be. . . . I don't try to write about the things I am ignorant of. If you want to take a historic period, or a geographic setting, to make fame or money, for you—or even —let us say, in the very extreme of liberality, to fulfill your mission toward rounding out literature—you are entitled to give them a fair bargain. . . . When you use Spanish names, it is your business as a decent woman, and as a writer, to have them right. . . . What would you think of yourself if, as a Californian, writing of California, you described seasons as they are in New England?"[14]

Although Lummis was less than ten years Austin's senior, he wrote to her as "my dear child" and adopted a paternal, if not professorial, tone. "Don't fill yourself with that Chautauqua idiocy about leaving it to the dreadful scientists to know anything," he advised, no doubt planting the seeds of her distaste for Chautauqua education. "It won't hurt you any more than it hurts other people to be right. There is a great deal to learn in this world, and most of it is expensive education. Where in some case a person who happens to have learned is willing to give you your examination for nothing, do not look on it with sneerness."[15] Whereas her own father and General Beale had been gentle figures of authority, Lummis was the stern father on whom Austin relied when she was turning away from Wallace. Like Beale, he admired her intellect and posed no sexual threat, even though he had a reputation as a Don Juan.[16] In every way Lummis proved a contrast to her indecisive, undirected husband.

In many ways Lummis's work became Austin's work, especially the

Eve Lummis in 1906. To her Austin dedicated The Land of Little Rain.

close observations of Indian life and the recording of their tales. Over the years his idiosyncratic way of life, his place as the cynosure of the western literary community, became goals to which Austin herself aspired. When her career was established, she emulated him by writing supercilious letters to those she wished to chastise for their careless understanding of indigenous literature.

Austin became fast friends with Lummis's first wife, Dorothea, and his second wife, Eve, whom he divorced Dorothea to marry. Eventually Eve divorced him because of his compulsive infidelities. In Austin's estimation, both women had received shabby treatment from Lummis. She kept in touch with them and confided to Eve something of how her own relationship with Lummis had changed over the years. "We had a sharp quarrel later, when I came to New Mexico," Austin wrote in 1929. "He wrote me the most insulting letter I have ever received; entirely unprovoked on my part, and without any excuse on his, except that he seems to have resented anyone [else] doing anything in New Mexico."[17] More damning to the friendship between Austin and her mentor was a review Lummis wrote of *The Land of Journeys' Ending* (1924), "which was so scurrilous that the editor of the Saturday Review, to which he sent it, refused to publish it."[18]

Austin's affection for Eve Lummis dated back to the very earliest years of her writing. She dedicated her first book, *The Land of Little Rain*, "to Eve, the Comfortress of Unsuccess." The dedication, she

modestly explained, was "plain enough so that all your friends will
know who is meant, and not so plain that you can not deny it to the
general public if you do not think it does you credit." She added: "It
is no more than fitting that this book should be dedicated to you since
you are the first western woman I met capable of inspiring me either
with affection or a very great measure of respect, I have met many such
since but you are the first and so I have imposed on you to the extent
of tacking your name to a book that I am a little afraid is more margin
than literature."[19] Many friends of the Lummises interpreted the dedication as an affront to Charles. Austin wrote that she herself did "not
know what to think of the book" and was "waiting to find out from
the reviewers"—an undisguised admission of her sincere anxiety and
uncertainty about the quality of her work, doubts unassuaged even by
the positive reviews in eastern and western periodicals.[20]

In view of Ina Coolbrith's active assistance to Austin in the early
1890s, the dedication of *The Land of Little Rain* is rather puzzling. Eve
and the Arroyo Seco group of artists and writers were probably more
important to her in 1904.[21] Still, her old friends felt the smart when
Austin, having achieved some success, neglected them. Indeed, Coolbrith showed a trace of bruised feelings when she wrote to Austin in
the summer of 1904 from San Francisco. She complained that she had
barely gotten a glimpse of her protégée during Austin's visit to the city
"and really thought (the conceit of me!) that, except dear Dorothea
Moore [the first Mrs. Lummis], I had a better right to you than any
woman in San Francisco!! I did not get one word with you alone and
I resent it."[22]

Mary's relationship with Eve had a very private and personal dimension. Eve's marriage to Lummis was not an easy one. His womanizing
was legendary, and as the second wife for whom he had thrown over
the handsome physician, Dorothea, Eve's position was painful. She be-
friended Mary and went out of her way to welcome her to El Alisal.
As Augusta Fink puts it, "A deep affection quickly developed between
the two women whose experiences had been fraught with disillusionment."[23] Eve was reserved in her confidences, but Mary did not require
a lengthy explanation to apprehend the domestic trials that she endured living with the talented but egocentric Lummis.[24] When Mary
and Ruth lived in Los Angeles near the Lummis family, Eve was particularly kind to Mary's little girl and encouraged her five-year-old son,
Amado, to play with her. Amado was frail and Mary took comfort in
the love that bonded the two children. "On the night when [Amado]
died Ruth was talking to him in her bed and insisted that he was in

the room, and that he wanted her to go for a long, long walk, away off," Mary recounted to Eve years afterward. After Ruth's death in the flu epidemic of 1918, she wrote to Lummis: "We do not know what these things mean, but to me it has always meant that back of [Ruth's] poor, imperfect body my child's soul waited its deliverance, and I am glad she will find one child who loved her in that country where they both have gone." [25]

First Successes

After returning to Independence in 1900, Mary settled down with Wallace to the task of planning and building a home while they boarded Ruth, now eight years old, with their neighbors, the Skinners. Mary called the place they built in Independence "the brown house under the willow tree" and the private corner of the house in which she wrote so prolifically the *wickiup,* a Paiute word for shelter. For seven years she applied herself to writing as never before, selling stories to such major publications as the *Atlantic Monthly, Cosmopolitan*, and *Saint Nicholas.* Many of these sketches and tales were brought together in 1904 as a children's book called *The Basket Woman.*

Mary had approached the editors of the *Atlantic Monthly* in early 1902 to publish her sketches separately or in a book. They responded favorably to the manuscripts she sent them and asked for more. In their congratulatory letter to the promising new writer, they mentioned "the charm and faithfulness" of her work. "It is not often that prose sketches of outdoor life have given us such unalloyed satisfaction." [26] The result was *The Land of Little Rain*, published in October 1903. Its elegant binding and format announced its appropriateness as a Christmas gift. Mary professed that she didn't much "care for the holiday books," referring to the handsome illustrations. [27] At least one reviewer agreed, writing: "None of these pictures, with the cunning of the artist's hand, bring out the country with its human and animal dwellers as does a single paragraph of Mrs. Austin's work. Indeed such illustrations of such fine descriptive work as hers seems [*sic*] almost an impertinence." [28] To Eve Lummis, who did extensive but unacknowledged editing for her husband's journal *Out West*, Mary self-consciously apologized: "You will agree that the illustrations of the Spanish Californians are ridiculous, no respectable girl of that class would go dressed like that—and to think of a Padre with a beard!" [29]

Mary and Wallace had put off the inevitable decision of what to do

with Ruth. The matter was not settled definitively until after publication of *The Land of Little Rain*. Mary reiterated throughout her life that
Ruth's illness was an expensive burden, and the Austins most certainly
lacked the means to place her in a private sanitarium before the success
of Mary's first book. In 1904 Mary took her eleven-year-old daughter
to Santa Clara and put her in Osborne Hall, a private institution run
by the noted Dr. Antrim Osborne, "where the difference between herself and other children, which was beginning to trouble her, would
not be felt, where it would not be known. Here the inability of other
people to bear her cross would not be taxed; where one could say if
questioned, 'We have lost her'; where her brothers would not be called
upon to make unwelcome admissions; where the pain could be borne
alone, as it was for another twenty years" (*EH* 295). Mary wrote to
Eve that she went to Santa Clara "to do something for Ruth, and
then to begin another novel which is already plotted."[30] The book for
which she sought material was *Santa Lucia*, a novel about marital strife
and suicide published in 1908. She may also have been gathering additional background for *Isidro*, which appeared in book form in 1905
after serialization in the *Atlantic Monthly*.

Is it more than coincidence that in *Isidro* the protagonist never makes
it to Santa Clara to fulfill his ambition of entering the priesthood?
Mary habitually drew upon her own life in writing her many novels;
it seems likely that if she could possibly have created a different future
for Ruth, she would have, just as she radically altered the fictional
Isidro's future by having him stray from his vocation on the way to
the mission of Santa Clara. With a certainty, the difficult journey to
Santa Clara with Ruth was much on Mary's mind when she wrote
Isidro.

If Mary took the lead in getting institutional care for Ruth, it was
because the responsibilities of parenting fell on her shoulders, not
Wallace's. He adamantly opposed committing Ruth, believing that "the
child should remain in the home even though all of the mother's time
and strength was [*sic*] devoted to her care." While townfolk gossiped
about Mary's neglecting Ruth and "farming out" the child during her
daily stints at her writing desk, Wallace remained exempt from their
curiosity and malice. As in Lone Pine, many people in Independence
pitied him because of his wife's "unnatural" behavior—her frequent
absences, friendships with the town's small Chinese community, and
perceived lack of maternal love for her unfortunate child.[31] In Wallace's
account of important events in their marriage, the date of Ruth's institutionalization is notably missing; he stops his chronology in 1901

and writes tersely, "Hope the list of events will help you recall the rest." Wallace was absent from the traumatic scene of parting that probably took place in Santa Clara during the winter of 1904. Ruth's final commitment did not take place until 1905; Mary alone signed the papers.[32]

Mary's unmitigated frustration in the years directly before this important event leaps out from her limited literary correspondence. To Charles Moody, the assistant editor of Lummis's *Out West* magazine and roughly her contemporary, she sketches a grim version of her domestic life. "Now about myself, there is no new trouble but the old one that sits at my table, lies in my bed, looks at me from my own glass, crumbles my heart to dust, and had at the last time I saw you confirmed itself as hopeless." Referring to the verdict of the doctors in Los Angeles that Ruth's case was hopeless (Mary probably never visited her daughter after 1905), she exclaims: "My house is left unto me desolate!" She asks Moody to read her story in the *Atlantic* for a better understanding of her anguish. "No Mother of a child like mine could write in that sustained lightheartedness who was not confined to it by a wolf of distress." Exquisitely sensitive about mentioning Ruth to any of her friends, she closes with a typical apology: "Mind, this is not complaining, it is not often I allow myself so much reference to it as this."[33]

Moody responded to Mary's letter with a generous assessment of her literary powers. "Night before last, I read the installment of 'Isidro' in the current 'Atlantic.' Last night, I read your 'Basket Woman' and this morning I have been preparing for the press the Christmas story with which you have honored us." Moody showed less restraint in his appreciation of Austin's work than Lummis. "I feel bound to say to you that I do not know of any woman in America who has the variety of literary power which you possess," he wrote encouragingly. Moody disagreed with the "western" tag that Austin's publishers had placed on her work. Speaking of *The Basket Woman*, Moody remarked, "Two or three of these little tales remind me of, and will match well with, Hans Christian Andersen at his best."[34]

Unlike most of Austin's literary friends, Moody remained acutely sensitive to her feelings about Ruth. "You seem to have been intended to do a certain work that no one else could; and could only achieve the power for that work under the pressure of a constant and not-to-be-remedied grief," he wrote. In what seems a questionable assessment from the perspective of late twentieth-century feminism, Moody attempted to console the writer by pointing to the specific way sorrow had nurtured her work. "It is surely true that the things you have done, and shall do, never would have been done if motherhood had given to you what mothers pray for, instead of what it has."[35]

Mary approached *The Land of Little Rain* with professional absorption. Since she was not teaching, writing was no longer avocational. Moreover, her work necessitated the services of a professional typist, a considerable expense in the Austin family budget. Wallace cooperated with the plan, even serving his wife breakfast in bed so that her train of thought would not be disturbed by mundane household duties.[36] Mary used her newfound freedom to explore the Independence area and to observe closely with her entire being as she had in the early Tejon days. Effectively ostracized by the town for many reasons—chief among them her advocacy of the Higher Criticism (close readings of Scripture that were not approved by the pastor and elders of the Methodist church in Independence) and her interest in minorities—Mary found herself "read out" of the church and ignored by many in the community. This suited her, as she needed time and solitude to write.

The Land of Little Rain

Austin reveals much of herself and of her literary project in the preface to the fourteen essays that make up *The Land of Little Rain*:

> I confess to a great liking for the Indian fashion of name-giving: every man known by that phrase which best expresses him to who so names him. Thus he may be Mighty-hunter, or Man-Afraid-of-a-Bear, according as he is called by friend or enemy, and Scar-Face to those who knew him by the eye's grasp only. No other fashion, I think, sets so well with the various natures that inhabit in us, and if you agree with me you will understand why so few names are written here as they appear in the geography. For if I love a lake known by the name of the man who discovered it, which endears itself by reason of the close-locked pines it nourishes about its borders, you may look in my account to find it so described. But if the Indians have been there before me, you shall have their name, which is always beautifully fit and does not originate in the poor human desire for perpetuity. . . . And I am in no mind to direct you to delectable places toward which you will hold yourself less tenderly than I. So by this fashion of naming I keep faith with the land and annex to my own estate a very great territory to which none has a surer title. (*LOLR* xv, xvi)

She admirably recognizes the empowerment associated with naming. Thus, the literary endeavor of *The Land of Little Rain* is bound up inextricably with the political project of restoring power over the land to the Indian. A related theme throughout the book is the sorrow of women. How fitting that Austin should find herself, against her will, in a town whose dominant mountain bears the Indian name Oppapago, which translates as "The Weeper." In the essay "Water Borders," Austin associates the image of the mountain with the "grave aspect as of some woman you might have known, looking out across the grassy barrows of her dead" (*LOLR* 129).

The importance of *The Land of Little Rain* and its immediately favorable critical reception have everything to do with Austin's singular power of description. She renders her impressions of this arid land with unprecedented clarity. The transformation of observation into precisely crafted and compelling prose constitutes the triumph of the text. Austin's prose holds the reader, as poetry does, with its carefully measured cadences and mystical insights. Through her imaginative revision the land is exposed as the site of ineffable mysteries—a locus that "breeds" language forms equal to the task of translating it for ordinary understanding. It is a place of fables, tales, and gossip.

> The palpable sense of mystery in the desert air breeds fables, chiefly of lost treasure. Somewhere within its stark borders, if one believes report, is a hill strewn with nuggets; one seamed with virgin silver; an old clayey water-bed where Indians scooped up earth to make cooking pots and shaped them reeking with grains of pure gold. Old miners drifting about the desert edges, weathered into the semblance of the tawny hills, will tell you tales like these convincingly. After a little sojourn in that land you will believe them on their own account. It is a question whether it is not better to be bitten by the little horned snake of the desert that goes sidewise and strikes without coiling, than by the tradition of a lost mine. (*LOLR* 12)

Animals hold secrets of the land to be decoded; they are in fact mystical creatures with special powers to see what humans, imprisoned in language, cannot or will not see. "The coyote is your true water-witch, one who snuffs and paws, snuffs and paws," Austin writes. The text attests to the timeless, cyclical process of nature, to the seeming brutality of the food chain in which animals and birds scavenge off the weak and the dying, the immutable cycle of life and death. This is her mediation on the rawness of nature in her essay "The Scavengers":

So wide is that range of scavengers that it is never safe to say, eye-witness to the contrary, that there are few or many in such a place. Where the carrion is, there will the buzzards be gathered together. . . . The way up from Mojave to Red Butte is all desertness. . . . In a year of little rain in the south, flocks and herds were driven to the number of thousands along the road to the perennial pastures of high ranges. It is a long, slow trail, ankle deep in bitter dust. . . . In the worst of times one in three will pine and fall out by the way. In the defiles of Red Rock, the sheep piled up a stinking lane; it was the sun smiting by day. To these shambles came buzzards, vultures, and coyotes from all the country round, so that on the Tejon, the Ceriso, and the Little Antelope there were not scavengers enough to keep the country clean. All that summer the dead mummified in the open or dropped slowly back to the earth in the quagmires of bitter springs. Meanwhile from Red Rock to Coyote Holes, and from Coyote Holes to Hawaii the scavengers gorged and gorged. (*LOLR* 37, 39)

When Austin turns her attention briefly from the "landscape line" and encounters a human inhabitant in "the land of little rain," she takes her readers along as companions and makes them privy to hidden lives. "He was a perfect gossip of the woods," she writes in "The Pocket Hunter," drawing us into the company of a man who wanders Death Valley and its environs looking for "rich ore." The Pocket Hunter has witnessed the destructive power of nature and of men "and felt himself in the grip of the All-wisdom that killed men or spared them as seemed for their good; but of death by sickness knew nothing except that he believed he should never suffer it" (*LOLR* 48, 47). The narrator encounters the Pocket Hunter after an absence of some years, during which the hunter left the desert with his newly found wealth to see the world. "The land seemed not to have missed him," relates the narrator, "but I missed him and could not forget the trick of expecting him in least likely situations. Therefore it was with a pricking sense of the familiar that I followed a twilight trail of smoke, a year or two later, to the swale of a dripping spring, and came upon a man by the fire with a coffee-pot and frying pan. I was not surprised to find it was the Pocket Hunter. No man can be stronger than his destiny" (*LOLR* 50).

Readers responded favorably to her detailed accounts of Indian life because Austin reconstructed in her essays a remote world they would most likely never gain access to, a world so pure and unspoiled that it seemed prelapsarian in its beauty. In "Shoshone Land" she captures this Edenic mood: "When the rain is over and gone they [the Shoshones] are stirred by the instinct of those that journeyed westward from Eden, and go up each with his mate and young brood, like birds to old nesting places. The beginning of spring in Shoshone Land— oh the soft wonder of it!—is a mistiness as of incense smoke, a veil of greenness over the whitish stubby shrubs, a web of color on the silver sanded soil" (*LOLR* 60).

Although Carolyn Merchant omits Austin from her analysis of organismic thought in *The Death of Nature*—preferring to demonstrate the influence of The American Romantics Emerson and Thoreau on the work of John Muir and Frederick Clements, pioneers of the preservation and ecology movements—Austin, as much as any of her American precursors found a profound spiritual insight in the wilderness.[37] She communicated this organismic strain of thought in *The Land of Little Rain*, a work notable for its unique lyrical power. This holds equally true for her other naturist works, most particularly *The Flock*, a book about sheep and shepherds in California that inspired the contemporary critic Henry Chester Tracy to write of the "magic of mood" characteristic of Austin's essays. A magic of mood, to be sure, but Tracy notes that "this magic in no way denies or distorts reality." He cites *The Flock* as an instance of the "true natural history of sheep, good natural history of the herder, and naturism of the human observer that lifts it out of the dull category of information." Tracy puts his finger on a workable definition of Austin's naturist realism, "a realism that does not break our mood."[38] The creative acts that Tracy brings to our attention in *The Land of Little Rain* and *The Flock* are those of the naturist, not the scientist. In both works Austin sets herself the task of creating a mood; mere facts are transcended and observations transformed into art. The natural phenomena she describes in "Water Borders" become palpably audible to the reader:

> The origin of mountain streams is like the origin of tears, patent to the understanding but mysterious to the sense. They are always at it, but one so seldom catches them in the act. Here in the valley there is no cessation of waters even in the season when the niggard frost gives them scant leave to run. They make the most of their midday hour, and tinkle all night thinly under the ice. An ear laid to the snow catches a muffled hint of their eternal busyness fifteen or twenty feet under the canyon drifts, and long before any appreciable spring thaw, the sagging edges of the snow bridges mark out the place of their running. One who ventures to look

for it finds the immediate source of the spring—all the hill fronts
furrowed with the reek of melting drifts, all the gravelly flats in
a swirl of waters. But later, in June or July, when the camping
season begins, there runs the stream away full and singing, with
no visible reinforcement other than an icy trickle from some high,
belated clot of snow. Oftenest the stream drops bodily from the
bleak bowl of some alpine lake; sometimes breaks out of a hillside
as a spring where the ear can trace it under the rubble of loose
stones to the neighborhood of some blind pool. (*LOLR* 127–28)

In her anthropomorphization of nature, "the lake is the eye of the
mountain, jade green, placid, unwinking, also unfathomable. Whatever goes on under the high and stony brows is guessed at"—a passage
that owes much to Emerson (*LOLR* 128). "The birch—the brown-
bark western birch characteristic of lower stream tangles—is a spoil
sport. It grows thickly to choke the stream that feeds it; grudges it the
sky and space for angler's rod and fly" (*LOLR* 135).

Mary probably gleaned much of the descriptive material in *The Land
of Little Rain* on the camping trips that Wallace found so invigorating
and she so exhausting. Although she complained about these expeditions to Dr. Doyle, it may be unfair for a biographer to suggest that
"their camping trips into the mountains, one of the chief outlets offered
in the way of entertainment, were marred by a secret antagonism, a
failure to co-operate." It seemed to Mary that "the plans for these out-
ings must always originate with Wallace," recounted Doyle, "and be
followed out according to schedule, even though it proved distressing
and aggravating for both of them." The fact is that Wallace enjoyed
botany as an avocation and "never willingly went [camping] without
her."[39]

Wallace's abiding interest in conservation suggests that he and Mary
felt a rapport in their mutual appreciation of the beauty of the California wilderness. Wallace worked diligently "to get government assistance for a Mt. Whitney trail . . . a good through trail over the
range at Whitney which would make a short hike from Owens Valley
to the grand Kern Cañon country and thence on by direct route to
Visalia's."[40] Camping was one activity the Austins could share, albeit
uneasily. One of the longest letters that Mary preserved from her
brother George gives a detailed and graceful account of a camping trip
he took with five other men in the San Fernando Valley. George wrote,
"I want to go up in the . . . meadows and camp one of these days
and climb the high peaks and to the lakes and follow the streams. It

is a wonderful place and I'll never be satisfied in the mountains with anything less."[41] Given the strained relationship between brother and sister, it seems unlikely that George, a felicitous letter writer and a practicing neurologist in Los Angeles, would write at such length about camping if he felt the subject was not entirely congenial to her.

Wallace's pride in Mary's work during this period cannot go unremarked. In her absence he assisted his wife in some correspondence pertaining to her literary career. In 1904, for example, he wrote to the editor of the *Mt. Whitney Journal* that "the book 'The Land of Little Rain' has met with very favorable mention from one end of the country to the other. I inclose [*sic*] a couple of clippings which will give you an idea of the character of her work. If she were at home and had the time I am sure she could do some good work for the 'Mt. Whitney Journal.'"[42] (Had Mary been at home, in fact, the idea of writing for the *Mt. Whitney Journal* might have appeared to her unacceptable, even ludicrous, in view of the recognition accorded *The Land of Little Rain* and the regular publication of her work by the leading nationally circulated periodicals.) Mary told of another occasion when one of her stories "was sent to *The Black Cat* by my husband, who thought it would please me to see it in print, which it did. But when about 1900 I began to seriously devote myself to a writing career, I made a list of magazines for which I meant to write in the order of their literary excellence, with *The Atlantic Monthly* at the top."[43]

Superficial as his concern may have been, Wallace cared about Mary's work and showed a sincere recognition of his wife's abilities. He retained generous feelings toward her over the years, remembering her with gifts and letters when he traveled and leaving an insurance policy to her when he died.[44] As for Wallace's paternal affection for Ruth, the phrase "my little girl" in his letter to the editor of the *Mt. Whitney Journal* testifies that he claimed the child as his, despite her affliction, in a way that Mary could not bring herself to do.

The raw, sensual power of nature is but one aspect of Austin's earliest book of essays. With the honed observational powers of the trained ethnologist she catalogs the method of the Paiute basket maker, Seyavi, one of the most memorable characters in *The Land of Little Rain*.

> In our kind of society, when a woman ceases to alter the fashion of her hair, you guess that she has passed the crisis of her experience. If she goes on crimping and uncrimping with the changing mode, it is safe to suppose she has never come up against anything too big for her. The Indian woman gets nearly the same personal note

in the pattern of her baskets. Not that she does not make all kinds, carriers, water-bottles, and cradles,—these are kitchen ware,—but her works of art are all of the same piece. Seyavi made flaring, flat-bottomed bowls, cooking pots really, when cooking was done by dropping hot stones into water-tight food baskets, and for decoration a design in colored bark of the procession of plumed crest of the valley quail. In this pattern she had made cooking pots in the golden spring of her wedding year, when the quail went up two and two to their resting places about the foot of Oppapago. In this fashion she made them when, after pillage, it was possible to reinstate the housewifely crafts. (*LOLR* 105–06)

Seyavi, the exemplar of the uninhibited creative mind admired by Anglo primitivists, rivets the reader of these essays. "Every Indian woman is an artist,—sees, feels, creates, but does not philosophize about her processes" (*LOLR* 106). In this sentence Austin gives away her own intense anxiety about creativity, for, as her many articles on the subject suggest, she was fascinated by the theory of creative process. In speaking of the individual style of Seyavi's baskets, she values her work and lifts it from anonymity.

Women like Seyavi, Austin writes, held deep within them "things to be learned of life not set down in any books, folk tales, famine tales, love and long-suffering and desire, but no whimpering. . . . But suppose you find Sevayi retired into the privacy of her blanket, you will get nothing for that day. There is no other privacy possible in a campoodie" (*LOLR* 111). In "The Basket Maker," Austin describes the quest for privacy that is common to creative women, but so often violated, whether in the Indian campoodie or the Anglo home.

Austin's account of writing her early masterpiece fuses practicality with mysticism:

I was languid with convalescence, I was lonely; and quite suddenly I began to write. I began at the beginning, and, with an interval of months for another illness, wrote straight to the end, practically without erasures or revisions. I remember the day very well—one of those thin days when the stark energies of the land threaten just under the surfaces. . . . There was a weeping willow whose long branches moved back and forth across my window like blowing hair, like my memory of my mother's long and beautiful hair. I think it was this which gave the reminiscent touch to my mood. For though I was there in the midst of it, I began to write of the

land of little rain as of something much loved, now removed. As I
wrote, two tall invisible presences came and stood on either side.[45]

Austin tries but fails to explain these puzzling presences. "Sometimes,
I felt them call me to my desk—sometimes I summoned them. I suppose they were projections out of my loneliness, reabsorbed into the
subconsciousness when the need was past." At the time of recollection,
Austin feels these presences only dimly, although she remains "occasionally aware of them inside of me."[46] It is tempting to speculate about
the identity of the two figures. Susanna Hunter, Mary's mother, may
be one—the memory of her flowing hair triggered by the fronds of the
willow tree. As for the other, several people from Mary's past emerge
as likely candidates: her father; her dead sister, Jennie; and Ruth, who
must have been always on her mind. The angels at her writing table
image the encouraging presences she longed for in girlhood and young
womanhood but failed to find except in her imagination.[47]

Austin certainly can be said to have "followed in the footsteps of
other naturists, Henry Thoreau, John Burroughs, and John Muir," the
usual string of precursors attached to her work.[48] In contrast to these
writers, whose imaginative capacity for creating stunning visual images
in language she capably matches, Austin has no peer in writing the
short sketch that captures the daily lives of the people of the West in
their ethnic diversity: the women she encountered in the campoodies;
inside the miners' cabins, and in the little houses built by the Hispanics
of "the little town of the grapevines," the title of one essay. In such a
town, by dint of the agricultural and culinary labors of the *senoras*, "you
will have for a holiday dinner . . . soup with meat balls and chile in
it, chicken with chile, rice with chile, fried beans with more chile, en-
chilada, which is corn cake with a sauce of chile and tomatoes, onion,
grated cheese, and olives, and for a relish chile *tepines* passed about
in a dish, all of which is comfortable and corrective to the stomach"
(*LOLR* 166).

Although Austin wrote this rich passage in her role of ethnologist,
she was accompanied by the domestically inclined Mary Austin who
was a skilled cook and gardener. Mary Hunter Wolf has remarked that
her aunt was much caught up in domestic detail, having absorbed all
too well the training she received in the domestic arts during her midwestern girlhood. Literary friends often remarked on her talents as
"an earnest hostess, absorbed in making things pleasant for her guests,
. . . the best of cooks . . . Mrs. Austin's cookery is famous among her
friends."[49]

But at times the desire to be the perfect hostess and cook conflicted with her equally strong desire to concentrate all energies on her literary work. Those closest to her felt her frustration; many a hapless secretary fled in tears after Austin vented her rage, displacing her anger onto them about matters that really had more to do with the interruption of the creative process than with deficiencies in typing or dictation.[50] Numerous letters in her typed correspondence contain handwritten comments about the "stupidity" of the secretary of the moment.

Antimodernism and the Appeal of Primitivism

In an illuminating essay that attempts to account for the shifting tides in the popularity of authors and their books, Cynthia Ozick has speculated: "A century, even a quarter of a century, dies around a book; and then the book lies there, a shaming thing because it shows us how much worse we once were to have liked it; and something else too; it demonstrates how the world shakes off what it does not need, old books, old notions of aesthetics, old mind-forms, our own included. . . . The world to the eager eye is a tree constantly pruning itself, and writers are the first to be lopped off."[51] Ozick's observation prompts a related question: What caused Austin's sketches about Indian life in the remotest areas of California to be acceptable to a large reading public and to critics in 1903? What aspects of American life have allowed these particular sketches to endure, while the majority of Austin's works have been pruned away, as Ozick would have it?

Like Henry Adams, born thirty years before her, Austin dissented from the commonly held belief in technological progress at the outset of the twentieth century. She followed the tack of many intellectuals and literary figures who "craved both the authentic experience outside the bounds of Victorian respectability and the intense spiritual ecstasy of communion with God"—cultural critic Jackson Lears's formulation of the crisis of antimodernism.[52] While many Americans turned to the old cathedrals and traditions of Europe, or even to the Far East, to alleviate anxieties emanating from an increasingly mechanized and technologized world, Austin found a solution in America itself. Turning to the Indians of the western United States, she sought relief from the banal elements of industrial America and the platitudes of organized Protestantism. In her encounter with California's Indians and Hispanics, Austin experienced a vitality compared to which her midwestern Methodism seemed pale and vapid. The critic James Rupert

argues that she found "in Native American dance, drama, music, architecture, poetry, and design an artistic response to the American environment which was socially and culturally effective."[53]

In *The Land of Little Rain* and *The Basket Woman*, Austin introduced
her readers to what Lears defined as an "antimodern quest for authenticity . . . not reducible to the raptures of military men or the slogans
of contemporary self-help manuals."[54] In so doing, Austin sounded
a rallying call audible to thousands of Americans who longed for a
simpler and more spiritual life unified by primitive myth. Such is the
unfettered, preindustrial world the writer represented for her readers in
the essays of *The Land of Little Rain*. When she describes heaven, as she
does in an essay about a Shoshone medicine man named Winnenap,
it is a place "worth going to if one has leave to live in it according to
his liking. It will be tawny gold underfoot, walled up with jacinth and
jasper, ribbed with chalcedony, and yet no hymn-book heaven, but the
free air and free spaces of Shoshone Land" (*LOLR* 65).

Similarly, in *The Basket Woman*, Austin establishes her linguistic and
ethnographic project in the preface, where she examines some Indian
words and customary usages. Austin the scientist, however, is only a
pose for Austin the storyteller and seeker of truth; her work differs
quite markedly in this regard from that of Charles Lummis. Her search
for the authentic permits her to suspend ordinary consciousness in
favor of the nonordinary or heightened consciousness of the Indian
and, by so doing, to enter into the spirit of the tale she tells. "I know
the story of the Coyote-Spirit is true, because the Basket Woman told
it to me, and evidently believed it," she writes, demonstrating her faith
in an informer whose way of life is timeless and essentially untouched
by the constraints of modernity. The narrator/writer and the Basket
Woman merge at certain points in the narrative, both being receptive
creative spirits: "She [the Basket Woman] said she had seen Coyote-
Spirits herself in Saline Valley and Fish Lake. In the same way she told
me about The Fire Bringer, and Kern River Jim told of Tavwots and
how it happens there are no trees on the high mountains. And if this
last is not true, how are you going to account for the fact there really
are no trees there?"[55]

In the harmony of landscape and inhabitants that Austin applied
herself to describe with such precision loomed an America that was
beyond the reach of many Americans entrapped in urban environments
in 1903, and beyond the ken of most Americans more than eighty years
later. Austin's quest for the real led her literally to her doorstep, and
it began at the command of her pen. She had what Lawrence Clark

Powell termed "the necessary equipment" to write classic prose about California. In addition to being on the scene, she possessed "a precise knowledge and a deep love of the land and its people, the capacity to absorb and transmute experience into literature, and the stamina to persist." Powell's assessment of her "deep drive for recognition" hits the mark in describing the personality behind the literary texts.[56]

Of the style that many critics have greatly admired in her first book, Austin insisted that "nothing was further from my mind when I was writing it. I had never exchanged a dozen words with anybody on the question of style, nor thought of it as being a writer's problem. When I wrote I tried always to write the way I supposed highly cultivated people talked to one another."[57] More important, perhaps, in establishing Austin as a major presence in early twentieth-century American literature was her exquisite sense of the alienation abroad in the land. As demonstrated in her earliest work, she retreated into the deepest recesses of the indigenous spirit, exhorted Americans to summon "the courage to sheer off what is not worth while," and reminded them that "life, its performance, cessation, is no new thing to gape and wonder at" (LOLR 78).

Twenty Mule Team Canyon, Death Valley, *by Ansel Adams. The photograph was reproduced in the 1950 edition of* The Land of Little Rain, *illustrating Austin's words: "To underestimate one's thirst, to pass a given landmark to the right or left, to find a dry spring where one looked for running water—there is no help for any of these things."*

Blackburn College class of 1888; Mary Hunter (Austin) stands at the extreme left.

Ina Coolbrith, poet laureate of California and an early mentor to Austin.

Charlotte Perkins Gilman, a writer whose feminism Austin admired. They met at the Lummis home.

Jack London (ca. 1906), Austin's friend and literary sparring partner in the Carmel days.

Mary Austin photographed by Charles Lummis in Los Angeles, ca. 1900.

Austin with James Hopper in her Carmel treehouse ("wickiup"), 1906.

Austin rehearsing the cast of her Indian play Fire *at Carmel's Forest Theater in 1913.*

Willa Cather, Austin's friend in New York and later in New Mexico, photographed by Nickolas Muray.

Mabel Dodge Luhan, Austin's confidante and fellow writer, photographed by Edward Weston.

Austin in her garden at Casa Querida in Santa Fe, ca. 1929.

Austin during a lecture tour in Santa Barbara, California, June 1929.

Ansel Adams working in his darkroom, ca. 1930, during the period of his collaboration with Austin. Photograph by Virginia Adams.

Austin in 1906, after she had settled in Carmel.

4
▲ ▲ ▲

AMONG THE CARMELITES

The modern Carmel is a place of resort for painter and poet folk. Beauty is

cheap there; it may be had in superlative quality for the mere labour of looking

out of the window. It is the absolute setting for romance.

—California: Land of the Sun

"Poor I am yet," Austin wrote to a friend in 1929, "but I never was obscure."[1] While living in the Owens Valley, she was already plotting how best to remove herself from the isolation of the desert. With the success of *The Land of Little Rain*, Austin began to reach out to the larger literary world and was gratified by its attentions. Her restlessness frequently took her away from home to visit friends in San Francisco and elsewhere. Wallace stayed on in the Owens Valley and struggled in vain to persuade the reclamation district to proceed with plans for irrigating the valley in the face of the disastrous announcement that construction of the gigantic aqueduct from the Owens River to Los Angeles could not be forestalled. Again he faced unemployment when the Desert Land Office was forced to shut down as a result of the aqueduct.

The water crisis of 1905 and 1906 hastened what had seemed inevitable almost from the beginning. The veneer of the Austins' marriage, cracked and chipped by the many crises they had faced, was further eroded by the tragedy of the defeated Owens Valley reclamation project. Mary, who had fought passionately to politicize the residents against Los Angeles, grieved over the plight of the valley and took pride in Wallace's efforts to expose "the collusion between federal agents and city officials."[2] She even defended him against "scurrilous stories" about his alleged sell-out to the Los Angeles business interests.

"The facts are," she wrote to a friend, "that Mr. Austin made a filing in the river which Mr. E. was not sharp enough to make, and [Wallace] refused to sell it to Los Angeles. . . . What my husband really did was to present the filing to the People of Inyo to help them in defending their homes."[3] However much Mary admired Wallace's integrity in this particular matter, and his temerity in writing directly to Theodore Roosevelt and other influential figures interested in preservation, she was willing to count the Owens Valley experience as a loss.

With Ruth gone and funds from her writing available for travel, Mary now had the means to separate herself from Wallace by stages. The marriage could shrivel to its natural death.[4] But it was not easy to withdraw. In a letter written from Independence, probably in 1905, to a young writer friend, she made excuses for planning to leave the desert. "I have been ill for some day [*sic*] and threatened with an attack like the one I had last winter, and I am making hasty preparations to get away to sea level for the rest of the winter. Perhaps I will be able to see you personally before I return to my desert and that will be so much more satisfactory." In the same letter she reports that she must "take heart stimulants every half hour," a routine that must have caused considerable inconvenience.[5] Constant domestic stress probably contributed to her heart problem.

One of the homes in San Francisco that Austin frequented in 1904 belonged to California historian Theodore Hittell and his daughter, Kitty. Austin describes the Hittell home in *Earth Horizon* as "a house of distinction, the center of an intimate circle of writers and painters of San Francisco: Ina Coolbrith; Charles Warren Stoddard; John Muir; William Keith; Carlos Troyer; Edwin Markham." Once again the old pattern of friendship emerged: she was drawn to the mature scholar's encyclopedic knowledge of California and San Francisco during and just following the gold rush, and "became a friend of the family—the old historian whose reminiscences trailed back to the eighteen-fifties; Kitty, whose interest took in the whole history of the Golden Gate; its intimacies; its undertakings" (*EH* 297).

It was to the Hittell family that Mary fled from the Palace Hotel when she intuited that an earthquake was impending on April 17, 1906. At five the next morning she felt "the crash of furniture, of falling chimneys, the pitching of tall old bureaus, the noise and confusion of the Earthquake" (*EH* 302). Mary found herself "standing in the doorway to see the great barred leaves of the entrance on the second floor part quietly as under an unseen hand, and beyond them, in the morning grayness, the rose tree and the palms replacing one another, as in a moving picture, and suddenly an eruption of night-gowned figures crying out that it was only an earthquake." The true nature of the seemingly benign "tremblor" became apparent as residents of the Hittell neighborhood flocked into the street "in bathrobes and kimonos" and discovered the fire which had started on Market Street. "But live wires sagging across housetops were to outdo the damage of falling walls. Almost before the dust of ruined walls had ceased rising, smoke began to go up against the sun, which by nine of the clock, showed bloodshot through it as the eye of Disaster."[6]

First Trip to Carmel Bay

Austin had fortuitously discovered the Carmel Bay area in the summer of 1904, while doing research on the Mission San Carlos Borromeo in connection with her novel *Isidro*. When she first tramped around the beaches with her friends, she found "a virgin thicket of buckthorn sage and sea-blue lilac spread between well-spaced, long-leaved pines. The dunes glistened white with violet shadows, and in warm hollows, between live oaks, the wine of light had mellowed undisturbed a thousand years."[7] Austin found that this spot had changed very little from the description David Starr Jordan had filed in 1880 to the United States Census Bureau. "Of all the undulations on the coast of California the most picturesque and charming is the little bay of Carmelo which lies just south of the Point of the Pines between this point and the rocky cape of Lobos," wrote Jordan, an ichthyologist, the president and first chancellor of Stanford University. He further observed that the bay's "blue waters [are] sheltered from the northwest trades by the pine-clad peninsula which ends in the reefs of the Point of the Pines. No one lives on this bay at present except a farmer and his little colony of Chinese who have a 'pescadero' or fishing camp in the edge of the pines, and a little group of Portuguese who watch for whales on a rocky ledge near Point Lobos."[8]

On a camping trip on the Monterey peninsula in mid-July 1904, Austin began to take extensive botanic notes of the Seven Pines area on the Carmel side that Jordan had investigated. She was particularly impressed by the "effect of dark earth and light diffused through the upper sky but not reaching us, a world of light beyond our world . . . the flowing effect of the night air like a cool stream bathing the sleeper." She found in the unspoiled Carmel a source of creative inspiration as others had before her, notably Robert Louis Stevenson, whose "Treasure Island" it was. Echoes of Coleridge reverberate in her account of the genesis of one of her stories. "Going to sleep one night to the sound of voices I had the first part of a dream being the story I shall call 'The Seals,' I seeming to be part of the story myself and hearing the water and the pine trees talk of a secret matter which concerned me very much. A day or two later I fell asleep in the afternoon and completed the story in a dream."[9] Austin, influenced considerably by Henri Bergson and William James, seemed open to psychic phenomena throughout her career, particularly in the 1910s. In 1918 she wrote to a medium named Sonia Levien in regard to a prophecy about the Russian Revolution that she had formulated the previous year. "Remember these intimations seem to come to me from the outer rim of consciousness, as sounds which one might hear moving in a fog. I make the best interpretation I can of them and try to avoid giving them the color of my conscious conclusions."[10] Austin became quite interested in automatic writing in 1920 and, upon the recommendation of publisher Henry Holt, attended four sittings in New York conducted by Dr. Wilbur Franklin Prince of the Society of Psychical Research.[11]

Her experience of dream writing in Carmel, however, appears to have been triggered by the ineffable beauty of the land itself. This was a land of bush and brook lupines, of tiger lilies and castillia, of the wild parsnip and "chapparral pea in the fern in best bloom." The wildlife included roadrunners, quail, rattlesnakes, sidewinders, and, she noted, "one gray long tailed rat in [the] swamp on [the] willow tree. Not shy." During the day there were hummingbirds, at night bats and nighthawks. Always on the alert for the rightful inhabitants of this beautiful place, her eyes ferreted out the timeless "traces of sheep and shepherds all among the rocks. . . . Traces of sheep visible for very many years." *The Flock*, which Austin called "my sheep book," was taking shape in her imagination. Carmel's natural beauty pleased and inspired her.[12]

Austin's decision to live and work there was confirmed by her infatuation with George Sterling. When she met the handsome young poet in 1904, he had just written his much-admired *Testimony of the Suns* and was being hailed by his California following as "a new poet of Keatsian promise."[13] Sterling and the group of poets in the "cosmic California school" (a term derisively applied by the Imagists and the "Eastern critics [who] considered their rhetoric old-fashioned") preferred to distance themselves from the East and its cynical literary judges. Staying their western ground, they became, in effect, a mutual admiration society.[14] In 1903 Mary had received a note from Sterling after the publication of *The Land of Little Rain*, and she visited him in San Francisco the next summer when she traveled to Monterey and Carmel.

By then Austin was enough of a celebrity to warrant a notice in the press of her arrival in the city, accompanied by speculation about her future plans. In an interview she had spoken rhapsodically of the beauty of Carmel and its desirability as a location for artistic work. By her account, Sterling read about her arrival in San Francisco and called upon her, although it is altogether possible that Austin, bolstered by her newfound success as a literary figure, alerted him of her arrival. She found the poet a romantic figure, "handsome as a Roman faun, shy restless, slim and stooping," exuding a youthfulness even though he was in his mid-thirties. He invited her to dinner at Coppa's, a favorite hangout of San Francisco's literary bohemia. Later she recalled the meal in vivid detail: "Such heaping platefuls of fresh shrimp for appetizers! Such abalone chowder, such savory and melting sand-dabs, salads so crisp, vegetables in such profusion, and pies so deep and flaky. Such Dago red, fruity, sharp and warming! And all for thirty-five cents! At Coppa's that night there was also spaget', and, replacing the ubiquitous American pie, little almond crumbly tartlets well filled with whipped cream."[15] Among the party on this gala evening were Henry Laffler, "the literary editor of the *Argonaut*" and "impresario to young talent on the Pacific Coast," the journalist Jimmy Hopper, Stanford biologist Vernon Kellogg, Lincoln Steffens, "and other such students of the creative arts who adventured so gloriously along the coasts of Bohemia."[16] These people were to form the nucleus of the Carmel artistic community a few years later.

The day after this memorable dinner, Sterling and Austin walked to Portsmouth Square on a literary pilgrimage "to fill the [Robert Louis] Stevenson galleon with violets, and after that to take tea and kumquats in the Chinese restaurant, and to sit for a while in the room that had formerly been Stevenson's at the Clay Street hotel," a sort of literary shrine to the man who had immortalized San Francisco in *The Wrecker* (1892).[17] As Sterling read aloud passages from his *The Testimony of the Suns*, Austin experienced romance, perhaps for the first time in her life. However, it was not until late in the summer of 1905 that their paths crossed again, this time in Carmel, where Sterling had built a home and "ruled the roost" of the budding bohemian colony that had taken root there.[18]

Carmel as an artistic community was the brainchild of a real estate executive named Frank Powers. He hit upon the scheme of offering free lots to "any artist who would build," according to Ella Winter, an

English journalist and Lincoln Steffens's second wife. Winter snidely refers to Carmel as the town of "too many lampshades—by the sea" and comments on the ingrown nature of a place where everyone knew everyone else's business. Powers recognized that the presence of artists would attract the public to buy property at premium prices on the virtually uninhabited and unfashionable Carmel side of the Monterey peninsula. In offering lots to Sterling, Austin, Jack London, Ambrose Bierce, and Steffens, among others, he launched Carmel's commercial development, which would mushroom to include not only the artists-in-residence, but socialites and speculators as well. "Small as it was, Carmel had three separate personalities," Winter observed.[19]

The first wave of artistic Carmelites included Joaquin Miller, Charmian Kittredge (who later married London), Harry Leon Wilson, Charles Warren Stoddard, John Muir, and Upton Sinclair. The second wave clustered around Robinson and Una Jeffers, close friends of Sterling, who settled in Big Sur a few miles south of Carmel around 1914. (They built their famous Tor House in 1918.) Winter and Steffens did not arrive for their extended stay until 1927.

Although Austin claimed that she conceived the idea of an art colony at Carmel, it was Sterling who first accepted the offer of property from Powers. He and his wife were settled in by 1905, when Austin returned from Owens Valley.[20] Bierce dubbed Sterling "the High Panjandrum of the Carmel crowd," and his home became the scene of what seems to have been an extended house party for literary personalities. H. L. Mencken, Theodore Dreiser, Sinclair Lewis, and Van Wyck Brooks are among the many who wrote their names in his guestbook. The Sterlings' comfortable redwood living room provided the ideal setting for a fish chowder they called "Thackeray stew," washed down with quantities of drink—ale and a rich, sweet muscatel, the beverages of choice among the Carmelites.[21]

Sterling came from an old Sag Harbor family and possessed the resources to build two places. The cabin of his dreams, which served as the gathering place of the art colony, was built "upon a . . . point of pines, all but islanded by meadow looking toward Santa Lucia and Palo Corona." To reach it from the town of Carmel his friends climbed through the pines and up a hill, "threaded the close encinas, skirting a lovely lake of herd grass all afoam with flowers, and went along a ravine made secret by dark, leaning bays." Holding court in his cabin, the poet cut a vital, "arresting figure," almost magical in Austin's eyes. "George was supposed . . . to resemble a faun," she recalled after his suicide in 1926. His physical looks intrigued her, especially his expressive face. "The poet's smile had always a lightly sardonic twist, and the tip of his thin nose was mobile and inquiring."[22]

What a contrast they were! Sterling was agile and light, Austin heavy, her nose blunt and figure squat. Whereas "he was easily tamed," even though he became agitated easily, she was volatile and held grudges. He played hard and drank heavily; she was unused to play and was by training and habit a teetotaler. By reputation he was a hedonist; she believed that women's sexual needs could be denied. "I never needed a love affair to release the sub-conscious in me," she proclaimed in her autobiography (*EH* 303). But they were in communion on the subject of work, for "he would never, never descend, however badly he had been used, to doing anything less than justice to his work." If Austin saw herself as a "woman of genius," Sterling was a "man of genius," a poet she compared with Shelley.[23] In him she saw nothing less than her soul mate.

Sterling possessed a mythic and luminous quality that Austin had never before encountered in a man of her own age, certainly not in Wallace, whom she chose to see as a sort of troglodyte. She believed in Sterling's genius, even when he took himself rather lightly. Once he wrote to her in a tone of self-mockery of his "local and rather tenuous fame," stating that what little he had moved him to "apathy. So real fame, I think, would be torment."[24] Eulogizing him years later, she judged that he had been "over-faithful to his locality, publishing at San Francisco almost exclusively, resting upon a local réclame which narrowed his public and, perhaps, the scope of his genius." Finding New York inhospitable, Sterling had returned to appreciative Carmel, for his "was never a competitive nature."[25]

"George and I were very much alone in that first year," Austin remembered (*EH* 298). This comment suggests an intimacy between them that may have been realized sexually but probably was not; as David Starr Jordan wrote in 1907, California was dominated by "the old Puritan Conscience, which is still the backbone of the civilization of the Republic."[26] Mary Austin was not a handsome woman, and Sterling had a reputation for affairs with beautiful women. Their private hours together were probably spent walking and talking. Sterling loved to walk, and he discovered in Austin an animated intellectual companion. "Of all our walks he loved best the one on Point Lobos, no poet's stroll, but a stout climb, dramatic, danger-tipped, in the face of bursting spray-heads torn up from primordial deeps of sea gardens, resolved into whorls and whorls of lambent color. Interrupting or terminating such excursions, there would be tea beside driftwood fires, or mussel roast by moonlight—or the lot of us would pound abalone for chowder around the open-air grill at Sterling's cabin. And talk—ambrosial, unquotable talk!" (*EH* 299).

Where was Sterling's wife while these frolics went on? Austin remained on affectionate terms with Caroline Rand Sterling until "Carrie" committed suicide in 1918. It was no secret that Sterling had been unfaithful to her. "We all of us knew that George required the stimulus of sex to have a releasing effect on him," Austin recorded, adding that Sterling's friends "lived in a kind of terror of what it might bring on Carrie his wife, for whom we all had the tenderest affection, and combined to shield."[27] After Carrie's suicide, Austin confided to Charmian London some of the precipitating factors in the couple's divorce. Certain friends had "made a point of telling [Carrie] much more than she had found out for herself [about George], affairs which had passed wholly unsuspected by her," resulting in Carrie's feeling "publicly betrayed, as she was, poor dear."[28]

Sterling, London, and Bierce

Sterling's homoerotic attachments—especially to Ambrose Bierce, his mentor, and Jack London—are brought into rather clear focus in Austin's account. Indeed, her version of their acquaintance indicates that Bierce caused her some jealousy.

> Never having seen Bierce but once, at Sterling's house, and having known him through young people who had passed under his hand, I judged him to be secretly embittered by failure to achieve direct creation, to which he never confessed; a man of immense provocative power, always secretly—perhaps even to himself—seeking to make good in some other's gift what he himself had missed. . . . I thought him something of a posturer, tending to overweigh a slender inspiration with apocalyptic gestures. I am sure he left as many disciples sticking in the bog of unrealized aspiration as ever he drew out on firm ground. Which leads me to suspect that he did not feel altogether sure of their surpassing character. In the end they drifted into an attitude of slightly veiled antagonism over George's acceptance, chiefly on the authority of Jack London, of Jack's version of Socialism.[29]

In the tangled context of Carmel politics, Austin surmised that Sterling was reluctant to have her meet Bierce because he "dreaded that I would uncover to Bierce the extent to which Sterling was implicated with Jack London"—a reference to London's socialism and Sterling's great admiration of him (*EH* 299). According to Bierce's letters to Sterling, he could not bring himself to go to Carmel during the early years, and he never built a house there.[30] A generation older than Sterling and his contemporaries, and caring neither for Carmel nor personally for Austin or London, Bierce was an unwelcome intruder as far as Austin was concerned. He may have been the only enduring member of the old guard, as Franklin Walker remarks, but Austin knew that California literature belonged to the new generation of writers, and thus had little use for Bierce.[31] Because she knew that Sterling wanted desperately to please the older man, Austin found Bierce's influence deleterious.

Interestingly, Bierce admired Austin's work and wrote an enthusiastic letter to Sterling about *The Land of Little Rain*, which Sterling had recommended to him in 1906. "The best of her is her style. That is delicious. It has a slight tang of archaism—just enough to suggest 'lucent sirups tinct with cinnamon,' or 'the spice and balm' of Miller's sea-winds. And what a knack at observation she has! Nothing escapes her eye." Bierce wanted to know what else Austin had written and what she was going to write. "If she is still young she will do great work; if not—well, she *has* done it in that book." His acute sensitivity to the problem of recognition for western writers inheres in a final comment on Austin: "But she'll have to hammer and hammer again and again before the world will hear and heed." Like other western writers, Bierce keenly sensed his own lack of celebrity in the East, and cynically referred to his "notoriety as an obscurian."[32] He harbored justifiable doubts that Austin could succeed where he had failed.

Sterling immediately replied to Bierce's letter, bringing his friend up to date on Austin's two novels-in-progress, *Isidro* and *Santa Lucia*. Although Bierce expressed a keen interest in her books, Sterling's report prompted a testy observation from Bierce, whose forte was short fiction. "She's a clever woman and should write a good novel—if there is such a thing as a good novel. I won't read novels."[33]

The Carmelites of the early days sought to get past a definition of higher culture that historian Henry May has described as "a bizarre and unbelievably innocent mixture of Mission Days and Chautauquas, fiestas . . . false exoticism and genuine uplift."[34] Austin thought of herself as being at the center of the Carmel trio. Her relationship with London and Sterling stimulated her probably more than any subsequent association in her career. "They were to me, these two—Jack and George—the first professional literary men that I had known, a

George Sterling, Mary Austin, Jack London, and James Hopper on the beach at Carmel in 1906. Photograph by Arnold Genthe.

source of endless intellectual curiosity. They were, for example, the first people who could get joyously drunk in the presence of women they respected. For in the outlying desert regions where I had lived this was not done. Partly because of this novelty and partly because I myself had developed a psychological and physiological resistence [*sic*] to alcohol far in excess of its reported delights, I gave myself with enthusiasm to discovering what others got out of it." [35]

With some superiority, she realized that her creative powers needed no lubrication by stimulants to prod creativity, while Sterling's and London's energies required "exaggeration of sensation to find their natural outlet in creative expression." Sterling, in particular, "could not give himself either to composition or to intellectual exposition of an idea, nor even sit and lounge comfortably until by one of three ways his genius had been eased into its appropriate path. When he had been plunging about for an hour in the stinging surf, or wrestling pine knots with an ax, or pounding abalone which had been strenuously gathered from the rocks, or had several drinks in him—then would talk pour from him gloriously," she observed. His friend Jimmy Hopper, journalist and fiction writer, "had the same high effect on him." [36]

She allowed Sterling and London a latitude in their personal behavior for two reasons: they were writers and should be permitted lapses; and it was Carmel, where the ordinary rules of society were suspended for a time. In a romantic poem about Carmel, Austin celebrated the magic place where the trio discovered one another and experienced the happy, sensual pleasures of childhood. Captured as well in this verse is the spirit of writerly solidarity that Austin had found in the colony.

> How white the beach at Carmel was that
>   day!
>   Woman white and curving
> round the discarded sapphire-shot, silk dappled
> heap of her garment
> That lisped and lifted, bowed full
>   to the wondrous long line of her,
>   lapse and revealed her.
> Behind us the dunes breasted shoreward,
> Moon cusped to the tussocks of tawny pale,
>   trumpet shaped minulus
>   and apple-hued sea grass.
> Low on the foreshore, Jack London and Sterling
>   and I together.
> Flickered the drift wood fire,
>   copper, steel blue, and splints of emerald.
> Voices of women dartled and swerved like swallows
>   or poised for our question and answer.
> For one of us was a poet, and one
> New come from the Sea Wolf's adventure,
> And one had walked with the Trues
>   in the land of Lost Borders.[37]

How did London, Sterling, and the other men of the colony come to see Austin? If we are to believe the account that Jimmy Hopper, one of her closest friends in Carmel, shared with one biographer, "she was always pretending love affairs." Another version (Hopper again the authority) has it that "the men fought shy of her. Lincoln Steffens ran away to Mexico, scared of her advances."[38] These stories may be hearsay; then again, they may be true. Similar reports of Austin's romantic aggressiveness were repeated so often that they have become a part of nearly every biographical account. Austin's humiliation must have been considerable if she heard these anecdotes at her expense;

she was a woman of great pride, and her bluster was often a mask she wore to hide her anguish stemming from family problems and many uncertainties.

Sterling had written colorful letters to Bierce, then residing in Washington, D.C., about the good life and high jinks of the Carmelites, in hopes of enticing him into their community. But Bierce was reluctant to return to the area after the San Francisco earthquake, which sent so many creative people packing to the peaceable haven of Carmel. (Austin herself had fled San Francisco only ten days after the earthquake and fire.) [39] Despite his declaration of "affinity" with the "settlement" at Carmel, Bierce wrote: "I should have to see the new San Francisco—when it has foolishly been built—and I'd rather not." In response to one of Sterling's exuberant letters, Bierce could express only reticence about the prospect of being personally associated with Carmel. "I'm warned by Hawthorne and Brook Farm," he wrote, comparing himself to a literary precursor's disastrous utopian adventure.[40]

The creative community in its earliest days established "a settled habit of morning work, which it was anathema to interrupt," but the afternoon was given over to hiking and sunning, to bathing, cavorting, and talking—in short, to physical pleasures of every description. London had committed himself to churning out a thousand words each day.[41] Austin preferred to dramatize in her reminiscences the halcyon days before Carmel's metamorphosis into the full-fledged success that realtors and business interests had intended; it appears that the routine of work and play broke down in later years.[42] In 1910 Sterling stated unapologetically to Austin his commitment to hedonism: "Probably the trouble is that with me my art is entirely secondary. To live and be happy are my only real concerns."[43]

Residence in Carmel

Austin moved into a rustic log cabin when she returned to Carmel in 1906. Augusta Fink has colorfully sketched her routine in a book about the Monterey area; she describes Austin's studio as "a platform high in the branches of a great oak." Austin was much talked about among the Carmelites, who watched her climb up the "rickety ladder" to her worktable in the tree, "dressed in long Grecian robes, with her hair hanging to her waist."[44] This is, of course, the mythic Mary Austin. Curiously, in this town of eccentrics, where nonconformity ruled the day, few had achieved freedom from the double standard as it applied to gender in the first decade of the twentieth century.

The stimulation of Carmel, unfortunately, could not offset frustrations that she was experiencing with Houghton Mifflin, her publishers in Boston. In July 1907 she was doubting her abilities to work through her novel *Santa Lucia*, an anxiety closely linked to Ruth's institutionalization in Santa Clara. Financial distress gnawed on her, even though she had been writing steadily and well up to this point. In what was to become a refrain throughout her career, she advised Houghton Mifflin that the novel was stalled. Her letter stopped just short of blaming them for the delay. "I do not know when I shall get the novel finished. I began it with great hope just before I lost my little girl, and since that time I have been so overworked at making a living, I can never get sufficient vitality at one time to go through with it. If you could have made me a thousand dollars from The Flock, I might have managed it this year."[45] These were the secret sorrows of Carmel, the dark underside of the merry times with her friends in the colony. Freedom from Wallace had engulfed her in financial distress that diminished her creative powers. Guilt over her daughter threatened to overshadow the relief of having her away. When she wrote to Houghton Mifflin to demand better contractual arrangements, they wrongly interpreted her importunities as the unreasonable ultimatums of an unseasoned writer. W. S. Booth, her contact at Houghton Mifflin, hinted in a note passed among the editors that the writer needed "an impresario" rather than a publisher, someone who would " 'finance' her and 'promote' her." After receiving several letters from Austin expressing dissatisfaction, one indicating her desire to have her "desert books brought out in a uniform edition," the editors debated the idea of politely telling her to take her work elsewhere.[46]

The house Austin built in Carmel in 1907 with the proceeds from the sale of the Independence house was without a view except (as she records in her notes) "a bit of the sea rim visible, the white dunes, and midway of the canyon a line of eucalyptus." When she chose property to build on, the requirements of her writing schedule dominated decisions about the house. Wishing to free herself from the bother of meal preparation, she opted for the convenience of living near the Pine Inn, where a hearty dinner cost a mere twenty cents.[47] She rationalized not having a spectacular vista like Sterling's, declaring that she "preferred to go to the view and so keep it fresh, also knowing that a fine view from a study window is a great distraction." Even so, after seven years of intermittent residence in the house, she conceded: "At times now I do regret being absent from the lovely flowing lines of the hills and the flaming surf."[48]

She kept careful notes of her garden, one of her great pleasures. "I have planted many things here," she wrote in 1913, "seeds of native plants—columbine, malilija-poppy, golden rod, (nemophilia) [*sic*], lupine, and (bush) poppy. Also long cherished seeds of *unus andersoni* brought from the desert, of red haw from Long Island, of Chinese wisteria and more than all, of the Italian cedar from the garden of the Decameron."[49]

Austin was never an attractive woman, but dressed in one of her favorite costumes, "the leather gown of an Indian princess," she was an exotic one. Her legendary idiosyncrasies, such as writing in her Paiute wickiup (sacred shelter) perched in a tree, endeared her to her many male companions in Carmel, most of whom were more than a little eccentric themselves. "There was always in her make-up a blend of sincerity and hokum, of spontaneity and playing-for-effect," according to one literary historian.[50] Bound by familial ties and barely able to support herself by writing, Austin established her identity as a writer in Carmel, a place that gave her access to the world of ideas on a continuing basis. Yet at times she felt the atmosphere of the little village too rarefied. Despite the many profound geographical and social shifts she had experienced in her life, Austin remained firmly rooted in midwestern pragmatism. Often she longed to reach out beyond idyllic Carmel to the world of those "men" making their mark in the practical realms of the professions and engineering. Provided with a letter of introduction to Mrs. Herbert Hoover, she began a friendship with the Hoovers, who introduced her to "what she called the 'outside world.'"[51]

The "ambrosial" conversations in which the writer steeped herself during the early Carmel days centered mainly on problems inherent in the play of genius and the peculiarities of the male psyche. Her observations were gender-related in that she found that only "*men* of genius" required "a drink or a love affair to unlock the fountain of the deeper self." Neither Austin nor Norah May French, whom she described as "the only other woman in our circle whose work came near to the class of London and Sterling," needed such spurs to creativity. That neither man asked her why this was so Austin ascribed to the male's "profound, accustomed indifference to what goes on in the mind of any woman who has not personally stirred him." Another topic that absorbed their circle was "why women in general are so attracted to men of creative capacity."[52] Austin caustically observed that "Jack had material enough, God wot, upon which to base a conclusion," and he bent his energies to the subject in his autobiographical *Martin Eden* (1909). London's novel about the plight of creative men appeared a year after her "problem novel" about women, *Santa Lucia*.

In their ongoing debate, Austin argued that women were acculturated to "parasitism" and trained to be "inspirational" as compensation for "their failure to produce creative gifts of their own." She called this an "illusion" that helped male artists to soar creatively.[53] What she leaves unresolved is how Sterling and London assisted her in wrestling with her own problem: achieving an identity as a woman artist in a masculinist society. She often referred to "an ideal mate" when speaking of others' marriages, yet this ideal partner was clearly absent from her own life. Were Sterling and London responsive to their friend's problem? Or, in their concern with the plight of the male artist, were they oblivious to Austin, who functioned as neither parasite nor inspiration?

Austin carried on a long-term and lively debate with London about women in fiction. In the character of Ruth Morse in *Martin Eden*, he provided an example of the "new woman" that she fought against portraying in her own work. However, in becoming a proponent for the essentialist argument—that is, in prescriptively defining the essence of what Woman should be—Austin was entrapped by the cultural assumptions of her time. "The trouble is that [men writers] seem to choose the most unfeminine types, the back of Broadway and Washington Square types, and try to persuade themselves that this is the new woman . . . barren and unproductive types, when the whole essence of any type of woman that will survive is fecunditity [*sic*]," she argued in a letter to London after she had moved to New York.[54]

Santa Lucia: *Marriage, Divorce, and Suicide*

In part, Austin may have worked out the resolution of this problem about genius in her writing, not in the fanciful novel of 1910, *Outland*—where Sterling's wild nature is captured in the character of Ravenutzi (described as "faun-like"), along with a host of other recognizable colonizers portrayed in a heavy-handed allegory of Carmel's social order—but rather in the largely unread novel *Santa Lucia*, published in 1908.[55]

While writers such as Edith Wharton "assumed a marked hostility that implied a great deal more than comic distaste" when they imagined the West,[56] Austin represented the West in a sympathetic light in *Isidro*, *Santa Lucia*, and *The Ford*. The vulgarity of the West, which

Brooks suggests Wharton magnified in such novels as *The Custom of the Country* (1913), did not find its way into Austin's writing. When Austin concentrates on the Anglo world of California, as she does in *Santa Lucia*, she infuses it with culture and gentility rather than illiteracy or vulgarity, leaving all the rigid class and gender roles intact, as they are in Wharton's fiction. *Santa Lucia* comes closer to being a novel of manners than any of her other works. She called it her novel about "how to be happy though married," but added that "the problem seems to be rather escaping me and the story taking the middle of the stage."[57]

In this minor novel Austin chose to focus on the married lives of three young women: William Caldwell, Serena Lindley, and Julia Stairs. Not surprisingly, she cast the female character bearing a male name in the most favorable light. William was named for an uncle who died at Antietam and embodied "all that was heroic, romantic, and nobly minded" (*SL* 272–73). William's father, a physician in the small college town of Santa Lucia, California, had hoped to bestow the name of his beloved brother on a son. Instead, he called his daughter William. Through her the name acquired "an association of so much that is sweet and tender that the figure of the dashing soldier has grown quite dim beside it." Thus, Dr. Caldwell informs William's prospective bridegroom that "William is a girl's name forever in our family" (*SL* 273). In Austin's Caldwell family, daughters can aspire to be sons, at least through the process of naming. William, an amateur scientist, has assisted her father in his practice. Her marriage promises to be the happiest and most egalitarian of the three major characters'.

William's relationship with her father bears more than passing resemblance to the relationship Austin fantacized she might have had with her own father. Before her wedding William half apologizes to her mother for having seemed to prefer her father over the years. " 'And there were times, dear ma, when it seemed more to me that I made more of a point of loving dad, and was more open about it, and I was afraid you might think I loved you less, though it was not true; and I could never understand why you never minded it. But I think I understand now, that if I should have a daughter I should want her to love—I should want her to feel that way about her own father, for it would only be another way of my loving him through her' " (*SL* 276). Perhaps this was the writer's way of coming to terms with the abortive relationship she had experienced with her mother after her father's death. But this is where Austin's similarity with her character ends, for

William enjoys the tenderness of a home where the grown daughter can comfortably crawl into bed with her parents on the morning of her wedding day. The home Austin created for William, with its visible and frequent displays of affection and emotion, represents the home she longed for in youth and in her own marriage. It was the sort of home that her own emotional inadequacies and those of people closest to her prevented her from realizing.

When the novel opens, the secluded setting of Santa Lucia has been somewhat disturbed by the recent arrival from the East of the young, preoccupied biology professor, Dr. Antrim Stairs, whose romance with the most beautiful and reckless young woman in town, Julia Hayward, is to culminate in a tragic marriage and Julia's suicide. As for the aptly named Serena Lindley, she resigns herself to a placid marriage with the dull lawyer, Evan Lindley, having gazed on Julia's fate when she tries to escape from her marriage. Serena "saw herself and all women moving on them [Stairs and men like him] by the way of colorless, unimpassioned marriages, by fatigues and homely contrivances, by childbirth and sorrow and denial—oh, a common story! She thought of William, upon whom happiness descended from the skies, ushered by wild risks, long thunder, and the drumming rain, and brought on her own face a rain of tears as she knew herself, with so many women untouched by any color or romance. Then she thought of Julia, flaming with tormenting passions as she drifted to disaster; she threw up the sash, and [in] the quieting touch of the night and the drifting film of the fog the pang of unfulfillment passed in the sense of saving commonness" (*SL* 345–46).[58]

When Austin began to write *Santa Lucia* in 1904, she had not yet separated completely from Wallace. Her move to Carmel resulted in his charging her with abandonment from October 1907, though their intermittent separations began much earlier.[59] Hence, marriage as a theme obsessed her mind as she contemplated her own choices and those of the women around her. The scenes from the two unhappy marriages that dominate *Santa Lucia* must have served a "therapeutic" purpose, as Augusta Fink suggests, for the men portrayed in this novel caricature some of the traits Mary found most irksome in Wallace.[60] Antrim Stairs had done his beautiful wife "no offense but the unforgivable one of not being able to make her love him" (*SL* 291). Evan Lindley's business schemes bring financial indebtedness into the marriage and humiliation to his wife, Serena, when the repossession men come to collect their furniture and piano, the result of their failure to meet time payments. From Serena's perspective, Evan "had never had any sensible appreciation of the pertinence of his wife's point of view to the conduct of his business, but now he was made to see that there was no smallest move of his in the game he played with men but had infinite and unsuspected capabilities of reacting unhappily on [Serena] and the baby" (*SL* 207).

It may be too reductive to conclude that many of the scenes appear to be direct transcriptions from Mary and Wallace Austin's unhappiest marital moments, especially the intimate details of their financial problems. Yet Evan, like Wallace, "instead of using the proceeds of his law business to clear the indebtedness occasioned by his marriage, . . . assumed new and alluring opportunities for turning his money quickly," speculations that ended disastrously in Wallace's real life and in Evan's fictive one (*SL* 191). Mary had never forgiven Wallace for being less than frank with her in the early days of their marriage about his mounting business debts. She recounted many times the embarrassment of being evicted from their San Francisco boardinghouse during Wallace's absence because he had failed to pay the rent—a duty Austin clearly assigned to the husband (*EH* 234–36). In Austin's value system, husbands owed their wives candor and deference. In fiction this took the form of Serena's blaming her husband for his irresponsibility in neglecting to pay the servant's wages after the birth of her baby. Serena reflects that "it was incredible that he [Evan] should not be able to get the money for a contingency so long foreseen, and amazing that he should respond with so little alacrity to his wife's wounded insistence that the debt be satisfied at once; and this at a juncture when merely to ask for considerate attention argued a dereliction" (*SL* 177).

The narrative of *Santa Lucia* provides its author with many opportunities to critique modern marriage by employing arguments later amplified in her journalism. Among the injustices she decries are the social ostracism that compelled mismatched couples to stay together out of respect for convention, society's unfair denial of suitable employment to competent married women, and the assumption that men should handle financial affairs despite their wives' demonstrated superior capability for managing money, even though in her own marriage she judged Wallace financially irresponsible. In sum, *Santa Lucia* inventories the countless inequities Austin found in her own marriage and in the institution itself.

Serena Lindley embodies Austin's argument that the well-educated woman more often than not has been shielded from the dire truths of men and marriage. "At twenty-one [Serena] was well read, well schooled, spiritually placed though not poised, not bodily strong, clean, reasonable, and pretty; but she had never handled a baby, never been kissed by any but her own people, was not learned in the practice of propping moral insufficiencies of those in whom it is a heart-break to admit the need of props; and at twenty-two and a half she was married" (*SL* 47–48).

Nevertheless, the emphasis in *Santa Lucia* is clearly on the misery of Julia, who is terrified of leaving her husband for her lover because of the social stigma of adultery. Julia's paralyzing fear prevents her from taking any decisive action. Her obsession "to escape into the larger possibilities of living" (*SL* 244) should strike a familiar chord for readers of Kate Chopin's 1899 novel *The Awakening*. It dismayed many readers who rejected the heroine's assertion that she would shed "the inessential" in her life, even her money, "but she would never sacrifice herself for her children."[61]

Edna Pontellier of *The Awakening* and Julia Stairs of *Santa Lucia* are cut from the same cloth. Both are regional characters, Edna bound to the southern traditions of Louisiana, Julia to the imported eastern strictures of California bourgeois society. Both are tortured women who resort to suicide as the final solution to unhappy marriages with men who lack understanding and sensitivity. Ultimately, for Edna and Julia the only way to speak out is through an act that paradoxically renders them forever silent. That Austin uses the device of suicide for Julia—in the form of a vial of deadly poison secreted in the folds of her wedding gown—expresses quite clearly the association of marriage and tragedy. Certainly it recalls the last details of Lily Bart's preparation for death in Edith Wharton's *House of Mirth* (1905), when she caresses the folds of the white Reynolds dress that she was wearing when Selden first realized his love for her.

Although both Wharton's Lily and Chopin's Edna are more clearly portrayed and more compelling suicidal heroines than Austin's Julia, an interesting question arises from these three novels written around the same date. Assuming that Lily Bart intentionally ingested a lethal dose of sedative, why do Wharton, Chopin, and Austin deploy the suicidal ending for women enmeshed in scandal? No facile answer works equally well in each case, but a pattern emerges if one examines the extent to which cultural roles restricted women writers at this time. Edna, Lily, and Julia run head-on into financial and moral boundaries that are defined more certainly by gender than by class or geography. Their anxiety might be summed up in Julia's predicament: "Her soul, hunting forever in its secret fastness, hiding its face from what it pursued, lest to name it was to grow afraid and give over following, perceiving dimly that its satisfaction must be also doom, fled crying in the dark" (*SL* 244–45). What Julia pursues is freedom, even recklessness. Her character is flawed by what R. W. B. Lewis termed "a wholly insufficient moral constancy" in his anatomy of Lily Bart.[62] In view of Wharton's and Austin's unhappy marriages, and Chopin's status as a widow in a society that privileged marriage, it seems pertinent to suggest that Edna, Lily, and Julia reflect the conflict that their creators experienced in attempting to reconcile the roles of writer and woman.

The portrait of the adulterous woman at the turn of the century, or the suggestion of sexual impropriety in Lily Bart's case, demanded a different treatment than that employed by mid-nineteenth-century American writers. In an important study of American social values, David Brion Davis found that by 1850 "the literary ideal of feminine perfection had become inflated to a point beyond even the dreams of realization," alarmingly out of synchronization with the economic reality that had once assured unchallenged male hegemony in the home and society at large. His examination of texts in which jealous husbands murder unfaithful wives demonstrates how "a husband's loss of prestige and power could best be symbolized in the outrage of sexual dishonor."[63] The heroines of Wharton, Chopin, and Austin suggest that the penalty for infidelity had moved out of the hands of the outraged husband. The woman herself, an altogether more sympathetic character than the immoral woman of nineteenth-century fiction, now internalized her own guilt.

The homicidal tendencies of the jealous husband had been transmuted into the suicidal impulses of the guilty and confused woman. A "general anxiety over the changing status of women," which Davis perceived in the nineteenth century, still surfaced in fiction.[64] At the beginning of the twentieth century, however, the increasing complexity of American marriage, stemming from the greater expectations women held of their husbands and their quest for personal fulfillment, was reflected in the alternatives open to women who were presumed to be outside the moral norm. Fear of adultery was as apparent in the first years of the twentieth century as it had been fifty years before; the most notable difference was that women now took responsibility for their own moral actions and destiny. In the fictions of Austin, Wharton, and Chopin, the woman moves to center-stage as a fully realized character, while the male suitor, lover, or husband becomes flatter and less individuated.

Santa Lucia catalogs in scrupulous detail Wallace's peccadilloes and oddities filtered through various male characters, at a time in the Austin marriage when permanent separation and divorce was at issue. Yet the novel renders with equal precision choices that were quite unavailable to Mary, who, despite her intellectual and artistic gifts, was constrained by the cultural assumptions of her time. The ideal marriage in *Santa Lucia* is the marriage of true minds, as demonstrated by William and George, rather than the compromise that Serena and Evan are forced to make when at last he comes around to considering her an equal partner. Serena, resigned to her marriage, banishes "the pain of unfulfillment . . . in the sense of saving commonness" (*SL* 346). Juxtaposed with Julia's suicide, her resignation can be taken as a moral victory only if we deny that writers' texts are nurtured by cultural assumptions and personal psychological agendas.[65] Austin was fighting in her own life *against* resignation to her marriage.

Yet Serena finds peace in renouncing the intellectual life she had fantasied with Antrim Stairs. Her more unfortunate friend Julia cannot summon the courage to take an unconventional path and break the bonds of marriage for the freedom her lover offers in the Philippines. Neither can she face a life of renunciation in a marriage without passion. The resolutions of Julia's and Serena's plights present two paths that Austin rejected in her own life. She continued to write *Santa Lucia*, leaving her husband behind for a new life in Carmel. Her friendship with George Sterling and, above all, the experience of being a writer and living among writers moved her toward the personal liberation she yearned for.

Nevertheless, the argument that *Santa Lucia* is a consciously feminist novel cannot be sustained. Austin urged Jack London to write "the big feminist novel," explaining that no woman could do so convincingly because "the woman must not be seen from the inside, like a piece of machinery, but as existing solidly in space."[66] What Austin meant by this is not entirely clear. Perhaps she foresaw the silly suffrage novel *The Sturdy Oak: A Composite Novel of American Politics*, which she wrote collaboratively with fourteen other authors, among them Fannie Hurst, Dorothy Canfield, Kathleen Norris, Mary Heaton Vorse, and William Allen White.[67]

While marriage is the chief theme of *Santa Lucia*, the other major motif concerns the superiority of the West to the East. Austin envisions California as a seductive woman,

> tolerant, full-natured, of ample-bosomed, courtesan charm, permitting [herself] to be loved with openness and acclaim. To one entering it in the eighties or early nineties, the land was full of belt-

loosening, breath-easing sound as men accommodated themselves to its largeness. Men of the East, and sons of Easterners, they were who went about stubbing their toes over business ventures for the joyous prick of the nerves arousing from sleep. Business villainies obtained a kind of public sanction if they served her; towns tricked and decried one another to become the bright particular jewel of her bosom. There was, around the centres of settlements, a continued ebullition in affairs of trade, through which bright bubbles of great ventures rose and broke with a singing sound. Men who went through those years got a kind of renewal from their very slips and failures, but it was very hard on their women, especially if they were, like Serena, from the East, and expecting to maintain in Santa Lucia the ideals of Bloomsbury, Connecticut. (*SL* 176–77)

Austin's evocation of the land differs from the female aspect of the land evoked by other writers in her imaging of anthropomorphized feminine power. Unlike real women, who are excluded from the male adventure, be it conquering the wilderness or achieving commercial success, Austin's land has a "courtesan charm" that permits her to trick and betray those who are unable to perform to her satisfaction. Austin's blatantly sexual imagery presents not a land raped by men but rather the land imagined as a dominant mistress. The writer had witnessed the success of the "business villains" who had unscrupulously taken the water rights from the Owens Valley ranch owners to transform Los Angeles into a garden. California was "all woman to the men she draws to serve her," for, unlike the nineteenth-century wilderness adventure, success with the land in the twentieth century depended solely on the shrewdness of those with the power to profit from her charms (*SL* 176).

In *Santa Lucia* Austin pits the scholar from the East, Antrim Stairs, against the new type of businessman, Evan Lindley, representing the West. When Evan takes his wife to see the parcel of land being prepared for the erection of "a row of cheap houses," Austin writes that "his facile imagination leaped forward to the largest possibilities to come out of her aptitude for planning, and his skill in disposing of houses after they were built." As Evan "read aloud to [Serena] magazine articles on plumbing and ventilation," a sense of power came over them both (*SL* 259). Serena must compromise her ideals in order to make her marriage succeed; indeed, she must give her husband's business scheme her whole-hearted support and cooperation. Though Austin was of two minds about development interests in California, in this novel building seems to carry the positive connotation of growth and optimism.

The business scheme that the Lindleys collaborate on is remote from the interests of Stairs and his tragically passionate wife. Neither the scholar nor his wife is suited to a land keyed to prodigious growth. Similarly, Lily Bart's association with the real estate tycoon Rosedale proved untenable in the milieu Edith Wharton created. Stairs returns to the East after his wife's suicide, having understood that he was not cut out to participate in "the ebullition in affairs of trade" in Santa Lucia (*SL* 176).

The cleavage between business and intellectual pursuits that preoccupied Austin in *Santa Lucia* suggests a dilemma she faced as a writer who "had no notion of a literary career, of how success was attained and a standing among other writers secured." Carl Van Doren had criticized Austin for failing to "combine all [her] gifts in one characteristic piece of work." In *Three Worlds*, Van Doren recalled that he "had written about her, for the Century, praising the abundance of her spirit but saying that her art seemed inferior to her prophecy." Austin, whom Van Doren esteemed as "one of the most perceptive and reflective minds in America," asked him, "Shall a writer take his direction from within as I do . . . or shall he plan a career as a business man plans a business in view of the main chance?"[68] She deplored the idea of art's commercialism, just as she found the commercialism of California abhorrent. Yet she needed to make a living from her literary work and yearned for success, in the same way that the citizenry of her imaginary Santa Lucia hankered after material success represented by growth and development.

Although Austin shared the view of many Westerners that the land belonged to the industrious, her work evinces a disturbing ambivalence about the corrupt forces of commercialism. She characterized California as "permitting [herself] to be loved with openness and acclaim" (*SL* 176). In using the metaphor of the courtesan, was Austin criticizing the California she had known, castigating the land for its promiscuous welcome to all comers? Or was the courtesan image emblematic of the accommodation that California made to individuals of so many backgrounds, of the land's generous and free reconciliation with her inhabitants, and thus symbolic of her strength? In *Santa Lucia*, Austin seems to embrace the latter view. If the novel is, in part, a commentary about the direction her career was to take, it is useful to refer to her own statements about choosing a middle ground. "If you have found out any way in which an American writer can be really learned and still get printed," she declared to Van Doren, "I wish you would pass it on to me, for I can't find it."[69]

Austin knew full well that she was not writing what people commonly expected of a Western, even though her "books were always of the West, which was little known; and always a little in advance of the current notion of it." It was a source of frustration to her "that people used to fret . . . because I would not do another 'Land of Little Rain'" (*EH* 320). In a sense, Austin had been typecast from the success of her early work. Thus, while the *New York Times* praised *Santa Lucia* for its author's "delightful art in the depiction of some of her characters" and her "exquisitely beautiful" evocations of nature, Austin must have been disappointed with the reviewer's conclusion that "one grieves to note a falling off in that distinction of style which has marked her previous work." Lukewarm as this review was, however, it was more positive than the *Outlook*'s which damned the novel for its "painfully deficient . . . construction" and its "positively depressing" dénouement.[70]

Europe and England, 1908–10

Despite the renewal Austin had experienced in Carmel, the 1905–06 period was a disjunctive and disturbing time for her. "She was stricken; she was completely shaken out of her place," she wrote in her autobiography (*EH* 308). She had been diagnosed as having breast cancer and, believing that she had only nine months to live, "wanted to enjoy some of the things that had been denied her."[71] When she had the opportunity to travel in Europe with her friends Vernon Kellogg ("then Professor of Bionomics, or something equally imposing at Leland Stanford University") and Charlotte Hoffman, who were to be married in Rome in the summer of 1908, she decided that her royalties would be well spent in seeing something of the world.[72] She stayed in Europe for two years. In Italy, even with "pronounced" symptoms of breast cancer, Austin "evaded" it by praying, by which she did "not mean the practice of petition, but the studied attitude of the spirit of transaction with the creative attitude working within" (*EH* 310).

London was the high point of Austin's tour abroad. She had never before had the leisure or the money to travel as a tourist. In England she met many literary figures whose work she had admired, including H. G. Wells, Hilaire Belloc, Shaw, Yeats, Henry James, and Joseph Conrad.[73] Austin particularly admired Conrad; she had first read his "Heart of Darkness" in 1902. Conrad's Marlowe provided the sort of narrative filter that she herself employed with such success in *Lost Borders*. He had read the copy of this collection that Austin had sent to him before she visited him in Kent in 1910 (chauffeured by Herbert Hoover), and she was immensely flattered by his admiration for her work. Feminist though she was, Austin was a writer first, so she was not put off when Conrad expressed astonishment that a woman could write so well.[74]

Staying with the Hoovers in London, she struck up a friendship with her fellow houseguest Anne Martin, an American feminist who was working with Emmeline Pankhurst. Martin, who remained Austin's friend when they returned to the U.S., esteemed her "as a profound and versatile woman of letters." Nevertheless, she found Austin trying at times in her role as celebrated author. "Mary Austin was a lonely, disappointed woman with an empress complex. She thought she was so important! Once when she traveled east tourist, for lack of funds, she called herself Mrs. Graham. She said she did this so that people would not annoy her as they would if they knew she was 'the great Mary Austin!'"[75]

Lost Borders

Austin's new publishers, Harper and Brothers, brought out *Lost Borders* while she was in London in 1909. Dissatisfied with Houghton Mifflin, she had offered it to Harper's and completed the sale before settling permanently in Carmel. This slim volume contains many of her best tales, several of which took up themes of the desert that she had introduced in *The Land of Little Rain*. The favorable critical reception accorded to *Lost Borders* reflected the public's appreciation of her skill with regional material.

The opening essay, "The Land," describes a waterless place that is filled with beauty and silence because "the best part of it remains locked, inviolate, or at best known only to some far-straying Indian, sheepherd, or pocket hunter, whose account of it does not get in to the reports of the Geological Survey" (*LB* 9). Austin hints that the theme of the land as woman will predominate: "Shall the tender opal mist betray you? The airy depth of mountain blueness, the blazonry of painted wind-scoured buttes, the far peaks molten with the alpen glow, cooled by the rising of the velvet violet twilight tide, and the leagues and leagues of stars? As easy for a man to believe that a beautiful woman can be cruel" (*LB* 10). The land is sirenlike, too impassive to be evil, an invitation to men and a competitor to women. Again, the prophetic narrative voice of *The Land of Little Rain* becomes the reader's guide. "Mind you, it is men who go mostly into the desert, who love it past all reasonableness, slack their ambitions, cast off old usages, neglect their families because of the pulse and beat of a life laid bare to its thews and sinews" (*LB* 10). Later, Austin offers one of the most erotic descriptions of desert in American literature: "If the desert were a woman, I know well what she would be: deep-breasted, broad in the hips, tawny, with tawny hair, great masses of it lying smooth along her perfect curves, full lipped like a sphinx, but not heavy lidded like one, eyes sane and steady as the polished jewel of her skies, such a countenance as should make men serve without desiring her, such a largeness to her mind as should make their sins of no account, passionate, but not necessitous, patient—and you could not move her, no, not if you had all the earth give, so much as one tawny hair's-breadth beyond her own desires" (*LB* 10–11). Yet the eroticism here is cool, for the land is immovable, inspiring desire but lacking it. Barren, the desert wilderness presents an arid visage, oxymoronically voluptuous.

As in *The Land of Little Rain*, the narrator acts as a filter of the tales related to her by and about the desert's inhabitants: a motley collection of drifters, prospectors, explorers, entrepreneurs, and sheepherders, most of whom demonstrate an astonishing insensitivity in their dealings with the women closest to them. The last story belongs to a mystical presence called "Walking Woman," who "had walked off all sense of society-made values, and knowing the best when the best came to her, was able to take it"—"the best" being the work of sheepherding, the love of a shepherd, and the joy of their child. "But look you: it was the naked thing the Walking Woman grasped, not dressed and tricked out, for instance, by prejudices in favor of certain occupations; and love, man love, taken as it came, not picked over and rejected if it carried no obligation of permanency; and a child; *any* way you get it, a child is good to have, say nature and the Walking Woman; to have it and not to wait upon a proper concurrence of so many decorations that the event may not come at all" (*LB* 208–09).

Occasionally, the narrator of these tales indulges in a dispassionate digression just short of sociological analysis, as in "The Hoodoo of Minnietta": "Did I say somewhere that women mostly hate the desert? Women, unless they have very large and simple souls, need cover; clothes, you know, and furniture, social observances to screen them, conventions to get behind; life when it leaps upon them, large and naked, shocks them into disorder" (*LB* 19). At other moments the narrator is delphic:

> Out there where the borders of conscience break down, where there is no convention, and behavior is of little account except as it gets you your desire, almost anything might happen; does happen, in fact, though I shall have trouble making you believe it. Out there where the boundary of soul and sense is as faint as a trail in a sand-storm, I have seen things happen that I do not believe myself. That is what you are to expect in a country where the names mean something. Ubehebe, Pharanagat, Resting Springs, Dead Man's Gulch, Funeral Mountains—these beckon and allure. There is always a tang of reality about them like the smart of wood smoke to the eyes, that warns of neighboring fires. (*LB* 3)

The narrator at first appears to privilege the stories related to her by men over those of women, arguing, "A man's story . . . is always so much more satisfactory because he tells you all the story there is, what happened to him, and how he felt about it, supposing his feelings are any part of the facts in the case" (*LB* 93). Yet the majority of these stories related incidents of the cruelty of men to women. Further, the most interesting tales have been overheard by the narrator, who listens attentively to the women's gossip in the campodies and towns she visits. In differentiating the way men and women tell tales, Austin is working in a tradition of women's storytelling. One thinks, for example, of the way Zora Neale Hurston began *Their Eyes Were Watching God*: "Now, women forget all those things they don't want to remember, . . . and remember everything they don't want to forget. The dream is the truth. Then they act and do things accordingly."[76]

One of Austin's tales, "A Case of Conscience," has been pieced together by the narrator from the gossip of Shoshone Indian women. Saunders, "an average Englishman with a lung complaint," sets out on a journey of exploration into "the coast of Lost Borders" (*LB* 26). While drifting in the hills, he becomes lost in Shoshone land. He takes a Shoshone woman, Turwhase, as his lover, "first, because he was lonely and had to love somebody; then because of the way the oval of her cheek melted into the chin, and for the lovely line that runs from the waist to the knee, and for her soft, bubbling laughter; and [he] kept loving her because she made him comfortable" (*LB* 30). In every way Turwhase is pliant to his needs. When Saunders's lung condition is pronounced cured by a Los Angeles physician, he must deal with the problem of abandoning Turwhase for his own people. His health regained, he wants to slough off his life as a squaw man and to return to his patrimony and English society. His "case of conscience" is precipitated by his paternity. "It was then Saunders' conscience began to trouble him, for by this time, you understand, Turwhase had a child —a daughter, small and gold-colored and gray-eyed. By a trick of inheritance the eyes were like Saunders' mother's and in the long idle summer she had become a plaything of which he was extremely fond. The mother, of course, was hopeless. She had never left off her blanket, and like all Indian women when they mature, had begun to grow fat" (*LB* 32–33).

Saunders, believing his duty is to his daughter, resolves to leave the mother and take the child to England so that she can be properly reared, despite the "explanations" that the presence of his "half-breed child" will necessitate at home (*LB* 32–33). But he fails to calculate the force of Turwhase's maternal instinct. He explains his intention to her and assumes that she will acquiesce in his plan with the same passive good nature with which she has accepted his love. He begins his journey unmoved by any considerations other than his own convenience. "At the hotel at Keeler that night he began to taste the bitterness he had chosen. Men, white men, mining men, mill superintendents, well-dressed, competent, looked at the brat which had Shoshone written plainly all over it, and looked away unsmiling; being gentlemen, they did not so much as look at one another. Saunders gave money to the women at the hotel to keep his daughter all night out of his sight" (*LB* 36).

Finally, this "gentleman" who makes a point of following the code —first by fulfilling his paternal duty to his daughter, even if it means abandoning her mother (of whom he is ashamed), then by contriving to get her out of the way when she threatens to embarrass him— is foiled by a stronger code. Turwhase tracks him down and demands the child back, scorning the conscience money he offers her. "With a flirt of her blanket she scattered the coins on the ground; she turned with dignity and began to walk desertward. You could see by the slope of the shoulders under the blanket and the swing of her hips, as she went, that she was all Indian" (*LB* 36). The narrator shares Turwhase's contempt for her "husband's" interpretation of duty, "old, obstinate Anglo-Saxon prejudice that makes a man responsible for his offspring," an irrelevant code in the desert, where larger principles prevail (*LB* 37).

The man and woman in another tale, "Bitterness of Women," are locked in a different sort of power struggle. The story opens when

Louis Chabot, a shepherd who fancies himself an irresistible lothario, callously explains to the unattractive Marguerita Dupré why he does not return her love. After three years of playing her along, Chabot is savagely maimed by a bear. "If there was any question of the propriety of the care of Chabot falling to Marguerita Dupré it counted for nothing against the fact that nobody was found willing to do it in her stead" (*LB* 173). She contrives to shield him from knowledge of his ugliness by banishing mirrors from the house and keeping him close to her. A marriage ensues that hinges on convenience, Marguerita being a woman of means and also an excellent cook. Not long after, Chabot ventures into the town, where the stares of children and the shrieks of a former lover—"there was something more than coquetry in the way she ran," Austin writes (*LB* 175)—reveal his disfigurement to him. Chabot returns chastened and resigned to life with Marguerita cut off forever from the game of flirtation, "the delicious disputed moves of the game he loves. . . . Though he is only thirty-four, poor Louis is no longer possessed of *l'art être désiré* [sic]" (*LB* 177). In the final lines of the story, the narrator renders an intimate portrait of the couple's marriage "and the bitterness of women which has come to him."

Gossip in the Desert

The hyperbolical story of Chabot's disfigurement and Marguerita Dupré's response surely conforms to the suggestion that the literary function of gossip depends on "information or pseudo-information that has already passed through many ears, many mouths, acquiring authority and heightening in the process."[77] For how does the narrator obtain these intimate details of the marriage if not through the gossip of the townspeople? "Knowing what he does of the state of her heart, and not being quite a cad, he does not make her an altogether bad husband, and if sometimes, looking at her with abhorring eyes—the shaking bosom, the arms enormous, the shade of her upper lip no longer to be mistaken for a smudge—resenting her lack of power to move him, he gives her a bad quarter of an hour, even there she has the best of him. For however unhappy he makes her, with one kiss of his crooked mouth he can set it right again. But for Louis, the lift, the exultation, the exquisite, unmatched wonder of the world will not happen any more; never any more" (*LB* 38). Marjorie Pryse, who has written an illuminating essay about the tales in *Lost Borders*, is altogether right when she refers to the "high price" Marguerita Dupré pays for a man's love. "She has the satisfaction of knowing that her injured and scarred husband cannot leave her, but she faces the knowledge as well that he will refuse to love her."[78]

What is the reader to make of the literary content and form of these stories? How does the narrator become privy to the tales set down? How important is the narrator's interpretive function to the myths and stories presented? What attitudes does the narrator transmit about men's storytelling as opposed to that of women? And how does this suggest a gender-linked pattern, since the stories are mainly about the relationships between men and women?

Certainly Austin uses gossip as an important literary device to advance these stories. The narrator weaves her tales by drawing on the resources of those she meets. Hence, we learn in "A Case of Conscience" of the many opportunities afforded the narrator through overheard conversations. "What I like most about the speech of the campody is that there are no confidences," the narrator says. "When they talk there of the essential performances of life, it is because they are essential and therefore worth talking about" (LB 38). By logical extension, the tale is worth telling, for "in a campody it is possible to speak of the important operations of life without shamefacedness" (LB 39). The tale of Saunders and Turwhase, which is about women's power, owes its origins to the gossip of the women. At the end of her story, the narrator confides to the reader, "When Indian women talk together, and they are great gossips, three things will surely come to the surface in the course of the afternoon—children, marriage, and the ways of the whites. This last appears as a sort of pageant, which, though it is much of it sheer foolishness, is yet charged with a mysterious and compelling portent" (LB 39–40). Simultaneously, the narrator attributes a nobility and eloquence to the campody women's gossip with the word *pageant*, undercutting it in the next phrase with "sheer foolishness," and finally restoring its power by attributing to women's speech qualities described as "mysterious and compelling." Austin employs the device of gossip in the sense of women's privileged communication, implying that the most "subordinated group" in society speaks most freely in the intimacy of an uncritical audience composed of other unempowered listeners.[79] In this way, Austin subverts the meaning of gossip as the frivolous conversation of women and redefines it as shared information of the most vital nature.

In a recent study, literary scholar Patricia Spacks asks the reader to "think of gossip as a version of pastoral. Not just any gossip: the kind that involves two people, leisure, intimate revelation and commentary, ease and confidence. It may manifest malice, it may promulgate fiction in the guise of fact, but its participants do not value it for such reasons; they cherish, rather, the opportunity it affords for 'emotional speculation.'" When applied to fiction, according to Spacks, gossip may be translated as "fragments of lives transformed into story." Austin's *Lost Borders*, enmeshing the reader in its web of fact and fiction, of gossip, speculation, and concrete detail, involves the reader in a collaboration with the narrator. "The gossip both derives from and generates a need to know the facts of the case—generates that need in the reader as well as in the fictional society."[80] The narrator mulls over fragments of information gleaned from a variety of sources to construct the tale; the reader weighs the reliability of these sources one against another, fully realizing that "multiple consciousnesses" (to use Spacks's phrase) have informed the narrative.

Circumscription is an important narrative element in *Lost Borders*. The narrator in "A Case of Conscience" can tell us "no more of that than I had from Tiawa in the campody of Sacabuete, where there are no confidences" (*LB* 41). This phrase serves as the introduction to Austin's next tale, "The Ploughed Lands," about a young Shoshone woman given by her people to Curly Gavin, a "Swamper for Ike Mallory's eighteen-mule team." Tiawa tells the narrator that she was rejected by Gavin after she had tended him through a bout with desert fever and guided him out of the wilderness to the "ploughed lands" of civilization. The narrator interprets the story Tiawa has related: "In the end —as I have already explained to you—Gavin went back to his own kind, and Tiawa married a Paiute and grew fat, for most in encounter with the primal forces woman gets the worst of it except now and then, when there are children in question, she becomes a primal force herself" (*LB* 50). In Spacks's analysis, the three key elements—narrative, interpretation, and judgment—"dominate gossip . . . generate a characteristic rhythm of investigation . . . [and] create a story."[81]

On occasion, Austin's narrator actually witnesses the events of the story and then passes judgment, indulging in gossip herself to drive the narrative forward. One such story, "The Return of Mr. Wills," begins: "Mrs. Wills had lived seventeen years with Mr. Wills, and when he left her for three, those three were so much the best of her married life that she wished he had never come back. The only real trouble with Mr. Wills was that he should never have moved West. Back East I suppose they breed such men because they need them, but they ought really to keep them there" (*LB* 52). The process of mythologization in *Lost Borders* is contingent upon gossip. The narrator functions as both recipient and propagator of splintered bits of information. Reconstituted in the tales is a coherent community, a group distinguished by their ties to the desert, according to the testimony of the narrator, who has made a confidant of the reader.

The narrator offers the reader a promise at the outset of the collection: "If you cut very deeply into any soul that has the mark of the land upon it, you find such qualities [of desert] as these—as I shall presently prove to you" (*LB* 11). The barren desert that Austin successfully interprets in *The Land of Little Rain* is humanized in *Lost Borders*, where women emerge as survivors. Like Austin herself, the women who inhabit the land of lost borders—the Walking Woman is their exemplar —discover inner reserves of power and spirituality that are unavailable to them in the larger, more chaotic world of modernity.

In *Lost Borders*, the plot of the strong woman who guides a weak man has several variants. *Santa Lucia* attempts to grapple with similar material in a bourgeois setting. That *Santa Lucia* fails to fully engage the reader in the same way that *Lost Borders* does is partly due to the device Austin uses to set up the narrator's relationship to the reader. The gossip of *Lost Borders* serves to make the reader complicitous, to participate as a speculative presence along with the narrator. This method facilitates the reader's imaginative entry into the intimate lives of those who inhabit the desert in ways that the didactic, third-person narration in *Santa Lucia* prevents. Ambiguous and problematic as the literary vehicle of gossip necessarily is, Austin's reliance upon it as a primary source of information in *Lost Borders* charges these stories with a complexity and urgency that is absent from the sustained narrative of the more conventional *Santa Lucia*. For all its sensational aspects of plot, the novel fails to persuade the reader of the significance of what is being related.

The Arrow Maker

While Austin was in England in 1909, she showed a copy of her play *The Arrow Maker* to the American producer William Archer and Edmund Gosse, the British librarian and literary scholar. Both men reacted favorably, and Archer arranged for the play to be produced at the New Theatre in New York, where it opened on February 27, 1911, for a run of eight performances.

Austin described *The Arrow Maker* as "a folk play, written in the poetic rhythms of Indian verse; formalistic, and climbing up and up to a ritual." Unfortunately, she and the director, George Foster Platt, had differing conceptions of her work. Platt, she complained, "knew nothing of Indian plays or of folk plays either." Austin lectured to him, argued, and explained what she wanted, insisting up to the night of the premiere that the play should have a "ritualistic presentation." In the end the playwright had her way, but she declared herself "worn out" and "wanted no more to do with plays" (*EH* 315).[82]

The main character of *The Arrow Maker* is a sorceress known as the Chisera. She falls in love with Simwa, the arrow maker, and helps him become chief of their Paiute tribe. Having gotten what he wanted from the Chisera—a magic arrow—Simwa abandons her for another woman. The gods revoke the Chisera's magical powers as a punishment for breaking her vow of chastity. Simwa, however, still fears the sorceress and tries unsuccessfully to kill her with the magic arrow. Finally the Chisera regains her powers and saves the tribe from Simwa.

Reviews of the play in New York were mixed. "Mrs. Austin's Indians seem very sophisticated in their speech; and they talk a great deal," commented the *New York Times* in an interview with the playwright. "Yet, in spite of the serious handicap she has assumed in her choice of material, there is a genuine, if not sustained dramatic appeal in her play which has a distinct literary quality; and though its male characters bear all the earmarks of having been conceived in a feminine braine [*sic*], they and the principal women of the drama are consistently drawn and ably pictured."[83] Adolph Klauber was much less kind, finding the production "at times . . . ridiculous largely because it is pretentious" and lacking the "rhythm suggestive of Indian speech." Overall, Klauber faulted the play for its inauthenticity. "Not American Indians, but Anglo-American Indians they seem in great part, the sense of characterization never seeking deeper than the multi-colored and tinted robes."[84] Klauber's criticisms of "the trite love story and its badly unimaginative acting" were not shared by the Indian photographer and ethnographer Edward Curtis. After seeing *The Arrow Maker* a second time, Curtis sent Austin an appreciative note, remarking that he "enjoyed it if anything more than the first night" and praising her "wonderful work in making white men and women seem wonderfully like Indians."[85] (Although no Indians appeared in the cast, the songs and chants were "taken from phonographic records of Indian music." An Indian chief coached the cast in the dancing, and the American Museum of Natural History provided costumes and artifacts that were copied for use in the play.)[86]

One modern critic has called *The Arrow Maker* "abominable" because

Austin has the Chisera speaking as "if she had absorbed the slogans of the feminist press and the tense, breathless ideology of the 'common man' . . . and the heroine is given to exclamations straight out of the mass-circulation magazines."[87] This judgment seems overly harsh. In fact, Austin protests that hers is not a "drama of great primitive passions." The "explication of this primitive attitude toward a human type common to all conditions of society" in *The Arrow Maker* is her plea for an understanding of creativity—certainly her own particular talents as a "woman of genius"—rather than a transcription of aboriginal life.[88] Writing about the play some nine years after it was produced in New York, Van Wyck Brooks found in the Chisera "the key . . . to an understanding of Mary Austin's peculiar mysticism." He noted that Austin had merged "the role of a priestess, an inspired leader" with the role of an artist, "which she has always thought of herself as filling."[89] Delineating the character that many thought was her alter ego, Austin wrote:

> The Chisera is simply the Genius, one of those singular and powerful characters whom we are still, with all our learning, unable to account for without falling back on the primitive conception of gift as arising from direct communication with the gods. That she becomes a Medicine Woman is due to the circumstance of being born into a time which fails to discriminate very clearly as to just which of the inexplicable things lie within the control of her particular gift. That she accepts the interpretation of her preeminence which common opinion provides for her, does not alter the fact that she is no more or less than just the gifted woman, too much occupied with the use of her gift to look well after herself, and more or less at the mercy of the tribe. What chiefly influences their attitude toward her is . . . no less than the universal, unreasoned conviction that such a great gift belongs, not to the possessor of it, but to society at large. The whole question then becomes one of how the tribe shall work the *Chisera* to their best advantage.[90]

On another level, Austin is addressing the concerns of those of her time who saw drama as an artistic form of advocacy, "a socializing agency; a means for cultivating interest—passionate interest—in the things of social concern."[91] Austin's frequent lectures on aboriginal drama clearly demonstrate her commitment to using drama for this purpose. Simwa is a familiar type in Austin's work. In the novel *No. 26 Jayne Street* the male who selfishly uses women for his own purposes appears in the guise of Adam Frear (said to be modeled on Lincoln

Steffens). One of the chants Austin creates for the Chisera in the final act of *The Arrow Maker* speaks eloquently of experiences common to all women, and surely transcends being the "obsession of a protesting feminist" for which the play has been faulted.[92]

> And my heart is emptied of all
> But the grief of women.
>
> All the anguish of women,
> It smells to the gods
> As the dead after battle,
> It sounds in my heart
> As the hollow drums calling to battle,
> And the gods come quickly.
>
> Now I shall make a new song,
> A song of the grief of women;
> But for myself,
> But for all who have eaten sorrow
> Who are sick and ashamed
> And for love go ahungered.

A few lines later the Chisera sings "the song of the mateless women":

> None holdeth my hand but the Friend,
> In the silence, in the secret places
> We shall beget great deeds between us![93]

Austin in *The Arrow Maker* foregrounds her deep resentment over "the enormous and stupid waste of the gifts of women."[94] Because she knew that theater audiences would be reluctant to accept her premise "outside of primitive conditions where no tradition intervenes to prevent society from accepting the logic of events," she couched her deepest feminist thoughts (though she did not use the word *feminist*) in a play with "Indian color." The theme is one that had embraced her as she had embraced it from the early Carlinville years. It germinated anew in her heart in Carmel and in Europe. Her divorce from Wallace not yet final, she struggled to gain artistic and personal equilibrium, having eaten most heartily "of the grief of women."

5

▲ ▲ ▲

LITERARY NEW YORK

I have been treated badly by men, as have most gifted women. But in my quarrels with men of whatever nature, although they charge me with behaving unwisely from their point of view, irritatingly, unnecessarily tactlessly, they all in the end grudgingly admit a certain inviolable "nobility."

—Austin to Henry Seidel Canby, April 1, 1930

The whole of my life has been in the nature of a consecration.

—Austin to William MacDougal, October 22, [1923]

After her two-year sojourn abroad, Austin returned to New York in 1910 and took an apartment on Riverside Drive in Manhattan. For more than a dozen years New York would be a home, although she continued to travel to cities all over the country, even to England once again in 1921, on arduous lecture trips to supplement her earnings from journalism and book royalties.[1] Frequently short announcements would appear in the *Bookman* reporting on Austin's whereabouts; even so, her comings and goings were difficult for the public to trace. Letters followed her from New York to the West and back again. Commuting took a considerable toll on the writer. Each shift meant a strenuous cross-country trip by train. Packing up her work and personal things, arranging to be absent from her house or apartment, and settling into a new environment became a ritual enacted on the average of twice a year. Once in Carmel, or Santa Fe, or New York again, she was required

Austin in 1914, the year of her divorce.

to mentally shift gears, to configure a work schedule accordingly, and to see to the details of a professional life, such as having a typist on hand. Arranging her work to afford her the income she needed presented another crucial problem; much of the time she felt physically drained, and she was often ill.

What had precipitated Austin's move to New York City? She found that living there presented the best opportunity for arguing the importance of the West in person, a mission she had attempted in letters when she lived in Carmel. More important, living in the East would enable her to negotiate better terms for her books. Reading between the lines of her correspondence to her editors from California, Austin's ambition to make a reputation and earn a living from her writing emerges clearly early on. "I think I have it in me to do bigger novels than any body in the west is doing, but I can not do them and work at other things for a living," she complained to Houghton Mifflin in 1907. Unless the publisher could "manage some way to make some money" for her, she added, she would take her books elsewhere.[2] Later in the same year she expressed heightened concern about the treatment she was receiving from Houghton Mifflin. "I should be glad to have you continue the management of my books provided you can make a living out of them for me, and that means, I think, that you must adapt your times and occasion more to mine than you have done during the past two or three years," she wrote. Projecting "books and books, mostly novels, more of them named and planned than I can execute in seven years," Austin alluded to her impressive productivity: "the novel, about 100,000 words, ready in October . . . a book of three Indian tales, fifteen to twenty thousand words each, two thirds done . . . another book of forty thousand, half done." Along with her progress report she included an ultimatum: "If I am to turn in all my books to you, you must be prepared to turn them all out and not down."[3] The urgency of Austin's letters reflects the difficulty of managing both the business and the creative aspects of her career from California.

In New York, by contrast, publishers were more accessible and contacts in the periodicals world proved easier to cultivate. Simultaneously, Austin discovered the power she possessed on the platform when the public responded enthusiastically to her lectures on Indian reform, women's rights, and a range of literary and cultural subjects. Her royalties remained scant, however—never enough to live on—and her moves within New York were necessitated by the imperative of finding reasonable rent. "I lived first on Riverside Drive, at the Washington Irving house, for two or three years at the National Arts Club, and at No. 10 Barrow Street," she relates in her autobiography (*EH* 336). But one must turn to her letters for the details of her material circumstances during her years in the city. "This problem of living in New York grows more difficult every year," she wrote wearily to a friend toward the end of her residence there. "Rents appear to be higher than ever, and I have not been able to find a tolerable apartment for less than two thousand, which I can't afford."[4]

Austin could never come to terms with the gross disparity she perceived between the prodigious amount of work she was producing and the niggardly financial gain and recognition she had achieved. Between 1910 and 1922, she wrote four experimental social novels— *A Woman of Genius* (1912), *The Lovely Lady* (1913), *The Ford* (1917), and *No. 26 Jayne Street* (1920)—and saw her most important play, *The Arrow Maker*, staged in New York. Numerous and diverse works of nonfiction emerged from these years as well, including *Christ in Italy* (1912); *California: Land of the Sun* (1914); *Love and the Soul Maker* (1914), a long essay on love and passion in the form of a dialogue; and *The Man Jesus* (1915), a biography of Christ, whom Austin envisioned as a "small town man." *The Trail Book* (1918), a volume of animal stories for children, reflected her continuing tie to the West. Journalism poured from her pen, as well as poetic interpretations of American Indian songs.

Austin's attitude toward New York and the eastern literary establishment was characterized by ambivalence, if not outright hostility. Her earliest impressions of the city reveal mixed feelings of intimidation and fascination. In 1911 she began to keep a notebook of observations "at the instance of my friend Lincoln Steffens to prove to him that I can not write a book about the city as interesting as *The Land of Little Rain*. Steffy is saturated with the city. He can look at his watch any time of the day and tell you what is going on in any part of it at that particular hour, and he cant [*sic*] understand that it will take me more years to learn my way about it than were necessary to know the trails from Mojave to Lone Pine. And he does not know how slow I am . . . nobody knows that and if I tell them they do not believe it."[5]

While other Austin notebooks are dominated by references to nature and are vibrant with color, the New York notebooks are preoccupied with urban life. Fascinated by the violence of the city, she saved clippings describing electric chair victims "lying in state"[6] and other lurid events of the day. "The second winter in New York, when I was homesick for California and having a bad time financially, I used to wander about the drab streets of New York looking for beauty and color," she recollected. "I would spend hours in the silk department of the big stores, and would stand in front of the florists [*sic*] windows." One day she found in the window of a Japanese art shop "a large hand moulded bowl of glass, not quite crystalline but with an iridescence running like fire under the surface . . . and inside the bowl the gold fish flashed in and out of the streamers of green water grass." Her financial situation at the time was so difficult that the price of thirty-five dollars for "all this loveliness" was completely out of reach. "It might just as well have been a thousand," she wrote.[7]

The early notebooks show that she was much interested in the Jewish heritage of the city, particularly the origins of Jewish celebrations and their meanings. Purim, the feast of spring, intrigued her, and she wrote notes about Queen Esther saving her uncle Mordecai from the gallows intended for the wicked Haman.[8] The biblical Esther's attraction for Austin is consistent with the writer's admiration of strong women. Yet, despite her appreciation of cultural differences, Austin was not immune to the latent anti-Semitism of her period. Few writers expressed their feelings about this sensitive situation as openly as she did. An outsider herself, she recognized the plight of others in that position. To her, Jews were outside "*our* anglicized democracy," a situation brought about by the "tragic . . . desire of the young Intellectual in New York, particularly if he has a Hebrew strain, to make a tribe for himself."[9] Noting the "preponderance of Jews among our critical writers" in New York, Austin questioned whether "the Jew, with his profound complex of election, his need of sensuous satisfaction qualifying his every expression of personal life, and his short pendulum-swing between mystical orthodoxy and a sterile ethical culture," was suitable for the task. She further questioned whether the Jewish intellectual community ought to serve as "the commentator, the arbiter, of American art and American thinking."[10] She criticized Waldo Frank's 1919 book *Our America* for generalizing the idea of an America from his New York Jewish intellectual's perch, an ethnocentric vantage point she found neither valid nor illuminating.

> It is a country centered in New York, with a small New England ell in the rear and a rustic gazebo in Chicago; the rest of it is predicated from a car window. . . . There is interesting, discriminating comment on the New England writers, especially such of them as [are] already dead. The rest of the book is chiefly concerned with Mr. Frank's own coterie and those outside writers who have done selected work. This includes the younger Chicago group, Sand-

burg, Anderson, Masters, and Dreiser. Two women are mentioned
as having stimulated American thought; they are Amy Lowell and
Emma Goldman. There is also a footnote somewhere in the book
admitting the existence of other poets and critics, and "several
novelists." And in New York there are Mr. Frank's friends sol-
emnly engaged in "releasing the soul of America," "organizing an
American tradition which shall . . . bring to birth an articulated
people," "quite simply . . . creating a consciousness of American
life." The names of these gentlemen are Stieglitz, Stein, Ornstein,
Rosenfeld, Oppenheim, Mencken, Littell, Hackett, and Brooks.[11]

Austin's alienation from New York stemmed partly from anger: Why
should "a small New York group" of men have such power over what
was "to be written and thought?" In the work of Frank and his ilk
—whose analyses of America she viewed as bereft of any serious consideration of the American Indian and of such Western writers as Alice
Fletcher, Willa Cather, and Charles Lummis—Austin saw a demonstration of "utter blankness to the sources of form and social inspiration"
in America. How, she asked, was it possible for credible New York
critics to employ "studied neglect" in reviewing a story of Zona Gale,
leaving the reader in the dark as to "whether it happened in Wisconsin
or in Senegambia—since the important contribution that Miss Gale
has to make is the delimitation of life in the small American community?"[12] She found Frank's *Our America* sorely wanting in its attention
to race, class, and gender—a representative example of a problem that
could be corrected only if the New York publishing monopoly were to
be dismantled and decentralized.

Austin's scrutiny of the narrowness of American cultural consciousness in 1920 seems ahead of its time, perhaps because cultural criticism
has become integral to scholarship of recent date.[13] Much of her career
in New York was spent arguing with the publishing elite about an
America she was convinced they neither knew nor wanted to know.
Austin held that it was not she but rather New Yorkers who exhibited
provincialism. She found the editors of the *Nation* and the *New Republic* "lashed to their publications, able to talk of what was written,
of what was going on under their noses, and not able to talk of what
might be going on elsewhere; not *willing* to accept the idea that there
might be anything elsewhere going on."[14] New York to Austin "was
much too intrigued with its own reactions, took, in the general scene,
too narrow a sweep." More damning, New York "lacked pattern." Not
until she returned to the Southwest did she recover "the feel of roots,

of ordered growth and progression, [and] continuity" that was integral to her growth as an artist (*EH* 349).

Over the years it became increasingly difficult to suppress her irritation when periodicals consistently rejected her manuscripts, then called upon her to write reviews if they had a "raft of Indian and semi-Indian stories" on hand awaiting evaluation. Essays of this type usually ran to less than eight hundred words and paid far less than the 2,500-word articles that she preferred to write. "Quite as last year, the review is economically unsound for you," Ernestine Evans of the *New Republic* advised her, while asking her to send a review from Santa Fe to New York by airmail.[15] Irked by the marginal position the West occupied in the view of eastern literary lights, Austin could only conclude that her own work was equally peripheral, secondary to what New York considered significant and avant-garde in American culture.

Belated Recognition

Nevertheless, by the end of her New York period Austin had won a large measure of recognition in literary circles. Her belated acceptance was signaled by a dinner given in her honor at the National Arts Club on January 8, 1922. The tribute, occasioned by Austin's impending move to Santa Fe, was attended by a constellation of notables, including the writer Hamlin Garland, the publisher Henry Holt, John Lane (representing her London publisher), J. S. Watson of the *Dial*, Henry Seidel Canby of the *New York Evening Post*, Barton Currie and Ida Clyde Clark of the *Ladies' Home Journal*, Ferris Greenslet of Houghton Mifflin, Edward Wheeler of *Current Opinion*, Carl Van Doren of the *Nation*, John Farrar of the *Bookman*, and Witter Bynner, president of the Poetry Society of America. An honorary member of the National Arts Club since 1911, Austin was a frequent resident in the pleasant and stylish building in Gramercy Park. She often participated in animated discussions about American culture by the club's fireplace, "drawing from the contacts with other minds a challenge to her own principles, so often at variance with the swift stream of life in New York and other Eastern centers."[16] Many of her fellow residents, however, thought her aloof; she usually dined alone, as had been her habit even in social Carmel.

In his opening remarks at the testimonial dinner, William Webster Ellsworth observed that men outnumbered women authors in the United States by three to one. Nevertheless, he declared, "if you place

side by side the names of American men and women who are doing
today the best work that is being done in fiction, the women will out-
number the men." At a time when women writers were being charged
by some with feminizing American literature—a backlash against the
increasing visibility and influence of their work in the preeminent
periodicals—Ellsworth's words were especially apropos. Proclaiming
himself a staunch believer in women's ability in "imaginative literature," he pointed out that the American Academy of Arts and Letters,
"which President [Martha Carey] Thomas of Bryn Mawr has effectively dubbed the American Men's Academy—has so far considered
only Julia Ward Howe as worthy of a seat in its assemblage."[17]

To read Austin's report of the dinner is to understand more fully
the extent of her struggle to be recognized by literary New York. The
most detailed personal bulletin went to her close friend and frequent
correspondent, Professor Daniel MacDougal of the University of Arizona and the Carnegie Institution of Washington, D.C. To him she
gloated that the celebration "was in a sense an admission of the complete subjugation of New York. It had taken twelve years to achieve
that recognition, she added, "but of course there was the war." Austin
described the dress she wore with girlish enthusiasm as "the most magnificent piece of color I could find, which would technically be called
rose color, but it was the rose of an Arizona sunset. It has a silver sheen
on it, took the light like flame and ran to lilac in the shadows. . . .
This with a Spanish comb and appropriate touches of black and silver,
gave to the whole gown the effect of having been made in a candy
shop."[18] Austin's interest in fabric and feminine apparel here and elsewhere suggests that, contrary to the view of more than one scholar,
she was interested in her appearance and, in the context of the times,
she was a "womanly woman."[19]

Austin always enjoyed affecting a touch of the theatrical, and in New
York she indulged herself to the hilt. The impression she consciously
contrived to make at the dinner accentuated her difference from the
assembled group. She delighted in underscoring her westernism by
the clothes and dramatic Indian jewelry she chose to wear—and by the
company she kept. To MacDougal she wrote: "I had invited the young
Indian painter to whom I introduced you, to be my guest and he arrived at my house about a quarter of an hour before the performance
dressed in quill embroidered buckskin, and wearing the most magnificent black and white flamingo feather head dress I have ever seen. He
said he hadn't any evening clothes, and would this do. So I took him

in the cab with me, and when the reception committee saw us come in together, I thought they would faint with joy."[20]

Austin appears to have relished her Indian escort's exhibition of "natural contempt for white men which all Indians at bottom feel on this occasion." With a flash of wicked humor she reported that "one kind lady asked what those teeth were in his necklace. 'Aligator,' he told her. She said 'How horrid!' but hastily and kindly added, 'I suppose they are the same to you as my pearls.' 'Not at all,' said my Chickasaw friend, 'any fool can take a pearl away from an oyster.'"[21] As this facetious story indicates, Austin still perceived herself to be an outsider in many New York circles, despite the kind speeches that flowed that evening from "Uncle Henry Holt," who praised her for prophesying America's spiritual destiny; from Canby, who saluted her as "the one complete master of the American Environment"; from Van Doren, who noted that of all American writers, she alone possessed "a tap root"; and from the *Century*'s Glen Frank, who "said with unpremeditated earnestness" that he had learned more from her "about how an American literary magazine should be edited" than from anyone else.[22]

Despite these accolades, Austin could not efface the memories of what she called "the rather sordid struggle of my literary life" in a single night of festivities.[23] She took vicarious pleasure in her anonymous Indian friend's verbal sparring with New York's literary notables; his "primitive" status shielded him from rebuffs that she would certainly have suffered had she ever been overtly confrontational with this elite group. She anguished over the preparation of her speech, titled "American Literature as an Expression of the American Experience," and was pleased by the audience's receptivity to the ideas that she later elaborated on in her controversial book on Amerind verse, *The American Rhythm*. The day after the dinner she received a flattering letter from Van Doren, who wrote: "I do not exaggerate when I say that your speech seemed to me a masterpiece, one of the very best literary speeches I have ever heard."[24]

Before the dinner Austin had elatedly written to MacDougal that "people are writing in and demanding opportunity to 'pay tribute,' and editors omitted from the guest of honor list are 'feeling deeply hurt,' though it does not seem to occur to them that a practical application of interest to my work might have secured their inclusion."[25] After the event, she reflected somewhat dejectedly "that no one who spoke revealed an intimate acquaintance with my books, that two of the speakers seemed to be uncertain of just what books I have written, and that every one had got what they had by actual contact" (with Austin).[26] This realization must have soured the memory of the occasion considerably, reflecting as it did her worst fears. "The only sort of work the public has been willing to take from me is a thin, glittering kind of intellectual essay," she complained to MacDougal.[27]

Only the absence of Herbert Croly, the founding editor of the *New Republic*, who had promised to attend the dinner, somewhat marred Austin's night of victory. "Herbert Croly had a scunner, against me; I don't know why," she recalled. "He refused to give me space in 'The New Republic,' or if he did, used it unkindly, and forgot to come to my dinner" (*EH* 345). Croly came to symbolize the forces most resistant to her work in New York. The *New Republic* had not championed insurrectionist journalism, as some expected, but rather delivered liberalism to its readers decked out in what some writers, Austin among them, considered arrogant elitism.[28] In 1919 she had asked a friend to complain to Croly that the magazine had "discriminated" against her by rejecting several of her manuscripts and giving her books unfavorable reviews.[29] After the dinner, however, she wrote to MacDougal that one of the magazine's young staff members, Bob Hallowell, "gave them as he says 'hell' and won their consent to invite me to cooperate with them in any way I saw fit."[30] By 1924 Austin was receiving the kind of encouragement from the *New Republic* that she had expected years earlier. Croly praised a piece she submitted for its "subtlety, imaginative insight and the kind of beauty of fundamental conception which I myself find really exciting."[31]

Friendships in the Early 1920s

Nevertheless, Austin was correct in her assumption that she was misunderstood by literary New York. Canby, for example, praised her sensitive interpretation of the environment, but did not include her in his list of novelists who reached the peak of their achievement in the twenties.[32] Although Canby considered her a "great woman," it was Austin the "great eccentric" who dominated his evaluation. He argued that she was "potentially one of the great American women of letters" and that she had "won her right to a prominent place in American literature," if she would stay with creative writing and leave science to the scientists. He appears to have found what Austin termed "a new metrical medium based on intrinsic American rhythms" an amorphous concept, and pressed her to define "just what the essential qualities of an indigenous American literature" were.[33] That Austin insisted on appropriating scientific theories into her writing indicates her adamant refusal to be denied entry into a realm of discourse controlled by males —the "scientists" to whom Canby alluded.

It was a frustration to Austin that she found herself trying to do the "scientific" research of a psychologist in her investigation of rhythm without formal training or "access to a psychological laboratory."[34] Her interest in rhythm resided in creative work, she confided to MacDougal; the theoretical work on rhythm had ceased to be the compelling focus. "I like to dive into a rhythmic stream like a fish into the gulf current and go where it takes me. I like to be a sun swinging through space with all my seven planets disposed about me, and I like to be the green flush that creeps up and dies rhythmically along the sides of Palo Corona. Best of all I like to flash into the life rhythm of some other human being, and find myself suddenly knowing all about what it was, now and will be. Then I like to repeat some of these experiences by writing books or poems about them."[35]

Close though her relationship was with MacDougal, Austin apologized to him for her "queerness" in the beautiful, lyrical letter she had written about rhythm. Perhaps, finally, she had been persuaded by Canby and Van Doren that her true greatness resided in her creative interpretation of America. More likely, she was deeply divided within herself about her role in American letters.

Of western American authors, Canby had enormous respect for Willa Cather, whose "Gallic" mind "had the precision of a scholar's, the penetration of a critic's, and the warm intellectuality of a creative artist's." Cather occupied a unique niche in Canby's pantheon as a major literary figure who was able "to talk of the craft of good writing with only the most indirect reference to her own work." Gertrude Stein and Ellen Glasgow also appear on Canby's list of important woman writers: Stein, "one of the most daring of the experimenters," and Glasgow, who seized the great theme of "the wreck of a way of life in the South after the great war."[36]

Austin, too, admired Cather's work, although she had reservations about her novel *Death Comes for the Archbishop* (1926). Cather clearly champions her French protagonists and the building of a French cathedral in Santa Fe, and Austin found the older writer guilty of betraying the Southwest in her sympathetic portrayal of Bishop Lamy, the cleric who thought New Mexico backward. Ironically, Cather inscribed Austin's gift copy of *Death Comes for the Archbishop*: "For Mary Austin, in whose lovely study I wrote the last chapters of this book. She will be my sternest critic—and she has a right to be. I will always take a calling down from my betters." Cather's later insistence that she had not written a word of the novel in Santa Fe is puzzling; she claimed to have gone to Austin's restful home merely "to write a few letters."[37]

The generous inscription to Austin and Cather's subsequent denial of writing any portion of the novel in her friend's study remain a conundrum—unless Cather unconsciously suppressed that she and Austin had come to the Southwest for literary inspiration at approximately the same time. Quite possibly Cather regarded Austin as a competitor for the same literary territory.[38] After *The Professor's House* (1925), Austin found fault with the way Cather handled New Mexico. "The best she could do was to split her story wide open in the middle and insert a green bough of New Mexico in such a fashion that I suppose nobody but myself really knew what she was trying to do," Austin wrote to Ferris Greenslet at Houghton Mifflin. Flawed as Cather's approach was to the New Mexico Austin revered, she conceded that the New Mexico section of *The Professor's House* was more successful with the public than the rest of Cather's novel.[39]

In many ways, Austin and Cather shared similar views about the craft of writing and the theory of fiction. Both treated region as integral to their fictions, not merely convenient and attractive scenery. When Cather visited Santa Fe, Austin's niece chauffeured her to various nearby places so that she could complete her research.[40] Austin, who endeavored to "become folk, in the completest sense, of that larger environment which is for Americans the matrix of so many local intimacies and masteries," believed that Cather was engaged in a similar project. "Are not the novels of Willa Cather, with their imperfectly bridged intervals between episodes, and her seemingly naive rejection of the superior consciousness of the bystanding Intellectuals as a medium of integration, exactly what is to be expected of a folk attitude toward American society?" she wrote in an article on the "magnitude of the American scene."[41]

When Austin lived on Barrow Street in New York, she had been friendly with Cather and frequently took tea at Cather's nearby house at No. 5 Bank Street.[42] Linked by their midwestern heritage, the two writers held in common certain principles of creativity. Cather told her biographer that she never paid much attention to language, while Austin asserted that language came to her during the mystical process of writing.[43] Curiously, Cather and Austin were profoundly conservative in the sense that they often tended to distrust the intelligence of other women, even their own female characters, attributing to them stereotypical characteristics held by society at large. It was woman in the aggregate whose subordinate situation these writers saw clearly. Most strikingly, Cather, like Austin, was torn between writing like a woman and producing constricted fictions, or writing like a man and thus betraying her authentic voice.[44]

Another of Austin's friends in New York was Mabel Dodge (later Mabel Dodge Luhan), a wealthy socialite from Buffalo at whose Fifth Avenue apartment notable figures in the arts, radical politics, and society gathered regularly to discuss the burning issues and theories of the day. Influenced by Gertrude Stein's "psychoaesthetics" and the vitalism of Henri Bergson, Dodge had established an avant-garde salon in Florence before returning to New York in 1913. On her "Wednesday evenings," one might encounter the psychoanalyst A. A. Brill holding forth on Freud or the muckraking journalist Lincoln Steffens arguing the case for social reform. Austin was often present discussing birth control with Margaret Sanger, free love with the journalist Hutchins Hapgood, or anarchism with Emma Goldman.[45] It was in Dodge's "radical salon" that Austin met Walter Lippmann and Bill Haywood, "who came to tell us what the I.W.W. was about" (*EH* 339). Haywood, a Socialist and national secretary of the Industrial Workers of the World, was facing a twenty-year penitentiary sentence for sedition. Lippmann, recently graduated from Harvard, was a rising star on the editorial staff of the *New Republic*. Years later Austin would feud publicly with him about the Indian "as a factor in our National life and culture," claiming retrospectively that he never quite forgave her for "slapping his wrists" in print.[46]

Steffens recalled that Dodge's "great old-fashioned apartment" was "filled full of lovely artistic things"; her bountiful table and well-stocked bar were added attractions.[47] But Steffens attributed the success of her salons to her gift for organizing evenings around a theme and insisting that guests address their remarks to the subject at hand. Much of the talk during the intellectually exciting summer of 1913 centered on psychological repression. According to his biographer, Steffens was an ardent Freudian who had declared that "one of the few discoveries of our day of personal use to us is that of the danger of over-repression, over self-control; a new sort of tyranny, the misrule of one's self." Playwright Susan Glaspell, another frequenter of Sterne's salon, would later say that "you could not go out to buy a bun without hearing of someone's complex."[48]

Feminism was often on the agenda at Dodge's gatherings. Although not a feminist herself, she enthusiastically welcomed the leading intel-

lectual representatives of the movement into her house. Austin's feelings on the subject were mixed and often contradictory. A close friend
observed that "although in theory she was a feminist, believing that
women more than men carry the creative fire, she actually preferred
the society of men, and depended upon men for her deepest companionship."[49] Austin took the position that constructive social thought
should be a male realm to which she alone among women had earned
admittance. Even after women's suffrage had passed, she urged Dodge
"to invite thinking young men" into her house, particularly those interested in discussing the Indian "crisis."

Both privately and in print, Austin stated that men dominated intellectual life and that women were incapable of producing great literature
because of the patriarchal nature of their culture. "In the current periodicals where our American Intellectuals are actively in evidence,"
she remarked, "it is noticeable that there are few women's names, and
none that stand out as convincingly, femininely original." Arguing that
American cultural values as much as overt discrimination served to exclude women from scientific professions, Austin wrote: "Intellectual
women frequently fail to take into account the effect of the tradition of
sex subordination working from within. Always in the interest of a distinguished man, one finds them giving too much even while protesting
that so much is taken."[50]

Austin ascribed the failure of women to attain "the highest achievement in music and sculpture" to their "neglect of form." Charlotte
Perkins Gilman, among others, failed her intellectual litmus test. "Mrs.
Gilman is not without style," Austin wrote, "but it is the style of Mrs.
Gilman's mind, thin, vivid, swift as a lightning streak, rather than the
carefully finished instrument of communication." This sharp reaction
probably exempted Gilman's 1898 treatise *Women and Economics*, the
reformer's most significant work, criticized by one historian as "an un-
systematic, impatient, repetitive, but cumulatively stunning indictment
of contemporary attitudes and behavior."[51]

However, Austin admired the intellectual qualities of social reformer
Jane Addams and the work of ethnologist Alice Fletcher. "And among
creative writers," she wrote, "no name glitters with so clear a light
of intellectual illumination as Edith Wharton's." Austin appreciated
Wharton's formalism and endorsed experimentation with "a genuine
woman culture," especially if it fostered "new and necessary apprecia-
tions of intellectual form."[52] She failed, however, to specify the nature
of the experiment or even how and when such a female-centered culture might emerge.

*The botanist Daniel MacDougal with Mary Austin near Tucson,
ca. 1923.*

Always cool toward intellectualism, particularly of the East Coast
variety, Austin eventually became skeptical about Dodge's circle of
friends. After Dodge moved to New Mexico in 1917, Austin confided
to her that she considered those who had flocked to her salon a superficial lot. She had discovered "that the Intellectuals not only wanted
nothing, but were wrapped in complacence about themselves so vast,
so impenetrable, that it first amazed me, became comic, and at last a
little pathetic. . . . I supposed I was not very gracious after making
this discovery, I felt imposed upon. I thought they had no right to
offer me stale ideas and call them advanced."[53] These ideas included
the theories of Freud, Jung, and Marx. Although several of Austin's
friends were undergoing psychoanalysis, it is not surprising, given her
family history, that she found its tenets threatening. Her disenchant-
ment with the Fifth Avenue gatherings may well have constituted a
defense against problems so close to home—most strikingly, her own
nervous breakdowns.

One of the closest and most enduring friendships that Austin developed during this period was with the distinguished botanist Daniel
MacDougal. Affiliated with the Carnegie Institution, MacDougal di-

rected two research field stations, the Desert Laboratory at the University of Arizona in Tucson and the Coastal Laboratory in Carmel. Austin met him in California around 1914. Her interest in science— she was an enthusiastic amateur botanist—and MacDougal's dedication to humanizing the understanding of science gave their friendship a solid foundation. If Austin entertained romantic thoughts for him, MacDougal's marriage and the writer's moral scruples probably prevented them from sexually consummating their relationship. It did not, however, keep them from corresponding and making frequent sojourns together in New York, Carmel, Arizona, and New Mexico, where she enlisted his help on her book *The Land of Journeys' Ending* (1924).[54]

Unlike most men in Austin's life, MacDougal returned her interest with devotion and kindness. He expressed hope that she would build a retreat near his place in the Carmel Highlands. Austin's most recent biographer conjectures that her "intellect and accomplishments" fascinated MacDougal. Moreover, he discovered in her an attractive "forthrightness" and an "earthiness" that he had not previously encountered in women. She visited him at the Desert Laboratory in 1919, 1922, and 1923. *The Land of Journeys' Ending*, which she dedicated to him, is a monument to their shared love and understanding of the Southwest.[55] MacDougal offered Austin intellectually stimulating companionship that was at once romantic and flattering to her ego. Yet the relationship appears to have exacted no commitment from her, and the sexual reserve inbred by her small-town Methodist upbringing remained intact. This, coupled with the geographical distance between them, appears to have kept the relationship vibrant yet unthreatening to Austin, whose tolerance for interruption of her creative life was quite limited. MacDougal was for her a sort of colonized ear, ready to listen to her problems and to respond generously without burdening her with his.

Genius and Gender

Of all the problems Austin grappled with as a writer, none preoccupied her more than exploration of the nature of genius. She linked this preoccupation to her westernness, believing that close contact with "the genius process in the stone age of culture as exhibited by my friends, the Indians," entitled her to identify the elements of genius. Austin dealt with this theme in her novel *A Woman of Genius* (1912) and returned to it in 1925 in *Everyman's Genius*, a sort of self-help manual designed for the layperson to use in developing genius. Austin believed that genius could be tapped in each individual by reaching into the "deep-self" in order to build upon "racial inheritance," this being "the sum of capacities acquired by the ancestors of the individual, to which he has access in meeting the exigencies of his immediate life."[56]

Austin by no means restricted genius to a special group, however. In theory, at least, it was to be found in "the blacksmith, the forest ranger, the sheep herder, the village dressmaker who could take your things as they came from a mail-order catalogue, and with a twist and a tuck or two, make them over into something she had never seen except in pictures, which satisfied your utmost craving for personal expression in dress." In *Everyman's Genius*, Austin provided a glossary of such terms as *psyche, race, racial inheritance, talent, immediate-self, deep-self, intuition,* and *supernormal faculty*. Genius itself she defined as "the free, untutored play of the racial inheritance into the immediate life of the individual," a definition that owes much to Jung's concept of the "psychogenetic residual" or the racial unconscious. As for "talent," Austin defined it as "any capacity for successful activity in a particular direction, with which the immediate self of the individual is endowed."[57] More important, perhaps, *Everyman's Genius* reminds us of the special genius that Austin found in the inhabitants of the desert.

Exactly how the physical process of genius worked in the creative mind was addressed mechanistically in several rather bizarre studies during the first quarter of the twentieth century, though perhaps not with the same zeal that Austin applied to the subject. She was not alone in her conviction that the study of genius deserved serious scientific investigation. In 1927, following several bouts of serious illness, she procured the necessary forms to bequeath her brain to the Burt G. Wilder Brain Collection housed in Stimson Hall at Cornell University. The document, signed in Santa Fe and witnessed by Mary Hunter, her niece, Frank Applegate, her closest friend in Santa Fe, and Joseph E. Foster, her family physician and friend, set down the reasons that prompted the donation.[58] Explicit instructions in the document guided the physician "primarily charged by the testator to carry out the terms of the bequest" in the particulars of promptly removing the brain from the deceased and preserving it in formalin solution. An accompanying memorandum explained that Wilder had been a professor of comparative anatomy and neurology at Cornell, where he had amassed a sizeable collection for the empirical study of the "brains of educated persons." The Wilder Collection comprised the brains of many people who had "achieved success in a particular field."[59]

Austin's theories about genius emphasized the mystical and numinous aspects of the human mind. At the same time, she was influenced by the findings of neuroscience. She may have heard or read of the institute in Moscow where a German neurologist studied slices of Lenin's preserved brain in 1925, with the goal of establishing a physical basis for Lenin's genius in political philosophy. But *Everyman's Genius* was not about slicing up pickled human brains to discover what materially constituted genius. Rather, Austin approached the topic from the vantage point of the working artist and included several accounts of the methods creative individuals used to manage their genius, soliciting contributions from the poet Marianne Moore and the writer Fannie Hurst, among others. Dashiell Hammett's review of the book summarized Austin's findings and their applications to the artist: "The eternal problem of the creative worker in whatever field is to bring his whole mind, his every faculty, to bear on the task under his hand. To the extent that he succeeds, granted adequate equipment, he produces what we ordinarily call a work of genius. As he fails he has to rely on his talent, his craftsman's skill. . . . Mrs. Austin has some sound things to say on the mechanics of the creative mind, on autosuggestion, autoprayer, and meditation. These things, consciously or not, are the accustomed tools of him who tries to focus his mind in its entirety on any subject."[60]

Although *Everyman's Genius* appeared years after *A Woman of Genius*, the philosophy that Austin set forth in it also informed her novel. Austin never doubted that she was a genius. Nor did she waver in her conviction that circumstances—her family, her midwestern Methodist upbringing, the patriarchal culture in which she lived, her unfortunate marriage and maternity—had conspired to cheat her of the full realization of her talents. *A Woman of Genius* expresses most fully Austin's understanding of the cultural construction of gender during the crucial decade after 1900. In the estimation of the feminist literary scholar Nancy Porter, the novel "articulates the conflicts of a transitional generation of women who relinquished the perquisites of protected, genteel womanhood for the rewards and responsibilities of the pursuit of public achievement and service to the community."[61] The first-person narrative of *A Woman of Genius* suggests its affiliation to the autobiographical form in significant respects. Early on, the narrator addresses the reader:

> It interests me greatly to undertake this book, of which I have said in the title as much as a phrase may of the scope of the under-

taking, for if I know anything of genius it is extraneous, derived, impersonal, flowing through and by. I cannot tell you what it is, but I hope to show you a little of how I was seized of it, shaped; what resistances opposed to it; what surrenders. I mean to tell you as plainly as possible how I felt it fumbling at my earlier life like the sea at the foot of a tidal wall, and by what rifts in the structure of living, its inundation rose upon me; by what practices and passion I was enlarged to it, and by what well meaning of my friends I was cramped and hardened. . . . This is the story of the struggle between a Genius for Tragic Acting and the daughter of a County Clerk, with the social ideal of Taylorville, Ohianna, for the villain. It is a drama in which none of the characters play the parts they were cast for. . . . What I mean to go about is the exploitation of the personal phases of genius, of which when it refers to myself you must not understand me to speak of personal merit, like the faculty for presiding at a woman's club or baking sixteen pies of a morning, which distinguished one Taylorvillian from another; rather as a seizure, a possession which overtook me unaware, like one of those insidious Oriental disorders which you may never die of, but can never be cured. (*WOG* 4–6)

The narrative explicitly refers to Austin's Carlinville background. The Father of her novel was "one of those men who make a specialty of integrity and of great dependability in public service." Admired by everyone in the town and worshipped by his daughter, Olivia May, Father "had a brilliant war record" (*WOG* 31). Olivia says that her father's death constituted the tragedy of her childhood, compounded by the grim aftermath of her mother's widowhood and the loss of the material comforts that a father provided, especially their cozy "yellow house with the chocolate trimmings" (*WOG* 44).

In Olivia's eyes, her mother retains an attitude "characteristic of Taylorville women . . . a kind of untutored virginity" (*WOG* 125). When Olivia asks about the sexual side of marriage before her wedding, Mrs. Lattimore at first shrinks away, then confides, "I'm sorry, daughter . . . I can't help you. I don't know . . . I never knew myself" (*WOG* 126). Olivia's brother, Forester, assumes the role of "provider," occupying the position that belonged to Jim, Austin's older brother, in the Hunter household. Not surprisingly, Olivia resents her brother's privileged status, just as Austin felt deeply resentful when her mother conferred the mantle of patriarchal authority on Jim.

Austin chose to make Olivia a struggling actress whose talent was lost in provincial Taylorville. (One remembers that Austin's forbears on both sides were tailors.) The fictional Taylorville suggests a typical midwestern town of the later 1900s, where the Methodist church "left you in no doubt about things" (*WOG* 57). Like Carlinville, it was a village of conformity writ large. "You attended morning and evening service; as soon as you were old enough for it, which was before you were fit, you taught in Sunday school; you waited on table at oyster suppers designed for the raising of the minister's salary, and if you had any talent you sang in the choir or recited things at church sociables. And when you were married and consequently middle-aged, you joined the W.F.M.S. [Women's Foreign Missionary Society] and the Sewing Society" (*WOG* 57).

Olivia marries her hometown sweetheart, a shopkeeper named Tommy Bettersworth, only to experience the unhappiness of a passionless union with an unimaginative partner, accompanied by the discomforts of premature motherhood. Austin's rendition of Olivia's plight recapitulates, almost exactly, her own experience during her pregnancy with Ruth in 1892. In short, *A Woman of Genius* was nothing less than a dress rehearsal for Austin's autobiography, *Earth Horizon*, published twenty years later. Austin set great store in the autobiography as a tool for understanding genius, "where truth—often unintentionally!—manages in many cases to shine through."[62] Appropriately, then, Olivia sets the stage for her eventual exit from the marriage in the form of a memoir. Like *Earth Horizon*, it is cast in the third person.

> My baby was born within ten months of my marriage and most of the time I was wretchedly, depressingly ill. All my memories of my early married life are of Olivia, in the mornings still with frost, cowering away from the kitchen sights and smells, or gasping up out of ingulfing nausea to sit out the duty calls of the leading ladies of Higgleston in the cold, disordered house; of Tommy gulping unsuitable meals of underdone and overdone things, and washing the accumulation of dishes after business hours, patient and portentously cheerful, with Olivia in a wrapper, half hysterical with weakness—all the young wife's dreams gone awry! And Tommy too, he must have had visions of himself coming home to a well-kept house, of delicious little dinners and long hours in which he should appear in his proper character as the adored, achieving male. (*WOG* 129)

Unlike Austin's Ruth, Olivia's son dies in infancy. "It was the most and the best I was to know of the incident called maternity," she broods, "that whether it was bitter or most sweet it was irrevocable" (*WOG* 137). Turning to acting after the death of her child, Olivia frees herself gradually from her husband and discovers that she is obsessed with the creative life of a performer. "My new-found faculty ached for use. It woke me in the night and wasted me; I had wild thoughts such as men have in the grip of an unjustifiable passion" (*WOG* 219). Olivia's connection with a repertory company, necessitating frequent and lengthy absences from home, hastens the breakdown of her marriage. Tommy Bettersworth is a likeable enough fellow, though a bit of a philanderer. Lacking in genius and utterly incapable of sparking the autoerotic passion that Olivia finds within herself as an actress, Tommy has the good grace to die young, thus freeing her without the social opprobrium of divorce. The parallels to Austin's own failing marriage are rife; but she spares her fictional alter ego from dealing with a child who does not die and a husband who brings suit against her for desertion —two facts of her own past that Austin spent her life rationalizing.

At one point in the novel, Olivia/Mary indulges in a soliloquy on the sorrows of genius: "For to be a genius is no such vanity as you imagine. It is to know great desires and to have no will of your own toward fulfillment; it is to feed others, yourself unfed; it is to be broken and plied as the Powers determine; it is to serve, and to serve, and to get nothing out of it beyond the joy of serving. And to know if you have done that acceptably you have to depend on the plaudits of the crowd; and the Powers give no sign; many have died not knowing" (*WOG* 234). *A Woman of Genius* becomes a chronicle of female solidarity when Effie, Olivia's younger sister and a conventional matron and club woman, salutes her for having the strength to step "out of the ranks in some achievement of her own." Olivia, she says, gives women the "courage to live lives of their own" (*WOG* 451). While Austin was writing *A Woman of Genius*, she knew herself to be very much a woman alone who was stepping "out of the ranks" to pursue her writing career in New York. She seems to have derived little comfort from the fact that like-minded women surrounded her, among them the members of Heterodoxy, a group of radical, reformist, and creative women who met weekly in Greenwich Village for lectures and to discuss mutual concerns.[63]

Olivia ultimately discovers passion and fulfillment in an illicit affair with her old love, mining engineer Helmeth Garrett, but she recoils from marriage rather than compromise her successful career on the New York stage. This gives Olivia yet another opening for an analysis of modern marriage as it relates to the creative woman, an analysis that retains remarkably contemporary overtones: "It must be because no man naturally can imagine any more compelling business for a woman than being interested in him, that Helmeth failed to understand that he could as well have torn himself from the enterprise for which he had starved and sweated, as separate me from the final banquet of success. I had paid for it and I must eat" (*WOG* 449). Olivia's love affair with Garrett elicited some of Austin's more unfortunate prose. Possibly because she thought the book needed sex to generate sales, she included a stereotypical dime-novel rendezvous between the couple in which she imagines Olivia reflecting: "I could feel the yielding in his frame. He was my man and I did what I would with him" (*WOG* 457). The tryst reads like parody and is unlike anything Austin wrote before or after.

Perhaps it borrows something from what she thought Frank Norris, Jack London, and other naturalists were giving the public. Specifically, she may have had in mind London's enormously successful autobiographical novel, *Martin Eden*, chronicling a writer's struggle for recognition. Austin yearned for more acclaim than being called a "great stylist."[64] Hankering for a share of the notoriety and money that novelists like London had realized, she seems to be searching for the winning commercial formula in *A Woman of Genius*. Yet, much to her credit as a novelist, Austin's greater imperative was to speak truth, even though neither her readers nor the publishing powers, who could make or break her novel, cared for her unremitting lectures decrying modern marriage.

Austin had little patience for those who turned away from her message. As a self-proclaimed woman of genius, she believed that others should listen to the truths she interpreted for them. London, on the other hand, believed that no amount of persuasion could convince an unreceptive world of the injustices done to the creative spirit. He lectured Austin on the subject at some length in 1915, criticizing her "serious" approach to a "bone-head" world. "Those who sit alone must sit alone. They must continue to sit alone. As I remember it, the prophets and seers of all times have been compelled to sit alone except at times when they were stoned or burned at the stake. The world is mostly bone-head and nearly all boob, and you have no complaint if the world calls you the 'great stylist' and fails to recognize that your style is the very heart and soul of your brain . . . you should be content to receive what the world gives you."[65] This offered little succor to Austin, who knew that her friend wrote from his comfortable estate in the

Sonoma Valley while she struggled to get by in New York living in rented rooms.

Olivia's affair with Garrett in *A Woman of Genius* elucidated important feminist points that were being debated in intellectual circles in New York and elsewhere. Perhaps more cogently than any novel of the era, it raised issues about parenting and the use of women's skills— not merely bearing children but the much weightier task of rearing them. Olivia candidly admits to Garrett that she is unwilling to sacrifice her talent to keep house, look after children, and see to it "that they brushed their teeth and had hair ribbons to match their clothes." In brief, Olivia refuses to conform to Taylorville's definition of a proper wife and mother. Her assertion that she will marry Garrett on the condition that he marry her career effectively ruptures their match. He can neither adjust the demands of his business to her artistic career nor understand why she should ask him to do so, when it is so clearly her place to renounce careerism.

The public reception for *A Woman of Genius* was disappointing. Austin insisted that Doubleday "dropped the book" after merely four months because of her candid portrayal of Olivia's sexual liaisons (*EH* 320). Later she found out that the novel had offended the wife of one of the publishers, who thought Olivia's conduct "immoral." Although she tried to recoup by selling the book to Houghton Mifflin, sales still lagged. The problem of properly marketing the novel further plagued its commercial success, since "the advance publicity . . . frequently contradicted all my notions of how and why the book came to be written" (*EH* 320). Twenty years later William Allen White praised *A Woman of Genius* in the *Saturday Review* as the best of Austin's longer novels. "Her realism was regarded as rather advanced in that day; certainly she discussed matters that Mr. Howells would have avoided, and her philosophy was a rather militant feminism in the days when American women were seeking the ballot." White hit on a key point when he acknowledged that Austin's feminism was independent of the suffrage cause and in advance of its time. In his analysis, her literary work "was propaganda for the emancipation of women that came in the next decade."[66]

Ever since her days in Carmel, when the Progressive period ushered in the lively suffrage campaigns, Austin had been closely in touch with those working for the rights of women. Charlotte Perkins Gilman, Grace Channing, and Upton Sinclair had helped to shape and sharpen her political consciousness in California. Her observations of the radi-

cal strategies employed by the Pankhursts in England, and her friendships there with English and American feminist writers such as Inez
Haynes Irwin, Anne Martin, and Marie Stopes, had familiarized Austin
with the theoretical arguments of the women's movement.[67]

A Woman of Genius is a feminist novel, to be sure, but one that follows no party line. Austin stands as an independent thinker of the first
order. Receptive to the arguments for women's rights, she was inclined
to take the view that this national issue owed more to her ideas than
she herself derived from the organizational strategies and structure of
the women's movement. By the time Austin wrote *No. 26 Jayne Street*
in 1920, her distrust of organized reformist causes and the agendas of
their prime movers was well established. Despite its autobiographical
intensity, however, *A Woman of Genius* falls short of Austin's earlier
work. It has neither the tautness, nor the subtlety, nor the precision of
language that characterize her short stories. Nor does this novel about
the stifling realities of marriage for the exceptional woman bear even
passing resemblance to the stark beauties of her naturist works. The
contrived plot functions as little more than an excuse for Austin to
hold forth on the subject that truly engages her: the incompatibility
of women of genius and the social form of marriage, and the difficulty of creating intimate relationships in a social milieu that stymies
women artists at every turn. Hence, *A Woman of Genius* remains more
interesting as an autobiographical and cultural text than as a work of
literature.

In it Austin persuasively inveighs against the traditional boundaries
of small-town life. She describes turn-of-the-century American attitudes about women's protected place, emphasizing the mystification of
sexual matters that assured women's complicity in their own subjec-
tion. Olivia summarizes life in Higgleston (the town near Taylorville
where she and Tommy settle) that was so deleterious to her sense of
creativity and autonomy:

> Does anybody remember what the woman's world was like in
> small towns before the days of woman's clubs? There was a world
> of cooking and making over; there was a world of church-going
> and missionary societies and ministerial cooperation, half grudged
> and half assumed as a virtue which, since it was the only thing
> that lay outside themselves, was not without extenuation. And
> there was another world which underlay all this, coloured and
> occasioned it, sicklied over with futility; it was a world all of the
> care and expectancy of children overshadowed by the recurrent

monthly dread, crept about by whispers, heretical but persistent, of methods of circumventing it, of a secret practice of things openly condemned. It was a world that went half the time in faint-hearted or unwilling or rebellious anticipation, and half on the broken springs of what as the subject of endless, objectionable discussions, went by the name of "female complaints." (*WOG* 218–19)

Austin's frank allusions to birth control in 1912 shocked readers who did not expect this issue to surface in a novel by a woman. *A Woman of Genius* was equally singular for the ways Austin chose to deal with the choices available for the creative woman. Critic Nancy Porter perceptively links it to a tradition of American novels about working by women writers, including Rebecca Harding Davis's *Life in the Iron Mills* (1861), Elizabeth Stuart Phelps's *Story of Avis* (1877), Kate Chopin's *Awakening* (1899), Edith Wharton's *House of Mirth* (1905), and Willa Cather's *Song of the Lark* (1915). Cather's Thea Kronborg, a professional opera singer, closely resembles Austin's Olivia. Both characters possess indisputable talent and the drive to see it fulfilled. And both manage to escape, as Cather expressed it, "from a smug, domestic, self-satisfied provincial world of utter ignorance" by choosing the life of the artist. Personal life recedes into the background "as the imaginative life becomes richer."[68]

It is equally instructive to read *A Woman of Genius* next to another, quite successful novel on the same subject, Theodore Dreiser's *Genius*, published just three years later.[69] Dreiser's protagonist is the amorous painter and writer Eugene Witla. Reared in the Midwest, Eugene ignores his true genius as a painter to pursue fame as an illustrator in New York. He is turned down by an opera singer for precisely the reasons Olivia eventually forfeits her lover. Eugene's life, complicated by romantic adventures and eventually by marriage to Angela, a stodgy, uncreative woman incapable of nurturing his genius, parallels the marriage between Tommy and Olivia, with gender roles and expectations reversed.

Dreiser's solution to Eugene's crisis is to do away with Angela during childbirth. By this expedient, Dreiser releases his genius from his wife's middle-class ambitions and moves Eugene forward to realize his true destiny—the dedication of his life to serious, realistic painting. Dreiser's sentimental variation on the theme of the incompatibility of genius with domestic life found favor with the public, perhaps because the penitent Eugene emerges at novel's end as a devoted father who takes responsibility for Angela's infant while he continues to produce great works. By contrast, Olivia realistically assesses the liability of having children at a time when women usually assumed primary responsibilities for parenting. Her rejection of familial devotion in favor of a pragmatic, comradely marriage to a playwright and director reifies Olivia's overriding commitment to an artistic career. Society's expectation that married women will uncomplainingly nurture their husbands and children looms for Olivia as the formidable impediment to the realization of genius, just as the societal expectation that he will materially provide for his family threatens Eugene's cultivation of his talent. For both Eugene and Olivia, society exacted an unreasonable toll for genius. Dreiser's gender gave him more latitude, and finally more acceptance, in expressing the problem.

Olivia likewise claims kinship to Wharton's Lily Bart in *The House of Mirth*, though perhaps her truer sister is the gritty survivor Undine Sprague of *The Custom of the Country* (1913), Wharton's most misunderstood heroine. When Olivia needs money to advance her career in New York, she goes to her best woman friend, Pauline Mills, and to Pauline's husband, Henry. Their refusal drives her to take money from Morris Polatkin, a character not unlike Lily Bart's would-be benefactor Simon Rosedale. Both writers perpetuate the ugly stereotype of the wealthy but vulgar Jew. Olivia finds herself "merely a dummy on which to hang a fat little Jew's notions of acceptable contours; the offense of it; the greater offence from which by the opportune appearance of the Jew I had so hardly escaped." Years later, Olivia, now a successful actress, encounters Pauline, who is securely moored to a life of comfortable motherhood. She excoriates her friend for putting her through this humiliation in her time of need: "Have you any idea, Pauline, what it means to have a man invest money in you? . . . a man like Polatkin. I was his property, a horse he had entered for the race. He had a stake on me" (*WOG* 484).

Protected Pauline, having had no inkling during the intervening years of the price Olivia has paid for success, registers shock when Olivia exclaims, "If you don't know that there were days when I would have sold myself for something to eat, it was because you didn't take the pains to" (*WOG* 485). Though this passage stuns readers today more because of its unintended racial slurs than because of Pauline's insensitivity to her childhood friend, *A Woman of Genius* stands as a novel of its time in more ways than one. To what degree the hardships of Austin's personal life in New York are reflected in Olivia's is not entirely clear. But the writer's financial situation was always precarious, and by 1912 she had taken positions as a clerk, typist, and factory worker—just to gain experience, she said.[70]

Olivia elevates her career to a "completer way of loving," for it enables her to share her most intimate self through her art. "I wanted more ways for that, space and opportunity. I wished to lay my gift down, a royal carpet for Helmeth Garrett to walk on; I would have done anything for him with it except surrender it. Not the least thing that came of my condition was the extraordinary florescence of my art" (*WOG* 440). Olivia's refusal of the offer of marriage tendered by Garrett, who demands no less than the forfeit of the most creative aspect of her being, advances the plot of "the new woman" to a new plateau, for Olivia's choice is one of affirmation rather than unadulterated renunciation. Sacrifice is demanded of her, as it is of Cather's Thea Kronborg. The leap in narrative line in these radically new sagas of the New Woman permits Olivia and Thea to emerge as victors in their struggles rather than victims; both consciously cultivate their genius and willingly pay the price of living "an artist's life, every hour of it."[71]

No. 26 Jayne Street

The last novel of Austin's New York period—indeed, the last work of fiction she was to write for more than a decade—was *No. 26 Jayne Street*. Although it is in some respects a bold work, dealing with such urgent reformist issues as suffrage and organized labor, it was not a commercial success and it found only conditional favor with many of the important periodicals.[72] The *Dial*, for example, commented that "both in subject and treatment, Mrs. Austin's work discloses its kindship to the social novel of Wells," while Ludwig Lewisohn in the *Nation* compared her to Henry James. Others, however, found the story slow and uninteresting, a "novel . . . written primarily for some purpose outside itself." Henrietta Malkiel, writing in the *New York Call*, found the novel no more illuminating "of conditions among New York radicals than . . . the New York newspapers."[73] Austin, who considered it one of her best efforts, was so stung by these criticisms that she withdrew from writing novels for eleven years.

Set in New York during World War I, *No. 26 Jayne Street* portrays the epiphany of young Neith Schuyler, who has returned from Europe following the death of her invalid father and a period of relief work in France. Although two aging great-aunts offer her a comfortable home, twenty-six-year-old Neith seeks independence in her own place, "three rooms with bath and kitchenette at Twenty-Six Jayne Street," off Washington Square (*JS* 1). Moving away from the protective influence of the aunts affords Neith opportunities to meet a cross-section of New York's radical Left and to contrast her capitalist background with the lives of her newly found friends.

The plot pivots about a diverse group of activists she meets through Adam Frear, a labor organizer and advocate of free speech with whom she falls in love. After they become engaged, Neith meets a principled feminist named Rose Matlock, her rival for Frear's affections. Also central to her epiphany is a shirtwaist presser named Sadie Leninsky, a young, unwed Russian Jewess who has been made pregnant by an anarchist. Sadie's common-law husband, Hippolyte, dies a martyr's death at the hands of the police after being arrested in a street demonstration.

This rather complicated plot illuminates Neith's growing awareness of the dishonest "fundamental relations" between the sexes in two sets of relationships, each involving two women and a man. In the process she begins to question the ideology of political movements that are subject to the same lack of integrity. Rose Matlock is the instrument of Neith's education. When Rose, a gifted public speaker and social theorist, tells Neith the shocking news that Frear was previously engaged to her, and that he summarily dismissed her after falling in love with Neith, Austin's central issue becomes clear: the decency of conduct between individual human beings. Frear's cruelty toward his former love and subsequent dishonesty to his fiancée flagrantly violate the code of private relationships, suggesting that the principle of altruism intrinsic to larger social movements—Frear's commitment to free speech, for example—is jeopardized by hypocrisy. Rose's revelation affirms Neith's belief in a feminist social order where men and women cannot coexist with equality in the face of double-dealing and secretiveness.[74]

"'We've lived in a fool's paradise, we women,' said Rose Matlock —'in a stage paradise of 'made love,' 'influenced' idealisms, 'cultivated' culture. We've played upon men. We've played at civilization. Now and then comes something like this war and upsets the play. I, for one will play no more. . . . 'I will not,' she finished, 'be played upon'" (*JS* 315). Historian William Leach states Rose's agenda another way: "At the heart of [early feminists'] concern was a belief that the pressures and character of urban and business life and the important impact of possessive individualism had created conditions unfavorable to the best interests of both men and women."[75]

Austin ironically capitalizes the names of reformist causes, sometimes poking fun at the Greenwich Village in flux that she knew intimately during the late teens. Big Business and Capitalist interests, represented by Neith's aunts and her cousin-in-law, Bruce Harwood, battle against the interests of Suffrage, Child Welfare, Better Babies, Curing Criminalism, and a dozen other worthy new movements, the most important being feminism and the Peace Movement before the onset of the war. At one point Neith reflects that "there was nothing in [her] European experience to give her the measure of that vast, interrelated organization of women which is at once the amazement and the weakness of American feminism" (*JS* 202).

Austin had witnessed the disarray of women's organizations in her capacity as informal adviser to the United States Food Administration during the war, while she was planning and writing *No. 26 Jayne Street*. During 1917 she helped organize community kitchens and traveled around the country on behalf of the Department of Agriculture. These experiences gave her enormous sympathy for women in many walks of life. In her book *The Young Woman Citizen* (1918), Austin again argued that the experience of womanhood qualified women to make exceptional contributions to the national and world order, contributions for which their previously disenfranchised status had ill prepared them.

Writing from Los Angeles in 1918 to Herbert Hoover, who ran the Food Administration in President Wilson's first term, she reported her observations of the effect that war work had had on American family life, emphasizing the material needs of the population during the war. "The great problem to be met now is the accommodation of labor, the housing and feeding, not only of people who have to be taken from one place to another to work, but the accommodation of families where both the father and mother are engaged in war work."[76] Austin felt that her old friend (and, according to her niece, possible romantic interest) Hoover was unsympathetic to, and perhaps unknowledgeable about, the situation of women during these critical times. As a member of the Publicity Board of the Women's Trades Union League, a position that gave her "inside information" on strikes, she had taken it upon herself to keep him informed. In a letter about conditions in the textile industry, she advised him: "The textile strike is the thing I tried to tell you about a year ago, where skilled women workers are absolutely indispensable, and yet so many of them, with the improved wages, have married and had families, that they are unwilling to surrender. This is really the source of so much unrest in labor. For awhile this can be satisfied by increased wages. Then if there is no other method of accommodation at hand, and there will be more—and still more—disorganization."[77]

Much of the factual detail of the war period in *No. 26 Jayne Street* derives from Austin's intense involvement with the women's war effort after America's entry into the war. She incorporated traces of her personal experiences with the Food Administration into the novel in passages such as this: "Just as the food shortage had been met by a recession into primitive measures, of the scrapings of individual kitchens, a patriarchal distribution instead of a sweep forward into more possessive administration of the public board; so along the frontier of social organization there had been breakages and temporary dissolutions. The whole energy of social creativeness which for the first few months of the war had seemed to gather, and to be about to exhibit, tidal force, had lapped futilely about the blank encircling walls of the 'business sense' of the community, and returned to fret with a deeper insistence in the old and only open channels of organized labor" (*JS* 336).[78]

Some have suggested that the impetus behind *No. 26 Jayne Street* was Austin's personal bitterness toward Lincoln Steffens. When their relationship soured, she was left "a woman scorned" with a desire to expose his insincerity in the character of the duplicitous Adam Frear. Neith sees Frear's lofty reformism in eclipse, as demonstrated by his shoddy personal ethics in casting aside Rose Matlock. The issue Austin speaks to through Rose Matlock is not merely Frear's fickleness in love, but the position of power that men occupy in their most intimate relationships with women. This presumed superiority permits them to set women aside, expecting them to remain passive and submissive.

Yet Austin's feelings toward Steffens do not seem a sufficient motivation to inspire an entire novel. She deftly handles several other themes, foremost the dramatic changes in American economic and social life wrought by World War I. The war had transformed women's traditional relationships with each other. Austin demonstrates these changes in several ways: through the noncompetitive understanding that evolves between Neith and Rose Matlock (it has been suggested that her name translates as "mate-lock"); through Neith's friendship with Sadie, the tragic representative of the proletariat, transcending class divisions; and through Neith's admiration of her best friend, the actress Madelon Sherrod, who bears with dignity her lot as the wife of a philanderer. Even Neith's consideration for her befuddled, elderly, "spinster" aunt Emmeline and her compassion for the wronged Frances Rittenhouse (the wife of an aging peacock of a man who has wasted her fortune through financial deceits) call attention to the female bonding that pervades each separate plot of the novel.

In short, *No. 26 Jayne Street* shows how stressful situations, which could so easily pit these characters against each other, bring women closer together. For example, Neith finds comfort in the experiential wisdom of her older actress friend. "Always in talking to Madelon one had the sensation of breadth and a kind of buoyancy that was not a mere effect, like the sparkle of a glass of Burgundy. It was more like a realization of a power in life itself to hold you up and carry you along if you trusted it. Madelon hadn't made Neith's own situation seem more heroic, but it seemed of itself more reasonable, more a part of things. It was something that would be the more easily endured and come to a more satisfactory conclusion the less one felt about it, the more one simply and unaffectedly insisted on the principle involved" (*JS* 343–44).

The "principle involved" hinges on the freedom of Rose, Neith, Madelon, Sadie, or indeed any woman to chart her own course. Adam Frear attempted to prevent his discarded lover from speaking out against him to Neith; in so doing, he prevented his fiancée from making an informed choice in their relationship. More damning, he forced Neith, unwittingly, to act complicitously with him against the interests of another woman. Women are a class in this novel; their interests are class interests.

It is reasonable to speculate that Austin's interpretation of principled feminism—of women's solidarity—engendered a negative critical response typified by Van Wyck Brooks's review of *No. 26 Jayne Street*. "And while I admire its subtle style, its deft psychology," he wrote, "I do not feel in it the peculiar note of individuality that made Mary Austin's earlier writings so distinguished." Brooks, reviewing for the *Freeman*, rather aristocratically lamented "the glibness, the mechanicalness that overtakes every writer who consorts with magazines: it strikes me that if she had succeeded in these later years in really registering her personality in her fiction she would hardly have been impelled to produce such vague, restless speculations as she has given us in books like 'Love and the Soul Maker'."[79] Brooks's review, witty at Austin's expense and grossly insensitive to the financial imperative behind her extensive journalism, stung her deeply. His privileged eastern background shielded him from the privations she experienced daily in the city, nor would she have wanted Brooks to know about them. He lived with his family in a country place in Plainfield, New Jersey, commuting into the city when it suited him, one or two days a week.

For no apparent reason, Brooks dredged up a number of stories about Austin's life in Carmel, where he first met her, and New York.

She was mortified to see these in print. "In Carmel, the California village where she used to live," wrote Brooks, "Mary Austin is a legendary figure; and many of the legends about her are very revealing. Once, ten years or more ago, there was a forest fire near-by and the villagers gathered about the horse-trough to go out and fight it. Suddenly there appeared among them a woman dressed in a long white robe, riding on a white horse with her hair streaming over her shoulders. It was Mary Austin. Having suddenly conceived of herself in the role of a Joan of Arc and garbed herself appropriately, she placed herself at the head of the procession and rode forth to stem the flames. Her novel, 'A Woman of Genius,' is the story of a great actress and there is every evidence in her life and writings alike of a powerful theatrical instinct that has been thwarted perhaps by an inadequate physique. But this story illustrates Mrs. Austin's permanent conception of her career."[80] Brooks recalled an incidence of Austin's "peculiar mysticism" that allegedly took place at the Museum of Natural History in New York. Because "she was at one time given a pass permitting her to enter the Museum at any hour of the day or night . . . she used to go there at midnight and, standing among the Indian relics, fall into a trance that placed her in mystic communion with the Great Spirit and the souls of the dead."[81]

Brooks, contrite to have committed such "indiscretions and ineptitudes," weakly apologized to Austin in a note: "My impression was that my article revealed the great respect in which I know both you and your writings. . . . I had no malicious intent in using those anecdotes." Moving toward an apology and at the same time holding fast to his position, Brooks wrote, "I had reason to think [the anecdotes] were not false; it did not seem to me that they were silly, and I cannot now understand in what way they are discrediting."[82] Brooks expressed to another friend how "greatly perturbed" he was by the tempest his article caused, especially since it had been interpreted as "an attack on her character." He rationalized his use of the stories by invoking reliable sources for the offensive anecdotes and protesting his admiration for Austin's work.[83] Later, he again excused himself by suggesting that his method had been to blame. He had distanced himself from his subject, being unaccustomed to writing about "living writers." Nevertheless, he concluded, "the article was a blunder."[84] Austin eventually forgave Brooks, and although he evidently tried to avoid her, they carried on cordial correspondence when she was in Santa Fe and even in New York. Brooks usually pleaded that living in the country prevented him from accepting social engagements in the city. He apologized for not being able to attend her testimonial dinner at the National Arts Club in 1922, using the excuse that he had houseguests—a response that probably miffed Austin, who recorded neither his absence nor their literary friendship in her autobiography.[85]

Brooks's protestations of truth and absence of malice in his *Freeman* review seem superfluous. He appears to have had two specific points in mind. First, he separated Austin's feminist writings from her earlier nature writings, and judged *Lost Borders* and *The Land of Little Rain* worthy of comparison with the work of respected international male writers: "She knew Nature, the Nature of the desert, she had mastered it, as absolutely and familiarly, as Balzac or a Tolstoy has grasped society, as no novelist perhaps can grasp a society as kaleidoscopic as ours." However, Brooks prefaced this praise with an assault on Austin's feminism and mysticism, which he considered absurd. By extension, he viewed her writings on these subjects as inferior. Unconscious of making Austin appear somewhat ridiculous, Brooks revealed an anti-feminist bias in his appraisal of her work. "Like almost every other American novelist," he wrote, "she has failed to develop in a direct line, and her career is cluttered with unsuccessful experiments."[86] Yet he neglected to mention other writers who had also experienced failures as their careers matured.

Carl Van Doren assessed Austin's artistic development more favorably. "Faithful to her original vision, she has moved steadily onward, writing no book like its predecessor, applying her wisdom continually to new knowledge, leaving behind her a rich detritus which she will perhaps be willing to consider detritus if it helps to nourish subsequent generations," he wrote in *Contemporary Novelists* (1922).[87] Austin instinctively trusted Carl and Mark Van Doren's ability to appreciate fully the scope and nature of her literary work. This trust led her to confide to Carl the angst that she experienced while living in New York. In a letter written to him on board the train as she traveled to Santa Fe in 1923, she described the years of personal turmoil that she believed had impeded her literary success. Ever since moving to New York, Austin wrote, she had been "largely distracted by the necessity of mastering the new environment, and by the secret sorrow [Ruth's illness] which for twenty-three years made a pivot for my personal life, and kept pulling me back to California when my material interests lay in New York."[88]

The opposing forces that Austin felt were further manifested in a form of artistic schizophrenia that resulted in a complete "break-down" by the summer of 1923. But the roots of her malaise had surfaced the preceding year, when she confided to Daniel MacDougal that she had "lost the feeling for Art." Although she was working daily at the typewriter, she described herself as "an automaton" and complained: "There is not a trace left of that sense of rapport with the work by which the artist ordinarily knows the kind of work he is turning out." Austin described her crisis of creativity in terms of the Svengali, the evil hypnotist in George du Maurier's 1894 novel *Trilby*: "My intelligence plays the part of Svengali to the unhappy Trilby of my deep self."[89] Nina Auerbach has argued that Du Maurier's Trilby O'Ferrall "is not an anomaly but the quintessence of womanhood" and calls Svengali's power "fatal."[90] In the same vein, Austin's metaphor for her artistic predicament suggests a split between her brain and Self, a dichotomy that she identified as a separation between the "virile" and womanly aspects of her personality. "And between the struggle to make a living by it, and the sense of repression in not being able to find any acceptance for the kind of work I want to do, I am getting a hard surface shell."[91]

Alicia Ostriker has written lucidly about the contemporary woman writer's predicament, analyzing the nature of "the crust" that Austin feared was threatening to encase her creative self in 1922. To say that a woman "'writes like a man' does not mean she writes with all her energies." It means she can think, organize, judge, even argue, but will not embarrass us with messy female emotions." On the other hand, Ostriker observes, "whoever 'writes like a man' but *is* not a man is pretending not to have a body, or passions, unlike the men who write like men."[92] Austin, who had always admired and emulated the "virile style," found herself in crisis at this time in her life. The creative work that drew strongly on the experiences of indigenous women, producing the memorable mothers of Austin's early fiction, had given way to what Mark Van Doren called her "treatises." Writing about the plight of Indians and the faults of modern marriage, Austin had begun to believe that her work was sterile, and she blamed it on New York.

Austin's artistic predicament was mirrored in the physical pull that she felt between East and West. It is significant that the book whose rejection by the New York critical cadre precipitated her crisis—*No. 26 Jayne Street*—is one of her most speculative, philosophical, and overtly feminist works. That Austin may have anticipated the disapproval of Brooks and his colleagues is suggested early in the novel, when the actress Madelon Sherrod shares with Neith the secret of her success in putting over her ideas. Although her genius has been mediated to her New York public through men, a process of manipulation that she has learned to control over the years, Neith is shocked to find that the actress needs the services of less talented men to maintain her position. In a way, Madelon's account of what it has taken to achieve her goals is equally a summation of Austin's New York years. "Between you and your public there is a wall of men, a felted almost sound-proof wall of male intelligence, male reporters, critics, managers, advertisers," Madelon says. "Even if I knew how to write, and I don't, there would still be men editors, men publishers, men reviewers" (*JS* 6).

The truth of the words she put into Madelon's mouth must have engulfed Austin at the National Arts Club dinner in 1922. That evening formally marked the end of her immersion in the masculinist world of publishing in New York. Henceforward, she would bend her energies toward the West.

6

▲ ▲ ▲

THE SOUTHWEST BECKONS

Gard was, as most New Mexicans, susceptible to the Indian mode of investing

all things with a personal aspect and a mystical apprehension of unseen powers

beyond the veil of Things.

—Starry Adventure

Austin's ultimate decision to build a house in Santa Fe and take up permanent residence there was precipitated by Mabel Dodge's move to New Mexico in 1917. Among the Pueblo Indians of Taos, Mabel "discovered a culture that she had lacked in childhood, failed to recreate in Florence, and could not find in Greenwich Village." Resettlement in New Mexico was the culmination of her search for self. In her sincere longing for a more fulfilling existence, this restless woman had never completely shed the reputation she had acquired over the years as "something of a cross between a head hunter and a Venus flytrap."[1] Mabel's multiple marriages and affairs were notorious; even her third husband, the painter and sculptor Maurice Sterne, is said to have fled her on occasion, "claiming that he felt his matrimonial mission was that of a bull, that her erotic demands robbed his potency and suffocated his ability to create."[2] This image Austin later drew upon in fashioning the unflattering portrait of Eudora Ballantin in her novel *Starry Adventure.*

In the late teens, however, the relationship between the two women was just beginning to intensify. Visiting Mabel in Taos around 1917, Austin declared that one day she would "settle somewhere here."[3] She reiterated that intention in 1923 in a note congratulating Mabel on her marriage to Tony Lujan, a full-blooded Pueblo with whom she had been carrying on a scandalous liaison. Lawrence Clark Powell, the

Mabel Dodge Luhan and her husband, Tony Lujan, in Taos,
ca. 1924.

critic, claims that Mabel Dodge Luhan (she spelled her name this way
for the convenience of her Anglo friends) brought Austin permanently
to New Mexico just as she was responsible for D. H. Lawrence's residence in Taos.[4] In her autobiography, Austin recalls meeting Lawrence,
Robinson Jeffers, Georgia O'Keeffe, Agnes Pelton, and Carlos Chavez
at Luhan's "spacious house on the edge of the Pueblo allotment," while
she stayed in one of the "half a dozen guest houses" that Luhan had
built on an adjoining field (*EH* 354).

   On a considerably more modest scale, Austin built an adobe home
on the Camino del Monte Sol in Santa Fe. Begun in September of
1925 on a site overlooking the city, not far from other writers and artists, the seven-room home was spacious and seemed more so because
of its sparse furnishings. With its sitting room and small library for
reading and an office to write in, it was a home built for work. Austin
called it "Casa Querida"(Beloved House) and instructed Mary Hunter,

who acted as her agent and contractor, to see that it was faithful to the Spanish style in every detail, including timbered ceilings and traditional Hispanic fireplaces.

Luhan, Austin, and O'Keeffe—women with exceptionally strong personalities—resided simultaneously in New Mexico. That Taos became Luhan's preserve, Santa Fe Austin's, and Abiquiu O'Keeffe's assured a measure of mutual respect and peace. Austin cited three factors that drew her to Santa Fe: "It is a mountain country, immensely dramatically beautiful; it is contiguous to the desert with its appeal of mystery and naked space, and it supplies the element of aboriginal society which I have learned to recognize as my proper medium." Austin found Santa Fe "stimulating, informative, providing the key to and intensive understanding of the whole pattern of civilized society." The presence of "individuals of the rank of . . . John Galsworthy, Carl Sandburg, Willa Cather, Witter Bynner, John Sloan . . . William Allen White, Paul Kellogg, Sinclair Lewis, and other scores of welcome names" assured a creative atmosphere. If Austin enjoyed her prestigious acquaintances, she also valued the folk culture in Santa Fe that was "so often lacking in the American small town; the pageantry of the Indian dance-drama, the Spanish fiesta, the open rituals of the Church and picturesque survivals," all of which combined to offer "the relief of unusual entertainment."[5] Yet, as one Austin scholar pointed out in the 1930s, "folkness was not an exotic means of entertainment to her; it was a way of looking at and interpreting life in the United States." The way of life she found in the Southwest, especially the Indian ceremonies and arts, exemplified the West of folk—powerful because its origins sprang from "the integrated experience of a people."[6]

One student of Austin's life has compared Santa Fe to Carlinville and other small, turn-of-the-century midwestern towns, where "the simple pleasures of community life" were available. Taos, Santa Fe, and Abiquiu contained "no industries of consequence to smudge [the] skyline, no pressure of metropolitan life to mar [the] easy hospitality."[7] O'Keeffe had experienced such quiescence in Sun Prairie, Wisconsin, and Luhan while growing up in Buffalo, New York. The small towns of the West were the natural refuge of creative individuals who resisted the increasing complexity of technological innovation and the urban capitalistic enterprise in the first decades of the twentieth century. Shortly after the publication of *Main Street*, Austin asked Sinclair Lewis "why Willa Cather, Vachel Lindsay and I find one end of the rainbow in Main Street, and why you and Masters, Anderson, Sandburg, Dreiser and thousands of others who flock from Main Street to the cities can't find it."[8]

O'Keeffe, Luhan, and Austin had escaped into the last vestiges of hospitable and unspoiled American land, where the "experience called Folk, and . . . the frame of behavior known as Mystical" were still possible.[9] In a limited sense their conservatism bears comparison to that of Henry Adams; but instead of looking toward the cathedrals of Europe, as he did, they looked back to the ancient pueblos and earliest Spanish colonial churches. The crucial difference between the Europeanists and the transplanted literati of the Southwest was the cultural nationalism of the latter group. Austin and Luhan deplored the fact that "the things . . . our people [Hispanics and Indians] produce in the way of drama and poetry and music and particularly in the way of industrial arts, rugs, blankets, pottery and every sort of fabric which calls for design, are obliged to compete with European articles" for the American dollar. Was not authenticity to be found in indigenous America? Austin vociferously protested to the secretary of the interior as early as 1919 that "the greatest artists and writers of America have taken their technical training and very largely their ideas, from Europe, consequently their work, excellent as it is, is not always representative of Americanism." She added that "the men" who constitute the core of "eminent" creative workers "have been for the most part concentrated in New York, which has tended to separate them still more from the industrial and agricultural districts which make up the bulk of the population." Further, Austin observed, American art dealers were "choked with European goods and European influences."[10] Luhan, like her fictional counterpart Eudora Ballantin, commingled European and southwestern art in her home. Austin remained a purist and collected only authentic Indian and Hispanic pieces for Casa Querida.

Although Luhan was certainly more than a mere "culture carrier," in Austin's eyes she never gained credibility as an artist or serious writer. And while Austin freely availed herself of Luhan's hospitality, these two formidable women frequently disagreed on a variety of questions. Tony Lujan, who apparently served as a mediator in these disputes, chauffeured them and their guests around the state, particularly to the various pueblos the Anglos wanted to visit. Austin recorded these trips in her autobiography as "among the unforgettable experiences of New Mexico . . . journeys of exploration and recollection." While he drove, Tony often would "sing the accentless melodies of his people which fit so perfectly the unaccented rhythms of the machine" (*EH* 355). Austin considered Tony, Mabel, and their Taos home the emotional and practical nexus of her life in New Mexico.

Austin and Luhan saw eye to eye in their appreciation of Indian art and their assessment of Indian rights. Luhan—whose organizational abilities Austin admired—set up an array of special events to dramatize the plight of the New Mexico Indians. According to her biographer, in the early 1920s she induced Austin to make the necessary arrangements for a group of Indians "to perform in New York, where they managed to reduce the New York Stock Exchange to silence as they played their drums and danced." If New York would not attend to New Mexico, then Luhan and her friends would ensure that New Mexico commanded the attention of New York. She had begun a project of compiling Indian folktales, encouraged by the ethnologist Elsie Clews Parsons, a frequent guest in her home.[11] "Austin knew that her progress in placing her own Indian stories would interest Luhan. When *McCall's* accepted some of them, she expressed both delight and a sense of weariness with the "snobbish" prejudice against Indian material that she had often encountered on her lecture tours. In 1922 she complained to Luhan that students at the University of California summer school "dissented" when she suggested they study Indian cultures, as if they were "above anything the Indian has to teach them." She had run up against this attitude before among such close friends as Lincoln Steffens. "I think Steff would be big enough, if he ever had a chance to study Indians, to admit them to his philosophy, but I doubt if he will ever expose himself to conviction," she wrote to Luhan.[12]

With so many viewpoints shared, what lay at the crux of the difficulties between Luhan and Austin? Luhan's relationship with Tony was never quite acceptable to Austin, possibly because of the latter's reticence about sexual matters. Notwithstanding her vocal protests against modern marriage and her clear support of issues foregrounded by the Woman Movement of her day, Austin's Methodist background died hard. She wrote in haste to Luhan in the spring of 1923 to "protect" her friend from a newspaper scandal which she felt certain would explode at any moment when Luhan's liaison with Tony became known. Her advice "to go away and be married quietly where there are no newspapers, and stay away . . . two or three weeks" reflects her anxiety about "newspaper slander" against her friend as well as her concern to "save the Cause from the constant menace of the news."[13] As Richard Drinnon has written about Austin, her anxieties about Freudianism and premarital sex, among other references to sexuality, suggest "that sex mattered to her much more than she let herself realize."[14]

Austin probably never resolved her ambivalence about Mabel and Tony's relationship. Nor could she reconcile her affection for Indians in the abstract with her distaste for their marriage. While she liked Tony personally, it was quite another thing to accept her very Anglo friend Mabel being married to a Pueblo Indian. Especially difficult for Austin to comprehend was Tony's habit of returning to Taos Pueblo occasionally to renew the intimate conjugal connection he retained with his former wife—a practice not altogether congenial to Mabel in light of the syphilis she had contracted from Tony some years before their marriage.[15]

Another issue that separated the two women was Luhan's wealth. What Austin probably found most galling—and, paradoxically, most compelling—about Luhan was the fact that she did not need to earn her way. Mabel's wealth conferred privileges of leisure and solitude that Austin may have thought she could have put to better use. If Luhan wanted to write, well and good; but she had the freedom that Austin lacked of choosing her own subjects and deadlines. Luhan had the luxury of writing for her own enjoyment, while Austin struggled to finish projects that really did not interest her because she needed the income. When Luhan lived in New York, from 1913 to 1917, she churned out articles for Alfred Stieglitz's *Camera Work*, for the *International*, and for Max Eastman and Jack Reed's weekly socialist newspaper, *The Masses*, but always for her own amusement.[16] While on a camping trip in California, Luhan unashamedly referred to her laziness in a letter to Austin. "I may do some writing for the Hearst papers—but maybe not. I'm not very keen to." In the same letter she alluded to writing "one thing called 'all cultures' . . . good idea but I can't write lovely rich prose like you can. I am so stilted."[17] To Luhan, writing was an avocation rather than a profession that required daily discipline and dedication.

In Taos, Luhan continued to hold "Wednesday evenings," taking enormous enjoyment in the smug discovery that many of the participants "had no familiarity" with the theosophical ideas that often were discussed. She invited Austin to "come up next Wednesday or any following one & tell them something of your occult experiences."[18] Since the trip to Taos entailed an overnight stay, Austin effectively would lose two precious workdays. These overtures underscored the differences between the daily pressures each woman faced. Austin, whose constant productivity kept her only marginally solvent, naturally preferred to arrange her visits around her own needs.

The necessity to rely on Luhan for financial assistance further upset the balance of power in their relationship. In the summer of 1923,

when Austin stayed with Mabel and Tony for over a month while recuperating from her breakdown, she noted the predicament of the professional writer in ill health. "All the doctors are agreed in attributing
[the breakdown] to the psychic compulsion that I have been putting on
myself for the past four years." To recover from this nervous collapse
brought on by overwork and financial problems, Austin's physicians
had asked her to give up "the strain of any kind of work that I do not
naturally wish to do. At present I can see no way of accomplishing that
and at the same time providing myself with a comfortable home and
reasonably happy surroundings."[19]

Yet Luhan wanted very much to write and, nudged by her thera-
pist, produced rambling, personal accounts of her life.[20] *Winter in Taos*,
published in 1935, is more notable for its stunning photographs by
Ansel Adams and Edward Weston than for its prose. "The people who
live here are at home and at their ease," she observes. "They feel independent and sure of themselves, and nothing we can do or not do ever
shakes their security for they are not as sensitive as we hope. If we do
not eat with them, it is because our tastes are different, and each is welcome to his own."[21] Although Luhan's observations anticipate those of
therapists later in the century, Austin's writings demonstrate a greater
understanding of the "sensitivity" of American Indians. Luhan's description of the spirituality of nature tends toward the syrupy: "And
yourself, the vessel of spring, you need not be spilled if your balance
holds, contrive to pass back to the needy universe this light before it
thickens into heat and densifies in flesh."[22] Austin of the "virile" style
could not bring herself to praise Luhan's writing.

A Difficult Personality

The reserve that Austin maintained toward Luhan was reflected, in one
way or another, in most of the writer's relationships. Indeed, it must
have been difficult for anyone to get close to Austin. "My early life
may have made me stiff to know," she confided to Luhan, adding that
she had "a deep seated resistance to being personally liked. Nothing
stiffens me quite so much as being called 'charming.'" Romantic attachments were especially threatening to her. "I have just turned away a
friend of twenty years standing for getting romantic about me," she
wrote.[23] Austin's early novels do not capture the closeness in human
relationships as successfully as her early short fiction does. A compari-

son of her first and last novels, *Isidro* and *Starry Adventure*, illustrates the complexity of her feelings toward others, Luhan in particular.

Isidro is a particularly apt example of how mannered Austin's fiction could be and contrasts with her later regional fiction centering on New Mexico. A seldom-read romance set against the early California mission period (probably the 1830s), *Isidro* is an improbable love story about a beautiful heiress, Jacinta, and Isidro, a dashing young *hacendado* (rancho owner) who is about to enter the priesthood. Jacinta was spirited off as an infant by her sickly young mother, fleeing an embittered marriage. When her mother died, Jacinta was taken in and raised by shepherds, dressed in male clothing, her true identity shrouded in mystery for many years. Jacinta chances upon Isidro on his way to the mission to take vows, and their friendship flourishes in the wilderness. She becomes a companion and servant of sorts to the courtly young Isidro, but their relationship reaches a crisis when Jacinta's true female identity comes to light and their authentic male friendship gives way to an altogether different kind of love—an embarrassed affection.

Isidro Escobar's refined sense of honor permits him no alternative but to forgo the priesthood and marry Jacinta instead. As if to signal that normality has returned, Jacinta discards her male shepherd's garb and dons woman's clothing almost as soon as Isidro discovers her identity. In this confusing novel, with its Shakespearean manipulation of gender identities, Austin represents the initial friendship between Isidro and the young shepherd (variously identified as El Zarzo, the Briar, and Jacinta) as superior to this ensuing romantic love. "As often as [Isidro] thought of the Briar his heart warmed toward the lad,—always the lad,—never the cold, still girl by the pomegranate hedge in San Antonio."[24] Austin chooses to represent same-sex friendship as more comradely, more equal, than the traditional hierarchical relationships between men and women. Thus, Isidro misses his shepherd companion even after his chaste marriage to Jacinta. "If she were but stretched beside him on the brown litter,—of course that could not be since she was a girl,—but if the boy El Zarzo lay there beside him . . . they could watch the squirrels come and go, or read the fortunes of Urbano in the faces of his men" (*Isidro* 350).

In a provocative article about the use of clothing to disguise gender, critic Sandra Gilbert has suggested that twentieth-century women writers have frequently expressed the struggle "to define a gender-free reality behind or beneath myth, an ontological essence so pure, so free that 'it' can inhabit any costume." Although there seems little point in

claiming Austin for modernism (Gilbert specifically applies her argument to modernists), the reader cannot help but note that Jacinta's
degraded sense of self persists from precisely the point in the novel
when her identity is established as female and the "male dominant/
female submissive sexual order" is asserted.[25] "So she arrives at some
very mortifying conclusions. First, that by her boy's trappings, which
she had never thought to question, she had lost esteem of very many
people, among them Escobar; next, that much as he disapproved of
those, she was much more acceptable to him as Peter Lebecque's lad
than as what she now showed to be" (*Isidro* 246). Certainly *Isidro* is not
meant as an "exuberant" examination of "gender disorder," as Woolf's
Orlando was in Gilbert's view. When order is restored in the wilderness world Austin has created, Jacinta is transformed and "claimed"
as Isidro's bride. "Where Escobar put her in his thought she stayed."
Yet a prevailing sense of "anxiety," to use Gilbert's term, remains. In
the resolution to the novel, Jacinta submits modestly to the patriarchal
order of things and is restored passively to her husband and long-lost
father.[26]

Gender disorder is, of course, only one aspect of *Isidro*, but it is a
critical one. Cross-dressing in this early novel previews the technique
Austin uses in *Starry Adventure*, in which the second-person narrative
filters through the consciousness of the male protagonist, Gard Sitwell.
Austin consciously transcends her marginality as a woman writer to resist "oppressive male authority" by speaking through Gard and thus appropriating the dominant discourse.[27] Briefly, *Starry Adventure* chronicles Gard's growing up in New Mexico amid Protestant and Catholic
influences. The son of a strong mother and an invalid father, Gard
is, in one critical estimate, the "prototype of the central figures in all
of Mrs. Austin's novels"—an idealist and altruist searching for happiness in the natural beauty of the New Mexican landscape, centering
his hopes on the recovery of "a useable past."[28] Appropriately, then,
when Gard grows up and must find a job, he chooses to stay in New
Mexico. His position as an assistant to an architect who restores the
old Spanish colonial houses to their former glory provides him with
an opportunity to meet Eudora Ballantin, a wealthy divorcée who ex-
udes sensuality and sophistication, as well as false sensitivity toward
indigenous New Mexicans. Gard's affiliation with architecture implies
a mastery of design and material; his name suggests that he is on his
guard at all times against the wiles of Eudora. Eudora's rival is Jane
Hetherington, a wealthy young woman of sensitivity and sincerity. Her
genuine involvement with the culture of the Pueblo Indians and her

unusual understanding of Gard's brief dalliance with Eudora, which Austin depicts as destructively sexual, fit her to be Gard's soul mate and wife.

Starry Adventure combines many of the major Austin themes: the timeless beauty of "the landscape line"; the essential nobility of indigenous inhabitants of the land, contrasted with the shallowness and corruption of eastern literati; and the superiority of the essential woman over the so-called New Woman. It may well be the "summary of her aims and achievement in the field of fiction," in the words of T. M. Pearce, the scholarly critic who knew Austin best.[29]

Can it be coincidental that Gard's background resembles Austin's own? His infatuation and secret affair with Eudora almost destroy his chance for happiness, until he sees her for the shallow adventuress she is. *Starry Adventure* is fiction, to be sure, but the Eudora who eventually marries the Hispanic Eugenio and opulently restores his ancestral home, Huertas Cardenas, bears more than an accidental resemblance to Mabel Dodge Luhan. When the house is almost finished and ready to function as a playground for Eudora's fashionable eastern friends, Austin creates an important scene in which Gard observes Eudora in the setting she has created.

There were fires in all the rooms which were sufficiently near completion for Eudora to give them her attention, and the faint perfume of burning cedar. In the intervals when the cloud shut down over Huertas Cardenas, there was still the flare of candles in the punched tin *candeleros*—copied from old churches at Trampas and San Antonio de Quemado. And at every alteration from cloud to sun, Eudora moved about alternately lighting and snuffing them so that she might watch the pattern of the barred and spindled shutters on the walls. She had the happiest appreciation for the quality of the walls as they had come from the patting, practiced hands of the women plasterers. She went about studying with that pleased bright fixity of hers, the shadows shaped by swinging doors and leaping fires. Other moments her response would be of sure divination for the contents of her boxes of imported possessions, such as would accent and define mutual advantages of bronzes, Italian brocades, unframed modernist sketches, old Mexican glass whose highlights were deep rather than high. She had the gift for effects, for producing, out of essential confusion, intriguing juxtapositions which she called amusing. It was, as you were to discover, her sole term of approbation for the claim Things made on her attention. . . . You were caught up in it, not less certainly than the native workmen who looked where she looked, and admired, and dramatized their admiration with the naive divertisement [*sic*] of children waving colored whirligigs at fairs. You thought: this is the way it must have been in the old days; the really superior *patron* and *patrona* dramatizing in their superiorities everything their dependencies most admired. (*SA* 280–81)

The description of Eudora's carefully orchestrated environment is virtually a visual inventory of the objets d'art that filled Luhan's home in Taos.

Much of the attraction of Eudora for Gard—and of Luhan for Austin—resided in her wonderful sense of how things came together, a controlled sensuality. Ugliness in the furnishings of her mother's home had offended Austin as a child. Yet in *Starry Adventure* Gard realizes that the impact of Eudora and her "things" on his senses cannot be separated from her wealth. An element of corruption clings to the tasteful, expensive furnishings and ultimately to Eudora herself, much as it does to Gilbert Osmond in James's *Portrait of a Lady*, to Fitzgerald's Daisy in *The Great Gatsby*, and to Undine Sprague in Wharton's *Custom of the Country*.

Rich. That was the hard-ribbed fact, that in moments when you were away from her, laid weals across your soul. You knew that Eudora's things were beautiful and appropriate, even in their strangeness. You had a feeling for Things. Especially for Eudora's Things, their rarity, their uniqueness, which was, first and last, a feeling for their expensiveness. When you came right down to it, the unifying item in Eudora's Things was that they cost money. You knew it by the way she didn't tell you; by the sureness with which, out of a vast assemblage of things far off but purchasable, she chose what she wanted. 'Charlot,' she would say, 'will have something'—or, 'I know a little shop on Lexington Avenue.' You got to know, during that first week of Eudora's at Huertas Cardenas, you couldn't escape knowing, what it meant, to a woman furnishing her house, to be rich. (*SA* 282)

What Luhan thought when she read the novel can only be guessed. Eudora, who is merely a collector, functions as a foil for Gard, who has the knowledge and background to appreciate New Mexico's natural beauty and the significance of the Spanish colonial objects Eudora has amassed. Ultimately Gard realizes that he has become one of Eudora's "things," just as her husband has. He escapes the museum he has helped her to build just in time to save his honor and realize the potential of his spiritual "starry adventure." The novel turns around the Veblenian theory of "ornamental womanhood" and demonstrates how an idealistic man can become a trophy in the hands of a woman like Eudora.[30]

In perhaps the unkindest cut of her pen, Austin insinuates that in her quest for power Eudora becomes very much like a male dressed in drag (Sandra Gilbert's image), while Gard, once free of her clutches, represents all that (in Austin's estimation) true manliness should be—including chastity—as Jane's suitor and husband. The sexual consummation of their marriage is left for the future. The Indian workers at Huertas Cardenas snicker behind Eudora's back at her "transvestism," much as Austin had suggested Luhan's friends laughed behind her back when she married Tony.

Austin touches on chaste marriage and unconsummated love in other fictions, most notably *Isidro*. That Gard may be a fictional alter ego for Austin, and Eudora for Luhan, suggests the spiritual impediment in the two women's relationship. For Eudora's sensuality is ultimately unacceptable to Gard. This position is consistent with Austin's negative view of the representation of sex in the American novel:

> I do not mean to deny that there are thousands of people in the United States whose love is the sordidly restricted episode it is described as being in books like "Winesburg, Ohio" and "Spoon River Anthology." Or that there are millions whose experience is limited to the turgid, tormenting bounderism suffered in the novels of Waldo Frank and Ben Hecht. There are quite certainly any number of people who, while sedulously cherishing the earlier ideal, fail as completely as do the inhabitants of Zenith City and Gopher Prairie in registering its high mark. But one does not need to accuse any of these authors of anything less than entire honesty in order to prove that there may be more beauty and aspiration in American love life than gets into their books.[31]

Certainly Austin, woman of the world that she felt herself to be, appears to us as something of a prude about sexual matters in many of her writings.

The Circe-like female protagonist of *Starry Adventure* emerges as a stinging criticism of sensuous excess. But Austin's passionate denunciation may have contained a twinge of envy of Luhan. "As a fact Eudora was insatiable, never to be sufficiently conned and measured and responded to" (*SA* 288). Nor could Austin resist putting into Eudora's mouth a parody of the pseudospiritualistic utterance that she had often heard in Luhan's conversation. In an exchange with Gard about the Deer's Cry at Jemez—an Indian ritual in which deer were flushed out of the mountains—Eudora explains: "We get into the same vibration, if you know what I mean. I mean there's a sort of stream of consciousness, and we get into it. That's what I always say, that when we know people, really know them, and are spiritually intimate, it enlarges the consciousness" (*SA* 289).

Luhan, however, had the last word. In a "tribute" written ten years after Austin's death, she vented some of the anger she undoubtedly felt for the real and imagined slights inflicted by her friend. "Our women's egos are perhaps as overwhelming as hers but we have learned to cage them to prevent them from making us too ridiculous," Luhan wrote. She went on to describe Austin as "one of those whose legs are too short for her top side" and who "felt like the tall dominant queenly type." Austin may have looked regal sitting down, Luhan observed, but she cut a "ridiculous" figure when she stood up. Especially sensitive about criticism of her Indian husband, Luhan recounted an anecdote about a lecture that he and Austin attended in New York. Throwing "a shawl over her head" and "holding two bunches of flowers in her hands," Austin "assumed a portentous poker-faced expression that she felt was the way Indian women feel." Then she "turned to Tony and commanded the Corn Dance song" and, much to his chagrin, coerced him into assisting her in an Indian dance in front of the large crowd.[32]

On the other hand, Luhan praised Austin's "zest" and myriad accomplishments, remembering her as "one of the best companions in the world in a house or on a trip. She loved to put on a big apron and go into our big old kitchen and toss a couple of pumpkin pies together. She loved to hob-nob, to sit and spin out reasons for strange happenings, to hear and tell about all the daily occurrences in both our lives. She was a romantic and loved the romance of the mystical and the occult and often induced in herself peculiar symptoms. She could see and hear and truly experience more than the rest of us, so when she least knew it she really became fascinatingly delphic and sibylline."[33]

Even when they lived relatively close together, the two women carried on an extensive correspondence, and certain cruel letters from Austin suggest that Luhan had cause to store up a goodly amount of resentment over the years. In one particularly offensive letter written in 1925, Austin advised Luhan that none of her friends "has ever treated Tony with entire respect. I have never mentioned this to you before, because I did respect your relations with him; but you make it

necessary that I should explicitly tell you that not only is he a joke,—
a good natured and occasionally ribald joke—but still a joke to most
people who come to your house, but that many of them, along, with
my friends, have resented my being used 'as a nursemaid to Mabel's
husband.'"[34] In addition to raising questions about Austin's legendary
respect and fondness for Indians, this letter demonstrates her potential
for spitefulness when her ire was aroused.

Sparking this incendiary missive was a letter that Luhan had written
to Austin's niece at Wellesley College. Austin, with a certain paranoia,
interpreted it as interference. "You wrote maliciously to discredit the
only person on whom Mary [the writer's niece] has to depend for help,
utterly unmindful of the harm that might come to Mary supposing you
succeeded in prejudicing her against me." Luhan apparently returned
the letter, scribbling on it "Dear Mary, Snap out of it! M.L."[35] Mary
Hunter Wolf remembers several of her aunt's outbursts over the years
when she was growing up, tantrums that she and other relatives were
powerless to combat.

In the early 1920s Austin became convinced that her niece had "no
one but me able to give her the chance she wants in the world."[36] In
truth, young Mary was well looked after in Hollywood, California,
by her legal guardian, George Hunter, and her stepmother, Georgia
Hunter. She dreaded her aunt's unpleasant "rows" with her relatives.[37]
Austin persisted in believing that young Mary was in league with her
against the rest of the family, who stupidly and maliciously refused to
see that she alone could provide the social and cultural "advantages" the
girl needed. After Ruth's death in 1918, Austin adamantly demanded
control over her niece's life and longed to have young Mary come and
live with her. When it became clear that she would never have custody
of her niece, she poured out her distress in a letter to Luhan. "This is
the first time in my life I have ever rebelled against God," she wrote,
calling her separation from Mary "a cruel, senseless sort of thing."[38]

Despite the tension between them, Luhan's treatment of Austin was
characteristically generous. She understood Austin's straitened circumstances and was free with hospitality, transportation, and even money
—outright subsidies in the form of monthly checks. "All the things I
want could be secured by money," Austin candidly wrote to her bene-
factress. "What I want is a permanent home and a resting place for my
affections. If my heart was at rest I know I could do better work."[39]
Many of Austin's letters to Luhan refer to her financial problems. In
1920 she wrote: "I long for New Mexico as never for any other land.
. . . Always I have still this perpetual problem of money." She could

Austin and her niece, Mary Hunter (Wolf), in Santa Fe, ca. 1926.

not solve the problem without Luhan's assistance, for in Santa Fe there was "the problem of altitude. Otherwise I could go there and stay long enough to make up for the expense of travel."[40] In a letter written from Santa Fe when she was still commuting to New York in the early 1920s, Austin alluded to "utterly unprecedented financial troubles" and urged Luhan not to "let go of what you are doing for me. I need it more than ever."[41] She relied on her friend to recognize that she was wasting her talent in New York as a "hack." Before Christmas in 1922 Austin complained that she was "making more money than ever by doing magazine work, but not enough . . . to withdraw from that work and write the kinds of books and plays I would feel justified in writing."[42]

Ironically, when she was in New Mexico, Austin often complained bitterly about inconvenience and disturbance to her work. "I suppose after I have been away from New Mexico for a year or two, I shall recall only its picturesque phases," she wrote in 1924 while convalescing from a "dreadful chill" contracted during an October storm in Santa Fe before the furnaces were lit for winter, "but just now I can see it only as a land of bad roads, bad weather, inadequate living facilities, incompetent service and intellectual sterility. I shall leave for New York as soon as possible."[43]

Yet such impulses conflicted with her continuing ambivalence toward the East. Although she was published widely and enjoyed the company of the major writers and intellectuals of her day, Austin often complained of professional slights. "I grew weary of the attitude of young New York toward my work, and just served notice on them that I wouldn't put up with it," she told Luhan. Never unduly modest about such matters, Austin related her strategy for bringing "young New York" around in 1920. "I told them exactly where they got off so far as the rest of the world was concerned, and all but the *New Republic* group and Mencken and the *Smart Set* rushed over to my side declaring they had always been on my side," she gloated.[44] Not one to spare her friend a hefty serving of braggadocio—perhaps because she was at heart an insecure and fragile woman who was quite uncomfortable in New York—Austin exulted over her successes with the magazines. "So now *The Nation, The Bookman, The Freeman* and *The Dial* are all captives of my bow and spear," she wrote, mentioning articles coming out in the *Unpartizan Review*—"Supernaturals in Fiction" and "Automatism in Writing"—as well as articles to be published in the *Delineator, Harper's*, and possibly the *Ladies' Home Journal*.[45] Austin tirelessly lobbied editors and successfully placed many articles through personal visits to their offices.

By the early 1920s, Austin had begun to receive public recognition of her unique contribution to American letters. In addition to the National Arts Club dinner, she was featured in the *Bookman* in September 1923. "Hers is, to be sure, a mind made to the desert's order," the magazine editorialized. "It has the classic rigor to cope with austerity and desolation and the precise delicacy of perception which sees intimacy and loveliness where they are most subtly and terribly concealed." The article praised Austin for expressing her emotions, singling out *The Land of Little Rain*, *Lost Borders*, and *The Flock*. "When she comes down from her own standard and the desert's, her workmanship persists in all its beauty and sincerity; her inspiration abandons her. That is the decree laid upon her by her experience in the lonely West." The "great American" quality of her writing was due to "the chance that took her into the southwest and [by which] she reads her desert rhythms and symbols into all American institutions."[46] Flattering as this praise was, Austin longed for recognition of her works that were not connected with the desert.

Sinclair Lewis echoed the *Bookman* salute when he compared Austin to Whitman in her feeling for an "American rhythm."[47] He added that he "would emphasize her importance, even aside from the undoubtedly great intrinsic value of her own books, in her unfailing insistence on the dignity and importance of real American spirit in American literature." Lewis and Austin had had their literary rows, particularly over the character of Carol Kenicott in *Main Street*. Austin considered Carol "a parasite" and as such unable to "produce beauty and wonder. . . . The Carol Kenicotts are as lacking in spiritual perception as Main Street is in intellectual perception." She chided Lewis, "Sex and art and religion, the mystical experience of each I mean, these are the things that are missing from Main Street."[48] Although she deplored Lewis's want of spiritual understanding, Austin counted him among her good friends after he visited her in Santa Fe. By 1920 she was willing to forgive the author of *Main Street* the "spiritual impotence" he represented in American life, if he would collaborate with her on the "really illuminative American novel." Austin told Lewis that she had come to "this idea of a combination of essential knowledge" when she was writing *The Ford*. Every so often, she wrote, "my material disappeared into the intricacies of male life beyond my capacity to follow it."[49] Although Lewis graciously declined this invitation, they remained the best of literary friends. He was one of the few men ever to get close enough to her to address her as "Mary dear."[50]

Austin also outlined her literary ideas to Luhan, although she did not confide in her to the extent she did in Lewis. Perhaps she shared her material with Luhan because she valued her opinion; more likely, however, she hoped to harvest encouragement from her friend in the form of hospitality or financial assistance. For Luhan was known to her friends as a one-woman granting agency of literary sabbaticals. In fact, when she purchased the Taos property, she had envisioned her home as one day becoming "a creative centre—not just a place for people to retreat into—or to go to sleep in or to barge in for just another good time"; she urged Austin "to consider it ready" for her "any time."[51] At least once Austin asked to borrow the plot of a story Luhan had told about "the haunting of [her] house in Italy by the spirit of a young woman who had been in [her] employment. . . . Could you just note down the main facts for me," she wrote.[52]

Luhan became the only friend who was privy to the distraught and tragic side of Austin, which she carefully withheld from her publishers and New York literary friends. She was also alone in hearing about Austin's romantic affairs. In 1920 Austin responded cryptically to her friend's query about her love life. "All I can say is that if I had had as much attention when I was in my twenties or thirties as I am having in my fifties, it would have ruined me."[53] In a 1929 letter about her friendship with Lincoln Steffens, Austin wrote: "At the time [around 1915] we all thought Steff was a great man, a great reformer, a Jesus type. I believe he thought so himself, but his gentleness, which seemed to be so much to the fore in his public life, was only for men, as I came to know afterward he is cruel with the kind of cruelty that leads little boys to pull the wings off of flies and to torture caterpillars." Steffens, Austin wrote, "was jealous of the attainments of women" and couldn't bear the "attention" accorded to her as a celebrity when they went out together. He accused her of engineering conversations "in which he couldn't shine," although she granted that Steffens was not "singular in not being able to endure any expression of literary superiority in a woman."[54]

Austin was clearly attracted to Steffens, even though she disavowed any amorous feelings for him. After the death of his first wife, Steffens married the talented, young, and very attractive writer Ella Winter. The story persisted that Austin had stalked him; she flatly denied this gossip. "I told him once, when we had quarrelled about something that he had said about me, which wasn't true, . . . I cautioned him that if he didn't look out, somebody would say that the real source of his quarrel with me was intellectual jealousy," she told Luhan.[55] When Steffens tired of Austin's company and blatantly rejected her, she took to viewing him as one of New York's "pathetic" intellectuals, probably to salvage her pride.

A sensitive woman, Austin received shabby treatment from many men in her professional career. She dealt with it by lashing out, which invariably led to more of the same treatment. Whether she found invective a good strategy of ego defense is a matter that can never be definitively settled. It is certain that she felt a stronger alliance with women—if not an intellectual alliance (she usually refers to artists as "men"), then a spiritual one. She put it to her public this way: "What do you suppose the wives of American pioneers were thinking about as they trecked [*sic*] across the continent behind their husbands? Where do you suppose the unmarried English and American novelists—who are the only novelists ranking close to the greatest men novelists of the world—inform themselves, except out of the inexhaustible storehouse of woman lore, lore chiefly about men's ways with women, which, in America, social use has rendered incommunicable."[56]

However intellectually superior Austin felt toward Luhan, she also manifested feelings of jealousy toward her friend, possibly because of the many men in Luhan's life. A. A. Brill, Luhan's psychoanalyst, was a specific target of her jealousy. "Just now I am more interested in you than in any man," she wrote to Luhan in 1922. "I am worried for fear when Brill makes you over some of the most interesting parts will be left out." Austin distrusted psychoanalysis, which she called "the prevailing American obsession." In a 1923 article, she attributed its popularity to "the younger generation's way, by putting the responsibility on the Puritans, of excusing itself for finding sex a tormenting and unmanageable business." Austin's misgivings about psychoanalysis may be traced to her notorious arrogance, especially on the subject of genius. In *Everyman's Genius* she claims, "Though I have not read a psychoanalyst who did not suppose he knew all about the genius process, I have never read one who did not demonstrate his complete ignorance of it."[57]

As for Luhan, Austin diagnosed her problems as stemming from the lack of a specific calling in life. "Your not having anything to do, and my being steadier than you are, is all I have at present to provide me with occasions for feeling superior to you, as we all must occasionally feel with our friends. I have hardly any place in my life for a woman who is both rich and perfect."[58] Austin's proprietary tone toward Luhan raises the question of whether the two women had a sexually intimate relationship. The probability is scant that they did, given Austin's stern Methodist values and Luhan's indisputable commitment to heterosexuality.[59] Whatever their degree of intimacy, their friendship was intense and marked by twinges of jealous possession on Austin's side. In defending herself against Luhan's charge that she had taken it upon herself "to play the hostess" in Luhan's home during the mid-1920s, Austin rendered a pro forma apology—"it shall not happen again"—followed by a diatribe against Luhan's circle. "And as for the comment of your friends, well you do know, don't you that your friends comment upon you quite as much as they do on your other guests, but I never take them seriously and it is a little of a surprise to find that you do."[60]

Austin did not refrain from bluntly pointing out whom Luhan should invite to her place in Taos and whom she should not. Somewhat mysteriously, she wrote: "I can't tell you things I have learned by inquiry about the lady you asked about, and as they are things that I should hardly like to set down on paper with my name to them, I will say only that it would be better if you didn't have her at the house very much, or give her the excuse of plausibility for anything she might say about you, should she fall into the delusions under which she seemed to labor while here."[61] Austin envisioned herself as Luhan's protector and continued to remind her, sometimes with acerbity, of her vulnerability and need of protection. Perhaps this was Austin's way of reciprocating the many favors bestowed upon her by Luhan, as well as asserting her own brand of control.

At the same time, Austin depended heavily on Luhan to provide her with introductions to notable people outside her own circle. Writing from London in 1922, she asked Luhan for the names of people whom it would be "pleasant" to meet and instructed her to draft "a letter to the Duse," explaining that "I want a few words from her for something I am writing about the training of gifted young women." She may have hoped to gather material about Eleonora Duse's views to include in *Everyman's Genius*.[62]

Indian Affairs

Austin's and Luhan's involvement in the Indian rights movement brought them into contact with John Collier, organizer of the American Indian Defense Association. His dedication to the Indian cause, like theirs, complemented his resistance to the "disaster" of modern civilization. Together, Austin, Collier, and Luhan arranged speeches and large meetings designed to heighten the awareness of Easterners, in particular, about Indian affairs.[63] Austin considered herself an ethnographer in her creative work; she sought out those doing important scholarly work in the field and corresponded extensively with them. Frances Densmore, for example, was a special friend. An outstanding ethnomusicologist, she began collecting and recording Indian songs in 1920. During the Depression, when Densmore was struggling for funding, she found a staunch supporter in Austin, who made contacts for her so that she might continue her scholarly work.[64]

For all the work Densmore and others produced, Austin could not shake off the feeling that the burden of reformist Indian causes fell on her shoulders alone. "I suppose I am doing all that can be done by keeping forever at the New York editors and critics, making them see that they must admit the Indian among American influences," she wrote wearily to Luhan around 1920.[65] During the early 1930s Austin derived enormous satisfaction from invitations by Yale's School of Drama to lecture on American Indian dance drama. She contended that students in American universities learned almost as a truism that modern dance drama was derived from ancient Greece. Writing in the *Yale Review*, Austin noted that "the last thing that such an American student learns, if, indeed, he is so fortunate as to hear of it at all, is that here in his own land, accessible from Pullman car and motor bus, Amerind dance drama, recognizably of the same type as the pre-Aristotelian mysteries of fertility and increase, trembles on the forward edge of the oblivion of ignorance and neglect."[66]

Although politicking for the Indians vitally interested Austin, it was the subject of Indian dance and rhythm that seized her imagination. Just how she formulated her theories remains somewhat nebulous. She bristled because Americans seemed insensitive to and ignorant of what she termed the "American rhythm," the title of her controversial book on the subject. One of her close friends in Santa Fe, the poet Witter Bynner, took her to task. "Your main error seems to me to be in trying to connect what you call the American rhythm with the English rhythm of your translations of an original Indian rhythm. You could never convince me that your rhythms in translations have anything to do with the American soil in the sense that the original Indian rhythm belongs to it," Bynner wrote.[67] Austin, however, had proven to her own satisfaction that primitive rhythmic patterns had later surfaced in classic traditions throughout the world, as well as in the American poetic tradition. She felt no responsibility to resort to scholarly evidence to prove the existence of an "American rhythm."

When the poet Arthur Davison Ficke criticized *The American*

Rhythm, Austin responded that she considered herself a "creative thinker." Her research came from within herself, and her "higher obligation" transcended that of providing "stodgy and meticulous demonstration for the uninitiate, of what has come to me through the natural channels of scholarly experience." She went on to explain that the "whole trend of the book is to exemplify the multiplicity of rhythmic elements which go to make up anything that we call characteristic rhythm. . . . I have briefly sketched in review the case for rhythm as it is understood by specialists in that field." In her view she had gone beyond scientific knowledge to present a "fresh fund of new information as to the origins of poetry." If people failed to understand what she was doing, so be it. "I sometimes feel that this general snootiness of the classic tradition [to] primitivism calls for a response in kind on my part," she complained to Ficke. "It is true that in this particular book, which is my own field, first staked out and preempted by myself, I felt more than ever the right to complete freedom of expression without too much deference to other people's ignorances." She distrusted "man's intellectual explanations of his experiences," preferring instead "to wander pleasantly through all the known fields of research which interest me without any reference to what other people may find there."[68]

To Mabel Luhan fell many of the routine tasks and follow-up involved in work with the American Indian Defense Association; she also served as exchequer for the association. Austin counted on her wealthy friend for funds to pursue the projects that interested her. "It is a great trial to me that I can't afford to continue writing Indian stories and making readable versions of their songs, but I suppose somebody else will come along who can do it better," she wrote in a statement calculated to prompt Luhan's generosity. Luhan and Austin believed that the eastern Brahmins ignored the southwestern indigenous art tradition, judging it less worthy of attention than what was being purveyed in the Manhattan galleries. They resented the eastern critical establishment, which seemed indifferent to the "independant [*sic*] art movements which originate elsewhere." Austin took the *New Republic,* and in particular Walter Lippmann, to task for reflecting an "insufferable" attitude "in attempting to speak for all America."[69]

By 1922 Luhan, Austin, and Collier were heavily involved in a fight to defeat the Bursum Bill. Written by New Mexico rancher and senator Holm Olaf Bursum, the bill proposed to take away substantial tracts held by the Pueblo Indians in New Mexico, effectively divesting the tribe of grazing and agricultural lands in favor of commercial interests. "I wonder why it is that people always feel certain they know what is good for the Indians in inverse proportion to the length of time they have been interested in Indians," Austin wrote to Luhan. She was particularly exasperated by the women's clubs. Although lectures to women's groups paid some of her bills (and the clubs consistently championed Indian rights), she found many of the women she met boring do-gooders. What particularly rankled Austin was the disarray among opponents of Bursum, who were not "informed" of a new bill in response to Bursum which she reasoned seemed "calculated to divide the friends of the Indian" with little chance of passage.[70] Bursum was finally defeated in 1923, in part due to Luhan's well-orchestrated national publicity campaign. The "Protest of Artists and Writers Against the Bursum Bill" enlisted the support of many creative people, including Witter Bynner, Zane Gray, D. H. Lawrence, Vachel Lindsay, Edgar Lee Masters, Harriet Monroe, and Elsie Clews Parsons. Collier galvanized the support of monied club women in California, whom he had encountered when he was doing immigration work. The Associated Federation of Women's Clubs played a significant role in defeating the Bursum Bill.[71]

While the Bursum battle was raging, Commissioner of Indian Affairs Charles Burke banned Indian ceremonial dances on the grounds that they were harmful to establishing a sense of time management among the Indians. Furious, Austin marshaled Taos and Santa Fe Anglos to resist the order forbidding the Pueblo ritual observances. "The Protestant missionary has always insisted that Indian drama, Indian dance, Indian music, Indian poetry, Indian design, must be totally destroyed and their place filled with third rate expressions of these things, pieced together from various cultures of our European past," she wrote. "Missionaries have taught young Indians that the religion of their parents was not only contemptible but ridiculous." In a document about tribal customs drafted for a United States senator, Austin elaborated on the consequences of cultural misunderstandings that occurred when "outsiders, teachers or missionaries or other meddlesome persons" interfered in the "necessary ceremonials by which, according to tribal belief, the Pueblo is kept prosperous."[72] Austin apparently believed that the Washington powers were in league with the missionaries in an effort to obliterate important aspects of tribal culture.

Luhan and Collier worked together to defeat the proposed restriction of Indian tribal rites. Luhan made herself available to testify in Washington, and Collier frequently met with her at the Taos compound before and during his tenure as American Indian Defense Association executive secretary from 1923 until 1933, when he assumed the post of Commissioner of Indian Affairs in Washington. Even Lawrence actively worked to defeat the Bursum Bill, although he found Collier's presence an irritant and warned Luhan against his unrestrained militance. "There is a necessary balance," he told her. "Collier is utterly out of balance. The Santa Fe crowd is perhaps seeking a little balance in its own way. Learn to modify yourself."[73] Collier, by all accounts, was a brilliant advocate for Indian rights, but "he was also a ruthless and hyperbolic propagandist who consistently maligned the motives of his opponents," according to historian Lawrence Kelly. "He left behind him a trail of broken friendships and bitter estrangements."[74]

Austin, too, criticized Collier in the bulletin she sent Luhan from New York during 1923. Although a hard worker, Collier might benefit from her analysis of Indians as "exciting and romantic figures," which he seemed to be overlooking in favor of demographic and economic arguments. Austin judged Collier's approach "too philosophical . . . to catch the popular interest." However, Collier acknowledged his debt to Austin in a speech he gave at Cooper Union in late January 1923. He told the crowd "that he used to be annoyed when he was not simply mystified by what I used to say about Indians, but that knowing Indians had changed his whole life," Austin reported. In the late 1920s and early 1930s the Collier-Austin collaboration underwent considerable strain, especially with regard to the Indian Arts and Crafts Bill. Austin became miffed because of Collier's coolness toward the Indian Arts Foundation in Santa Fe. According to Austin, the foundation had taken on "the business of rescuing Indian artists from government futility, of fostering Indian talent, of educating the American public to appreciate it, and of finding a market for high quality Indian products." Believing Collier to be ill-informed, she invited him to join the foundation, lectured him about a "snootily" worded letter to her, and rebuked him for failing to consult the foundation on the Crafts Bill.[75] Austin again felt herself and the Santa Fe group being pushed aside in matters of Indian policy. Perhaps she was equally concerned that, by ignoring her, Collier was appropriating her power in the Santa Fe community.

The differences between Collier and Austin over the Indian Arts and Crafts (or Leavitt) Bill hinged upon their contrasting perspectives on preserving the Indian arts. Collier's concern was that subsidies be provided for producing Indian art. "So long as there exists within a group an institutional demand for beautiful products without any commercial motive, and so long as the group is economically self-sufficient,

[the] commercial factor is absent or negligible," he explained to Austin. She countered that the bill masked a darker motive, that of creating "another little Indian bureau to deal with Indian art, in precisely the same manner that Indian education has been dealt with in the past. . . . We objected to the Leavitt Bill, primarily, because what is wanted now is not a market for Indian arts, but a method of persuading Indians to produce art."[76]

Austin vigorously opposed government intervention on the grounds that the government's education programs had systematically destroyed the urge among the young to create Indian art. Instead, she endorsed "the creation, accessible to Indian workers, of a Museum of Indian Art for the Indians; the creation of a market for the best examples of Indian Art; the creation of a proper attitude on the part of the Indians toward their art; the holding of annual Indian fairs with prizes and credits for exceptional work; the study of Indian Art by itself; the education of the American public in Indian Art; the preparation of loan exhibits in American schools as part of this education; [and] special efforts for adapting the work of Indian artists to modern requirements."[77]

In the event, Austin's program for the Indian arts revival, thought by some to have been coercive and paternalistic, has been largely followed. Each summer, the Indian ceremonial dances and art competitions continue to be judged by Anglos using Anglo criteria, a source of frustration to many Indians, who object to the stereotype of the mystical race that has emerged from the commodification of their culture. Nevertheless, Austin, Luhan, and their friends considered themselves saviors of the Indians from the "evils" of wage labor. They saw the Bursum Bill as the first step in an overall strategy of depriving the Indians of meaningful work on their own land and forcing them to earn a living in factories and refineries. They argued that the Indians would be far better off making beads out of turquoise, doing shell work, and generally having "things to do during the winter months."[78] Presumably agriculture would occupy them during the summer. Austin and her friends were equally committed to the preservation of Hispanic culture. They founded the Society for the Revival of Spanish Arts (Colonial Arts Society) in Santa Fe and advocated a special curriculum for the Spanish-speaking citizenry at the El Rito training school in San José. They wished the curriculum to be restricted to the "manual arts," which would "enable the young people to avail themselves of their native genius and to find a market for their work as fast as they can produce it." In retrospect, efforts such as these appear paternalistic.

Austin and her group similarly attempted to raise public consciousness with regard to the "injurious" conditions under which American Indians lived. In a 1929 article hailing the appointment of Charles Rhoads to the chief position at the Bureau of Indian Affairs, Austin had called attention to the public health problems that were rampant in Indian schools and towns. "Briefly, the situation is this: every Indian community is a focal point for communicable diseases, chiefly tuberculosis and trachoma—diseases from which the Indian has developed no immunity and for which the Indian Bureau has provided no effective remedy," she wrote in *Forum*. "Along with this amazing condition, and contributing to it, is an appalling discovery that Indian children in government boarding schools are systematically underfed and overworked to a degree which would not be tolerated for a moment in any white community." Austin blamed the government's misplaced "energy—and incidentally, the taxpayers' money—which have been devoted to cajoling and compelling *our* Indians to behave like white men." Convinced that money "would, if rightly applied, have made of them the best of all aboriginals," she and Collier supported bilingual, reservation-based day school programs to keep alive the cultural heritage of the tribe.[79]

Austin had spoken out against the Indian boarding schools as early as 1900. In one story, "The Return of Sally Jack," she explored the issue of Indian assimilation through the eyes of a little Paiute Indian boy. Sally Jack is sent north to a school where he "pined for the campoodie and the golden slope where it lay looking out toward the Cosco hills, and in his white-sheeted bed longed for the feel of the earth under him, the free air and the stars; but most he longed for his mother." Austin allows her character (who was "No. 297" at the boarding school) to escape and beg his way home, fleeing the place where "the young bronze braves [are] cleaning yards or making bric-a-brac . . . and the files of unmothered youngsters [are] saying grace over their brown beans and dried apples."[80]

Quite probably it never occurred to these well-meaning Anglos that in concocting make-work projects for the Indians and manipulating a special curriculum for both Indian and Hispanic students, they, too, were depriving substantial numbers of people of a chance to become self-sufficient. Perhaps it never struck them that the term *our Indians* might have been offensive to many indigenous Americans. Undoubtedly, the idea that many Indians had no interest in recovering their tradition of crafts would have been unacceptable. Of course, Austin was correct in her assessment that white society's "fetish of bundling up the human body in cloth, the fetish of steam-heated houses, the fetish of substituting the fox trot and the bunny hug for the buffalo

and deer dances, the fetish of high-heeled shoes for women and of
$9.98 custom-made suits for men" were out of place in tribal culture.
She protested vigorously against such assimilationist attitudes. However, in attempting to revive the ancient Indian arts, Anglo intellectuals
and artists chose to dictate an idyllic way of life that pushed the Indians back into the past and denied them access to an industrial future.
Organizing the Indians to do the work that Anglos deemed appropriate was a laborious undertaking. In 1923 Austin conveyed to Luhan
something of the process: "I have . . . talked with San Ildefonso and
Tesuque [pueblos] about reviving the weaving which they say their
father's father's [*sic*] used to do. They can buy the fleeces very cheaply,
and all that will be needed is a loom and somebody to teach them for a
few weeks."[81] The distribution and marketing strategies that the Santa
Fe group conceived for these goods were naive. Austin and her friends
persisted in believing that a large, untapped market existed for Indian
crafts, particularly for blankets of high quality. Their major concerns
focused on ensuring "the quality of the goods" and "the integrity of
the workers," nebulous goals, to be sure.[82]

Austin, with a sense of self-righteous mission, continued to bicker
with other well-intentioned whites, especially Collier, over the best
means of fostering the Indian arts and crafts movement. In 1931, writing to Secretary of the Interior Ray Lyman Wilbur, she complained
that Collier, as Commissioner of Indian Affairs, had ignored the Indian
Rights Association, which she claimed spoke for the intellectuals of
America. "What I suggest . . . is that the Department make some public gesture to claim for itself the present high level of public interest
in Indian Arts. Do not let John Collier grab it off you and claim it
for his following. Have something written for one of the widely circulated magazines, preferably one of the women's magazines giving
an explicit account of what is being done in Indian arts and claiming
as co-operative with the Government certain authoratitive [*sic*] names
which I can easily furnish you." As a parting shot, Austin discredited
Collier's knowledge of the field, adding, "If I don't know about Indian
Arts, who does?"[83]

As Dudley Wynn observed in the 1930s, Austin "bowed to nobody
in respect for Indian culture and in comprehension of the wholeness
and beauty of the Indian way of life, but she could nevertheless see
that the concrete pattern of Indian life would ultimately be broken, the
religious and esoteric meanings of the poetry, decorative design, and
dance-drama lost." As long as these forms could be nurtured, America
would know an authentic culture, a culture of "wantlessness," as she

termed it; America would know the meaning of an innate sense of community.[84]

Doubtless, as Richard Drinnon suggests, Austin "shared with her contemporaries certain social Darwinian notions about 'primitives.'"[85] The correspondence between Collier, Austin, and Luhan abundantly documents the paternalistic attitudes held by many participants in Indian reform. Austin clearly believed that she was acting almost single-handedly to preserve the Indian arts by means of a highly directive program of education and persuasion. In an important communication to Collier, she alluded to a financial commitment that surely must have involved Luhan:

> About the general market for Indian blankets, I should tell you that I have been looking into that very carefully as I am financing a movement of Chimayo blanket makers. The Chimayo blankets, of course, are Spanish-Indian, but they pass with the general public as Indian blankets. About a quarter of a million dollars' worth of them go out of New Mexico every year, but these are second and third rate. The demand for first class blankets of this type is still so far from being satisfied that we expect to run along for a number of years without having to move to enlarge the market; and I have agreed to finance it up to fifty thousand dollars a year. All this involved a very careful study of the Indian blanket situation. I wouldn't hesitate to do as much or more than that for Navajo blankets except that I know I could not possibly persuade the Navajo Indians to make fifty thousand dollars' worth of first class blankets a year.[86]

Although her amateur analysis of markets for Indian crafts may have been based on dubious research, Austin rightly assumed that the Indians were bound to the environment in ways of which most Anglos were unaware. As Drinnon points out, she maintained enormous respect for the spiritual complexity of Indian rule and ritual.[87] But respect was not enough. What was needed was a more realistic view of the problems and poverty encroaching upon the Indians of New Mexico, whose interests could not be substantially advanced merely by the enthusiasm of the Anglo elite.

7

▲ ▲ ▲

THE PHOTOGRAPHIC
IMAGINATION

I am not sure that the other tourists saw anything but the changing

configuration of the cliff through the cloud-drift, but that was their misfortune.

It is only as they please that Those Above show themselves in the rainbow, which

when the sun is low is perfectly round here, or the moonbow, faint and

fluctuating on the level floor of cloud below the cañon rim.

—The Land of Journeys' Ending

"Because it was written about lasting things," Lawrence Clark Powell has praised *The Land of Journeys' Ending* as the literary work "that best embodies the essences of the region whose heartland is Arizona and New Mexico."[1] Published in 1924, a year before Austin returned to the West permanently to settle in Santa Fe, this book marked a temporary departure from the social and political concerns she had dealt with in *A Woman of Genius* and *No. 26 Jayne Street*, the theological and philosophical questions she had tried to answer in *Love and the Soul Maker*, the cultural analysis that undergirded *The American Rhythm*, and the reformist issues she had addressed in her journalism.

Instead, *The Land of Journeys' Ending*—which Austin intended as the companion volume to *The Land of Little Rain*—allowed the writer to unleash her visual imagination once again in a project of creative interpretation, this time of the southwestern topography: "Being a book of prophecy of the progressive acculturation of the land's people, this is also a book of topography. And the topography of the country between the Colorado and the Rio Grande cannot be expressed in terms invented for such purpose in a low green island by the North Sea. A *barranca* is terrifyingly more than an English bank on which the wild thyme grows; an *arroyo* resembles a gully only in being likewise a water gouge in the earth's surface, and we have no word for *canada*, half-way between an *arroyo* and a *canyon*, which—though, naturally, you have been accenting the syllable that best expresses the trail of the white man across the Southwest—is really pronounced can-*yon*" (*LOJE* xxviii).

The Land of Journeys' Ending was written after extensive research and travel in the Southwest culminating in an automobile trip of some twenty-five hundred miles that Austin took in the spring of 1923 with the artist Gerald Cassidy, his wife Ina Sizer Cassidy, and Daniel MacDougal. Despite ill health, Austin reveled in the outdoors and the congenial company. MacDougal led the group and explained the botanical features of the Southwest. Observing and hiking, sketching and taking notes during the day, at night the small party made camp and dined on the barbecued ribs that MacDougal prepared over the campfire. In the cool, dry darkness, Austin's companions listened to her "unwritten-down . . . always entertaining stories" before retiring "for the night in [their] bed-rolls on the soft hot sand . . . lulled to sleep by the song of nocturnal desert life." The stories Austin told around the campfire became her volume *One Smoke Stories*, so titled because she intended that each could be told "while one smoke lasts." Having put her distinctive interpretive "mark" upon the story, Austin occasionally warned Ina, one of her closest friends, not to encroach on the material that she planned to use in her forthcoming collection of short tales.[2]

Austin was in her element on this trip, complementing MacDougal's botanical explanations with information that she had researched before setting out, particularly on the folklore of the Papago and Pima Indians. Ina Cassidy recorded in her journal that "the role of mentor" suited Austin, adding, "Whether this role is prompted by a spirit of generosity, a desire to share her knowledge, a subconscious prompting of her old 'teacher' habit, or an exposition of egotism, one is never sure."[3] More probably, Austin's informal lectures served to rehearse ideas that she planned to formalize in *The Land of Journeys' Ending*.

The book that resulted from this pleasant trip was not simply the written recollections of a journey, however. It provided Austin with an opportunity to return to the literary form that had launched her career and to the descriptive prose that came naturally to her in *The Land of Little Rain* and *The Flock*. She took copious notes during the trip, later working them into the mellifluous phrases that distinguished her work from that of all other contemporary American writers. Her acute visual sense suggests the photographer's eye, though she fully intended that Gerald Cassidy illustrate *The Land of Journeys' Ending*, a plan that the Century Company found unworkable when it came to reproducing the artist's drawings.[4]

Like *The Land of Little Rain* and to some extent *Lost Borders*, *The Land of Journeys' Ending* recovers an authentic heritage of folklore and mystical beliefs from Indians, many of them elderly, that Austin encountered during this arduous trip through Arizona and New Mexico. In transcribing them, the writer purposed to revitalize them.

> From old Pecos come fireside legends, dating from later Spanish times, of a huge serpent appeased yearly by the sacrifice of a plump brown baby. Maria, our *cocinera*, says that once to the rancho of her grandfather, came a young Pecos woman concealing her *ninito* under her shawl, weeping and begging to be hidden until the festival of the Awanyu was past; and if confirmation were wanted, was there not a woodcutter, who, going early to Pecos after fresh snow was fallen, saw the track of a snake clear about the town, huge as if an ox had been dragged!
>
> Better evidence is the prevailing decorative pattern of the plumed serpent, frequently assimilated to the pattern of the lightning, associated with the life-giving water. At San Felipe I found it circling the baptismal font and the bowl of holy water. (*LOJE* 253)

Surely New Mexico was the perfect location for Austin to elaborate upon ideas of the "deep self" she had held for years. Observing festivals and rituals in the Indian pueblos, her own theories about myth and spiritual life were reified. As in *The Land of Little Rain*, Austin directly addresses the reader of the text as a participant/observer; in deploying this bold narrative act, she stirs the reader from his or her accustomed role as passive consumer of words: "For I have written thus far in vain if you do not begin to understand that New Mexico is still a place in which the miraculous may happen. All myth, all miracle, is in the beginning a notice of a Borning in the deep self; new ideas, new concepts of spiritual reality making their way to expression whatever stuff is current in the mind of the locality" (*LOJE* 337). While the terrain engages the writer's imagination, she invites the reader to journey with her "beyond the described scene to understanding and mystery."[5]

A Photographic Response

What assuredly can be termed a photographic technique charges Austin's written representations of the land. Many writers of her period and of the previous generation had felt photography's "jarring impact on society and culture during the years following its introduction to the world." Ralph Bogardus has argued persuasively that Henry James "possessed a photographer's eye and perception of reality." He attributes James's "photographic consciousness" to his growing up during the nascence of photography. In this "cultural atmosphere—with its peculiar perceptual/conceptual codes—[where] he evolved his perceiving/conceiving consciousness," James's visual imagination was nurtured. Austin's reliance on impressions and images, especially in her naturist works, demonstrates a similar awareness. Certainly her work follows in a tradition of American writers born in the nineteenth century whose interest in the photographic is manifested in their work: Edgar Allen Poe, Henry Thoreau, Ralph Waldo Emerson, William Dean Howells, and Stephen Crane.[6]

The language of visual representation abounds in *The Land of Journeys' Ending*. "Anywhere along the flood basins you are likely to see plump specimens of bisnaga uprooted from the rain-softened soil by their own weight, going on comfortably with their life processes while lying on one side," the writer/guide informs her reader, picturing the scene with the verisimilitude of a carefully composed photograph (*LOJE* 127). Words indicative of texture, size, shape, and color convey photographic immediacy; words relating to visual perception—*see, illusion*—emphasize the eye. "Over some of these *playas* the mesquite is so evenly spaced, and the low-branched shapes are so uniform that the illusion of traveling through peach orchards has continually to be brushed aside," Austin observes (*LOJE* 146).

Like the works of experimental photographers of her period—Alfred Stieglitz, Paul Strand, and later Ansel Adams—Austin's writing transcends mere pictorial description, yielding what Stieglitz termed "equivalents of my basic philosophy of life."[7] Stieglitz believed that "all art is but a picture of certain basic relationships; an artist's most profound experience of life"—an aesthetic shared by Austin. Her visual imagination puts before the reader a synesthetic representation of experience, each image informed by attention to technical matters of focus, composition, point of view, and depth of field. What begins as a photo-realistically imagined scene—an image of snowfall in the mountains, one of many in the text—develops into a metaphysical reflection and, more personally, a remembrance of things past:

> It is only at very high altitudes that it is possible to see snowflakes shaping level with your eyes, coming out of the thick grayness as a star comes out of twilight. There is a falling flash that gathers whiteness as it falls, and suddenly on the black cloth of your coat you catch a cluster of stemless, feathery blooms that under your breath dissolve and regather. . . . Snowflakes forming under such conditions are unusually large, probably because they cannot form at all except in the absence of all motion but their own. Those that come sliding down the long slopes of mountain being almost always clogged together, shattered in particles, or whipped by the wind into round, icy grains. Sometimes on the surface of heavy falls after warm days divided by cold nights, will be found a still more varied bloom of snow flowers in the form of hoar-frost, mingled with ice spicules which the Tewas call "seed-of-the-snow." It is, I think, of some such shape of matter it made the thin shell that far beyond the reach of man's highest flight of air, shuts in our world against the invasive universe. Well! What if science has not yet found it? Very clear spring and winter mornings, after long falls of snow or heavy rain, from heaven-reaching cumbres [crests] I have seen it, straining the blue out of the sun shafts, breaking and scattering them as heat and light. Now, I remember that when we were very young, the German housemaid used to bring us clear sugar eggs for Easter, with a peep-hole at one end, to an inclosed [*sic*] colored picture; so the earth ball within its shell might look, should there be seraph or any other creature to peep in. (*LOJE* 390–91)

Just as the photographer can "focus selectively to emphasize visual qualities and relationships within a composition,"[8] so Austin focuses with photographic precision and deliberation upon the natural phenomena she observes in the "cactus country," a series of compositions in *The Land of Journeys' Ending*. When her imaginative lens rests on the giant sahuaro rising "to a height of twenty-five or thirty feet, erect, columnar, dull green, and deeply fluted, the outer ridges of the fluting set with rows of lateral spines that inclose [*sic*] it as in a delicate grayish web" (*LOJE* 120), the resulting image possesses at once the clarity of a photograph and the ineffable quality that Stieglitz called "equivalency." Austin's work illustrates Stieglitz's theory of latent pictorial content that reaches beyond stark images captured by the camera or the words on the page.[9]

Her technical employment of the close-up in the sahuaro image reveals mysteries of light and texture beyond superficial description. "Between the ridges the sahuaro has a texture like well-surfaced leather, giving back the light like spears, that, seen from a rapidly moving car, make a continuous vertical flicker in the landscape" (*LOJE* 120). Austin's description owes much to the new aesthetic of photography in the early 1900s formulated by those photographers of the photo-secessionist movement, Stieglitz preeminent among them, who regarded photography as an art form akin to impressionism. The sahuaros in Austin's visual imagination appear impressionistically to be "marching together against the rose-and-vermillion evening . . . like the pillars of ruined temples" (*LOJE* 120). Although Austin still lived in Inyo in 1902, when Stieglitz orchestrated the pathbreaking exhibit entitled "American Pictorial Photography, Arranged by 'The Photo-Secession'" at the National Arts Club in New York, the writer could not have been ignorant of what this radical movement in photography was about. When she came to live in New York, she herself became a member of the club and was in touch, if not directly with Stieglitz, with those who frequented his gallery "291."[10]

Like many photographers, Austin trains her eye on the horizon in *The Land of Journeys' Ending*. Her image of a stormcloud is not unlike an Ansel Adams photograph: "Always from a fixed point on the horizon the gulf signals with great thunder-heads of cloud, glittering white, gray with withholden rain or taking fire with the sunset, blown inland" (*LOJE* 156). It may be going too far to suggest that Austin should be grouped with other "modernist literary and visual experimenters like Proust, Joyce, Eliot, Picasso, Griffith, and Eisenstein," as Bogardus argues for Henry James. Austin simply did not have an affiliation with avant-garde artists.[11] Clearly, however, her dexterity in composing verbal pictures and her attention to light suggest an appreciation of photographic possibilities and place her in the company of those photographers who saw the aesthetic potential of this relatively new technology for moving beyond mere image making.

Critic Vera Norwood has linked Austin with the photographer Laura Gilpin, suggesting that they independently created "their own female drama of life in the landscape." The two women shared the belief that any understanding of the people who inhabited the land began by understanding the wilderness itself. Gilpin, born in Colorado Springs in 1891, was more than a generation younger than Austin; although she often took photographs in New Mexico, she and Austin may never have met. Gilpin avoided the East and thus apparently escaped the anxiety of choosing between East and West that plagued Austin and other writers of her period. Norwood intimates that Austin's literary naturism was more typical than Gilpin's because of the inherent "difficulties women of the 18th and 19th centuries found in responding to the landscape . . . compounded by the cultural stereotypes which effectively excluded them from the world of visual landscape representation." [12] Even more critical, Norwood argues, was the problem women faced in carrying cumbersome photographic equipment into the wilderness.

Although W. H. Jackson and Edward Curtis had photographed the West, no woman before Gilpin had ventured into this terrain as a professional landscape photographer. Gilpin's interest in the land as an environment "distinguished her from such nineteenth-century photographer-explorers as William Henry Jackson or Timothy O'Sullivan, and from her contemporary, Ansel Adams, who photographed the West as a place of inviolate, pristine beauty," Martha Sandweiss maintains. Like Austin, Gilpin saw the West as "a peopled landscape" profoundly affected by the daily lives of its inhabitants. [13] Gilpin and Austin, both emancipated women, transformed the American vision of the West as previously seen through male eyes. Austin envisioned the strength of the feminine in her lyrical descriptions of the land, while Gilpin pursued the grueling art of photography, undaunted by the rigors of the environment, in the "tradition of Austin's 'Walking Woman,' drawn irresistably back to nature and yet not quite able to express succinctly the potential for successful life by a white woman in that landscape." [14]

Neither Gilpin nor Austin perceived women as passive participants in the interplay of land and human spirit. Gilpin's strong photographic portraits of indigenous American women surmounting the hardships of a harsh though beautiful landscape in *The Enduring Navajo* are the visual equivalents of Austin's prose portraits in *Lost Borders*. [15] Gilpin, too, embraced a pictorial style relying on black-and-white film (as did Adams) to move beyond a literal representation of her subjects. The freedom from gender constrictions that Austin and Gilpin discovered in their observations of the land and its native people, as Vera Norwood's study perceptively proposes, fed and strengthened both artists' work as they sought forms of representation adequate to the vastness and diversity of the American West. For Austin, *The Land of Journeys'*

Ending marked the beginning of a final spurt of creativity. In the Southwest she would recover something of the creative sustenance she had drawn from the California desert twenty years before.

Ansel Adams and Mary Austin

It is tempting to speculate whether Austin would have used photographs to illustrate *The Land of Journeys' Ending* had she known a collaborator of Ansel Adams's talent. The difference in these two artists' ages, of course, prevented their collaboration before the late 1920s. Austin was nearly sixty when the twenty-five-year-old photographer visited her in Santa Fe in 1927 with Albert Bender, a wealthy San Francisco insurance executive and patron of the arts. Driving "twelve hundred long miles, mostly on washboard roads," through the Southwest, Adams recalled that he "fell quickly under the spell of the astonishing New Mexican light. The magical transference from dusty wind and heat to sparkling vistas and translucent air was unexpected and felicitous. Summer thunderstorms create the dominant symbolic power of the land: huge ranges of flashing and grumbling clouds with gray curtains of rain clearing both the air and the spirit while nourishing the earth." [16] Adams, who was moving away from a career as a concert pianist and turning his prodigious energies toward photography, was impressed and somewhat intimidated by Austin. [17]

Although Bender had corresponded with the writer, they had never met before. His genial personality and committed philanthropy were well known in San Francisco; he took great personal pleasure in advancing the careers of western artists and writers. Bender backed Adams by arranging for his first portfolio to be published and sold. A steadfast friend of George Sterling, he was naturally drawn to Austin, and her appreciation of Bender no doubt eased the way for her collaboration with Adams. Their Taos Pueblo project seems to have had its genesis in Adams's enthusiasm for the photographic possibilities of New Mexico, combined with Bender's commitment to assuring that his young protégé have the opportunity to do a major project in the Southwest. In Adams's autobiography, written shortly before his death in 1984, he summarizes the influence of the Southwest on his work: "Those who have not visited the Southwest will not discover its true qualities in texts or illustrations. Very few artists have caught its spirit; the siren-calls of the theatrical are not favorable to aesthetic integrity." Like Gilpin, he preferred the "inherent abstraction" of photographing

*Albert Bender, friend and patron of Mary Austin and Ansel Adams,
photographed by Adams.*

in black and white, explaining that it "takes the viewer out of the morass of manifest appearance and encourages inspection of the shapes, textures, and qualities of light characteristic of the region."[18]

Two years intervened before Adams was able to return to the Southwest to photograph intensively. Before he arrived in Santa Fe in March 1929, this time with his bride, Virginia Best Adams, Bender sent a humorous letter to Austin forewarning her of the healthy appetites of her visitors. "I am writing you a confidential letter today about Ansel and Virginia Adams. These young people have practically every virtue in the catalogue of righteousness, and there is only one thing about which you should not be unaware, and that is their appetite. Please do not let them go hungry. They need food every hour in large quantities, and if you have no mortgage on your house now, you will have at the time of their departure. If the circulatory system permits, I think a special pipe should connect with Ansel's room, through which a cup of coffee could be furnished day or night."[19] Adams, struck anew by the rapid changes of light in the Southwest, wrote to his father that "the sunrise over the Sangre de Christo mountains was most extraordinary."[20]

Austin liked the young couple and entrusted Casa Querida to their care while she was away on a lecture trip. They stayed in the apartment that Mary Hunter had added to her aunt's home for the periods when she resided in Santa Fe.[21] The Adamses enjoyed the artistic atmosphere of Santa Fe and Taos. "In those euphoric bibulous days, the entire Santa Fe intelligentsia, a mélange of strange lifestyles, would attend [Witter] Bynner's bashes," Adams remembered in his autobiography. One evening at a typical Bynner gathering, "the potent bootleg liquor worked its charms early," Adams recounted. "I grandly played the piano, including my spoofs of a Chopin etude with benefit of an orange in my right hand and Strauss's Blue Danube performed both with my fingers and, for the emphatic chords, with my derriere."[22] Austin looked on with wry good humor. As the Adamses came to know her, the writer gradually seemed less daunting to them; it was her kindness and generosity that they remembered.

On the Lecture Circuit

Austin was not always appreciative of Adams's work. He had taken some photographs of her in Santa Fe during his first visit, and in January 1929 he sent the proofs together with an earnest note expressing his hope that she would "be utterly pleased with the prints."[23] No doubt he was disappointed to receive a sour reply saying that the photographs had arrived in New Haven but were unsatisfactory, in fact "impossible" to use for her purposes. "I dare say you can take away that dreadful smirk, and the drawn look about the mouth," she wrote, "but the carriage of the head, with the face thrust down and forward, and the slumped shoulders are not only not characteristic of me, but contradict the effect it is still necessary for me to make on my public."[24]

By her "public," Austin meant the audiences that she addressed on her wearying lecture tours during the 1920s and 1930s. She counted on the money she earned from speaking to finance her Santa Fe retreat. Knowing the lecture circuit as she did, she considered herself more than qualified to instruct the young photographer on the function of a publicity photograph. Her didactic letter to Adams illuminates the extraordinary pressures she placed on herself: "A photo for publicity must be something other than a likeness; it must convey something of the personal drive, the energetic index, the impact of the whole personality as it affects the public. What I know about that is always of an upright and forthgoing quality. Not what people who know me intimately are likely to see."[25]

During the winter of 1929, Austin traveled extensively in the East, giving lectures arranged by speakers' bureaus. The typical compensation ranged between $100 and $150. Her cross note to Adams was prompted more probably by exhaustion and illness than by vanity. On January 5 she had read her poetry at the Church of the Epiphany in Boston. From there she proceeded to Evanston, Illinois, where she addressed the University Guild about the American novel on January 8. Then it was back to Mount Holyoke, Wellesley, and the Twentieth Century Club for separate lectures on January 19. On January 21 she spoke to the Boston Ministers Meeting on the American Indian. Her longest period of time that winter was spent in New Haven, followed by lectures in Illinois during March on the way to research her autobiography in Carlinville. A brief respite came in April when she returned home to Santa Fe to work out arrangements with Adams for the Taos book and to prepare for a series of lectures called "The Pattern of American Literature" at the University of California in Los Angeles, scheduled for May. In addition, the contracts for her autobiography and the novel *Starry Adventure* weighed heavily on her mind.[26]

Adams, struggling himself during the first major phase of his career, was not insensitive to her financial situation. Before arriving in Santa Fe, he reluctantly asked for a partial remittance on his fee of five hundred dollars for the book they were to do (*Taos Pueblo*) to "cover all ex-

Ansel Adams's portrait of Austin in 1929. She thought it unflattering.

penses and permit me to proceed with the work in the most thorough manner." But, he added, "if this would cause complications, I will be able to make other plans for meeting the first expense." Bender, he reported, had "voiced his desire to lend his aid to the project, and he might be able to advance a small sum towards the first expense." Adams regarded Austin's text "as the dominant feature of the book" and urged her to name "a just recompense" for her work before they began.[27]

Although public speaking kept her busy, Austin's earnings were never enough to make her comfortable about money. The agencies, which took a 25 percent commission, often pressed her to give additional lectures for less than her minimum fee if they could cluster bookings in a given area. When Austin was invited to speak by the great universities, she found the platform more satisfying and was willing to accept a smaller fee. In 1928 she accepted an engagement at Stanford for a fifty-dollar honorarium. Earlier that year Berkeley had paid her $150, expressing regrets "that the auditorium was not filled, as it should have been."[28] Travel and preparation for these engagements represented a significant expenditure of time; events before and after her lectures—luncheons, receptions, and other social gatherings—further drained her strength for creative work. "It is a terrible hardship to me to have the company of commonplace minds crowded upon me when I am trying to write," Austin once confided to Daniel MacDougal.[29] She believed in the aristocracy of the intellect, something that she failed to find in the audiences of American women's clubs. As early as 1922 she disparaged the groups she encountered on the lecture circuit, declaring that the questions women asked after her lectures were not "indicative of the desire, or the sense of obligation . . . to enter into the creative struggle." She deplored the "circumstance that few women's clubs can be induced to pay to women artists the terms and attention that are conceded to men."[30]

It is fair to say that Austin despised the timidity she observed in women, even as she recognized the societal and cultural causes for their reticence. "Some day it will come to her, together with the horrid thought that she has been excluded this long time from cultural effectiveness, not by man's wish to exclude her, but because she has never learned the game," she wrote in an article on female passivity.[31] In the introductions that preceded her lectures—most of which she wrote herself, just as she wrote the blurbs for her book jackets—Austin underscored her identity as a western writer, an independent thinker aligned to no literary movement. One such introduction called attention to her best-known works:

Mary Austin has always been recognized as an acute and deeply intuitive thinker. That she has not yet received her proper estimate as a literary artist is due as much as anything to the extraordinary range and variety of her product. She has never been interested in building up a literary career, but in expressing in whatever form seems appropriate at the moment, her vivid interest in the American scene, in novels, essays, poems, plays, and a particular type of descriptive writing in *The Land of Little Rain* and *The Land of Journeys' Ending*, which she has made characteristically her own. At present Mrs. Austin divides her time between New York and Santa Fe, New Mexico where she is building up a permanent residence and a center for the wide range of personal activities all more or less influenced by her conviction that here, between the Rio Grande and the Colorado is to rise the next great and powerful culture.[32]

Taos Pueblo

Ansel Adams was elated when he and Austin arrived at an "enthusiastic decision to collaborate on a book of words and pictures."[33] To Austin he referred to it as *"your book."*[34] The subject they at last agreed upon was the ancient Taos Pueblo, where "still from the house tops the creation epic is chanted by the appointed head of the religious societies, in majestic rolling rhythms; still at the ceremonial times—not without sharp skirmishes with the Indian Bureau—the boys go into the kivas to be taught their tribal traditions, instructed in the ancient faith, and urged to make their hunger fast for the personal revelation, as it was in the Days of the New, the Days of the Unforgotten" (*TP* [13]).

Adams immediately wrote to Bender about the book that would launch his reputation as one of the West's most important photographers. To gain permission to photograph the ancient pueblo, virtually unchanged "in its two and a half centuries of White contact," necessitated delicate negotiation.[35] The Indians regarded many of the areas within Taos Pueblo as sacred, precluding photographers from working there. Further, a degree of tension existed between the pueblo and Mabel Dodge Luhan—and by extension her friends—because of her marriage to Tony Lujan. The tension eased somewhat when Austin arranged for Mabel to pay alimony to Tony's Indian wife.[36] Since the Taos Pueblo Indians did not recognize the white legal system, they never officially sanctioned a divorce between Tony and his Indian wife; nor did they acknowledge his marriage to Mabel.

Nonetheless, Tony retained enough influence to persuade the governor of Taos to assure Adams access to the pueblo. Following a council meeting, Adams was given unprecedented privileges to wander through the community and photograph at will. Fascinated by what he saw there and excited by the possibilities for creating distinctive photographs, he conveyed his enthusiasm in a letter to Bender in San Francisco: "It is a stunning thing—the great pile of adobe, five stories high with the Taos Peaks rising in a tremendous way behind. And the Indians are really majestic, wearing, as they do, their blankets like Arabs. I think it will be the most effective subject to work with—and I have every hope of creating something really fine. With Mary Austin writing the text . . . I have a grand task to come up to it with the pictures. But I am sure I can do it. Dear Albert—look what you started when you brought me to Santa Fe!"[37] After *Taos Pueblo* was published late in 1930, Adams wrote to thank Bender for his support. "It is you that succored a poor artistic fish from the dry land of moronic isolation, it is you that cleared the way for the individualistic expression of a highly technical art."[38]

Austin had introduced Ansel and Virginia to Luhan, and they stayed at her rancho, Los Gallos, while he was photographing Taos Pueblo. One of the most striking portraits in the book is of Tony Lujan, an androgynous figure with his head shrouded in a Navajo blanket, the stoic face only partially visible against the dark background. (Ironically, that photograph was taken in Adams's San Francisco studio.) When the book was finished, a copy was presented to the pueblo and housed in a sacred *kiva,* the structure where Indian rituals are performed.[39]

Although Adams's photographs formed the nucleus of the book, Austin treated him somewhat condescendingly. She insistently referred to him as "the illustrator" for *Taos Pueblo* and for a book about the Spanish colonial arts that he was planning to produce with her Santa Fe neighbor, Frank Applegate. "In the first place, you must realize that the illustrator is always a secondary consideration with the publisher," she wrote to Adams in the late summer of 1929. "The contract is made with the author, and then it is up to the author to use such influence as he may have to persuade the publisher to agree to a certain type and treatment of illustration."[40] Although it would take Adams months to photograph and to develop, print, and select the images for inclusion in *Taos Pueblo*, Austin asserted that her text was of paramount importance and that her schedule should take precedence over his. "I note that you do not intend putting the book together until next spring," she wrote in August 1929, "but as I go east in January not to return until April, I must do the writing soon or not at all. Besides your publisher will want to have the MS in hand in laying out the book."

Austin expected to spend only "about a week" writing the text; she had put off going to Taos that summer because Luhan was ill.[41] In September she explained that she needed "the inspirational mood" of Taos to write the text, but was still waiting for Luhan to recover.[42] When Adams informed her that the Grabhorn Press of San Francisco planned to publish "two hundred and fifty copies of [the] book at fifty dollars a copy . . . and a hundred copies at seventy-five dollars a copy," she was aghast and advised him to proceed with a cheap edition. "Do I understand that the Grabhorn Press wants to issue the cheap edition, or do you expect me to find you another publisher?" she asked. "My own regular publishers are pretty well loaded up with things I am doing now, a novel [*Starry Adventure*] in the fall and an autobiography as soon as I can get it ready."[43]

In fact, Austin wrote the text without seeing Adams's photographs. The elegantly produced book, with its henna linen binding, its exquisite typography, and the splendid prints shown to best advantage on heavy paper designed by W. E. Dassonville, prompted her to compliment the young photographer. "I agree with you that it is a superb piece of workmanship," Austin wrote in January 1931. "I think, however, that we can do a little better next time. . . . I should see your photographs before writing the text, so that between us, nothing should be left out. I would like the book to have an equal value for its content and its quality as a piece of book making."[44] She clung to the hope that the book could receive wider attention in an inexpensive edition, though Adams diplomatically countered that *Taos Pueblo* deserved careful design and fine quality. "In calling it an Art book, I do not mean that only in referance [*sic*] to the pictures; your text is as beautiful as anything heretofore done on an Indian subject, and should merit a fine typographic treatment," he wrote. In the end, a cheap edition was never issued; the expensive facsimile reprint did not appear until 1977.[45]

The twelve Adams photographs understandably received more attention that the text when the book was first published. "These photographic studies are really a joy for the beholder," declared *California Arts and Architecture*. "Ansel Easton Adams has had great success in showing the striking effects of the alternate blocks of light and shade shooting the buildings." Referring to Austin's text, the reviewer wrote, "Never has this accomplished lady done a finer piece of interpretation."[46]

Indeed, the marriage between Ansel Adams's photographs and Austin's prose was in every way felicitous. He captured the essence of Taos Pueblo in his images of the architecture—the ancient South House, the kiva, and the church ruins—and of the Indians going about their daily chores. The photograph entitled "South House, Woman Winnowing Grain" (Plate X) is an excellent example. Adams and Austin represented the Taos culture as "tap rooted." The text and the photographs eloquently celebrate the pueblo's enduring quality "even against the modern American obsession for destructive change" (*TP* [13]). Although Austin has been criticized for romanticizing the daily existence of the materially impoverished Indians, probably no better description of Taos Valley exists than Austin's, photographic in its intensity, poetic in its language.

> Pueblo Mountain stands up over Taos pueblo and Taos water comes down between the two house-heaps, North house and South house, with a braided motion, swift and clear flowing. As you look at the south entrance to the valley, Pueblo Mountain, bare topped above, and below shaggy with pines, has the crouched look of a sleeping animal, the great bull buffalo, turning his head away and hunching his shoulders. Beyond him the lower hills lie in the curved ranks of the ruminating herd. It is not so much the animal contours that give the suggestion as the curious quiescent aliveness of the whole Taos landscape, as if it might at any moment wake and leap. You look and look away, and though nothing has altered you are quite certain that in the interval the hills have stirred, the lomas [hills] have exchanged confidences. Far out, to the north, where Taos Valley ceases to be valley without having lifted again to hill proportions, there is a feeling of the all but invisible tremor of a sleeping sea. (*TP* [1])

In capturing the faces of the villagers, Austin and Adams seem to have looked through a single lens, freezing the same timeless moment. They were as successful as Anglos could be who attempted to interpret for the outside world the "impenetrable timelessness of peace" that pervaded Taos Pueblo, "as though the pueblo and all it contains were shut in a glassy fourth dimension near and at the same time inaccessibly remote" (*TP* [6]).

Or should you happen upon the pueblo in one hour of evening bustle, when the men are coming in from the field, young people lingering on the bridge between the house-heaps, the *pregonero* draped and authoritative as any Roman senator, announcing the day's news and advices of the day to come, from North house or South house—Hlauuma, Hlaukwima,—you become aware of something subtly excluding in the unfamiliar speech rhythms, the alien tonality, and the want of a revealing response in the listening citizens. You see them fixed by the voice of the proclamation in whatever position it finds them, fixed as prairie dogs at the sound of a snapped stick, on the housetops, in the *portales,* the women going to and from the creek, dripping water jars poised on their heads, the old men appearing automatically at the doorways, like those little figures out of wonder clocks, retreating as automatically. And in not one attitude anywhere a clue, a suggestion as to what it is all about. (*TP* [6])

Taos Pueblo allowed Austin to expand her ideas about women quite naturally in the form of an ethnographic description of the matriarchal structure of the Taos Pueblo Indians, a social order that she judged "perhaps the most stabilizing fact of [the] Pueblo Constitution. Every house is a Mother Hive, to which the daughters bring home husbands, on terms of good behavior; or dismiss them with the simple ceremony of setting the man's private possessions—his gun, his saddle, his other pair of moccasins—outside the door. To the wife—the soft voiced matron who trips about on small, white shod feet in fashions of three hundred years ago,—belongs the house, the furniture, the garnered grain, the marriage rights of her children. Peace and stability, these are the first fruits of Mother-rule" (*TP* [13]).

Not surprisingly, Austin was not nearly as interested in the art of beautiful bookmaking as in circulating her work. When Adams reported that the expensive edition had sold well in 1931, she expressed incredulity that he had "done so well to dispose of the book so successfully in times of depression such as the present."[47] The Adamses did not forget Austin's kindness. They kept in touch and occasionally sent little remembrances that she appreciated. "The cactus which you sent is doing well, so are the bulbs; and I was naturally delighted with the little Chinese bowls, out of which I take my raspberries every evening," she wrote in August 1931. In the same letter, Austin projected further collaboration with Adams, but her extensive writing commitments prevented her from realizing such plans before her death in 1934.[48] However, Adams expressed his appreciation of *The Land of Little Rain*, which he admired for its photographic depictions of the land and inhabitants of California's Owens Valley, in the form of a special edition of the book. Published in 1950, it contained his black-and-white photographs, accompanied by brief excerpts from her 1903 text.[49] Recalling Austin many years later, Adams said simply, "Seldom have I met and known anyone of such intellectual and spiritual power and discipline."[50]

Tender Ties

When Virginia and Ansel Adams returned to San Francisco in 1929, they told Bender about Austin's ill health and dire financial situation, which prevented her from having an operation that she had spoken of as necessary. Subsequently she wrote rather stiffly to Bender: "I am sorry that Ansel should have made you acquainted with my private troubles which he discovered only by the accident of being in the house, and by the fact of his being, like all the younger generation, less observant of the privacies and reservations of an earlier usage." She returned a check Bender had sent her, explaining that she could not afford to take time for surgery. "Even if the operation became an emergency, the contracts [for *Earth Horizon* and *Starry Adventure*] would remain and before I could earn any further income, they would have to be fulfilled."[51]

Central to understanding Austin's value system is her consistent refusal of financial assistance. She declared that she "was brought up . . . and lived in the prepossession of my generation that one should never accept monetary aid."[52] News of her deteriorating health and financial predicament inevitably prompted offers of assistance from Bender, Daniel MacDougal, and other friends. Although grateful for their concern, Austin rebuffed them for one overriding reason: a deep-seated anxiety about her strength and self-sufficiency. Apparently because Mabel Dodge Luhan was a woman, and because they were bound together in their reform work for the Indians, Austin was able to put aside her scruples and accept some money from her Taos friend, especially when she could justify it "for the Cause."

Austin's various illnesses remain something of a mystery. She insisted that she cured her breast cancer by the power of prayer and positive thinking; she also suffered from gallbladder and heart problems. Dependent as she was on her ability to speak and write, her fears about the consequences of illness were justified. No amount of assurance could persuade her that she was not critically ill. At the same time she insisted that her niece undergo psychiatric testing at the Menninger Clinic. Mary Hunter's problem was diagnosed as severe strain caused by living with her demanding aunt, whose invalidism required her to remain in Santa Fe. According to Austin's doctor, exhaustion and tension posed a real threat to her health. During the Santa Fe years, she suffered from high blood pressure, although not so urgently as to require surgical intervention.[53]

Austin's correspondence during the late 1920s and early 1930s is laced with medical terminology relating to her heart condition. From New York she wrote hopefully to Bender about infrared therapy: "This is a great relief, for though it will probably be as expensive as surgery —I have to buy an infra-red machine—it will take nothing else out of me and I can probably go on working just the same." Austin had gone to New York with her Santa Fe physician to investigate the latest treatment for her condition, which she considered no less than a "miracle." To Bender she wrote: "But think of the simplicity of it, a tiny invisible ray searches out my vitals, destroying what is evil and stimulating what is good!"[54]

Only after she arrived in San Francisco in the winter of 1928 did Austin learn that Bender had been working behind the scenes to arrange lecture dates and otherwise make her stay in California pleasant and productive. Thanking him after she returned home, she invited him to Santa Fe and expressed hope "that you won't feel that you did too much for me." Although his support was unsolicited, she needed to assure him "that whatever I receive I always make a point to pass it on"—another manifestation of her feeling that others might think ill of her if she appeared vulnerable or dependent.[55] Ever since the nervous breakdowns she had experienced as a student and a young married woman, Austin had struggled to create an illusion of independence and strength in the face of personal tragedies that left her psychologically fragile.

In attempting to reconstruct the etiology and progression of her various ailments, the possibility must be considered that from childhood into maturity Austin suffered from what has been called "survivor's guilt." The shattering deaths of her father and sister in her adolescence, the deaths of her older brother in 1917 and of her retarded daughter in 1918, and her distorted relationships with the living —mother, brothers, husband, daughter, and niece—suggest the stress inherent in the writer's life. Her own embittered communications with

Mary Austin, ca. 1930. Even during illness she continued to work.

her family contributed greatly to her mental anguish, a fact that does not diminish the extraordinary pain that scarred her personality.

By nature and upbringing Austin was an honorable, generous, and proud woman. Despite illness and financial distress, she took pleasure in doing favors for those she was fond of, provided the expenditure of her limited time and energies was not exorbitant. She much preferred to dispense help to others rather than to receive it. Possibly this is why she somewhat misleadingly spoke to friends about her financial obligations for her niece at college, when the truth was that a trust had been set up by Mary Hunter's father, James Hunter, at the time of his death in 1917.[56] Yet even as Austin's friends rallied to pledge financial assistance in her moment of need, she responded generously to her relatives in Illinois. For Christmas of 1929, for example, she sent her mother's half-sister money to replace a worn and irritating artificial eye.[57]

Frank and Alta Applegate, her Santa Fe neighbors, occupied a special place in Austin's heart. The Applegates hailed originally from Illinois, and the writer felt a midwestern kinship to them. She relied on them to take care of her house and garden when she was away and enjoyed their intimate friendship when she was at home. Frank, perhaps her dearest male friend in Santa Fe, was an unassuming artist who had amassed with his wife an outstanding collection of Spanish handicrafts. He was an ardent preservationist of the colonial arts—"the carved chests, the hammered tin, the weaving, and the decorative embroidery [which] were losing their market to the factory-produced objects which everywhere standardized American households."[58] Austin respected his knowledge of the folk art of New Mexico, which surpassed her own. His large collection of religious artifacts included the carved *Cristos* and *santos* (wooden figures depicting Christ and the saints), the stone *reredos* (altar screens), and other examples of ecclesiastical art that modern tastes considered crude and, hence, discardable. Together they worked closely as founders of the Spanish Colonial Arts Society to preserve and revive the lost arts of the colonial era in Santa Fe. With Austin's encouragement and promise to locate a publisher, Applegate had begun writing a book on the subject, illustrated by his own drawings and Adams's photographs.

The intensity of the friendship between Austin and Applegate caused some unwarranted speculation in Santa Fe, especially among those unacquainted with the writer's longstanding habit of developing close friendships with men who were experts in fields that interested her. From her earliest days in California, she educated herself by establishing intellectual or artistic links with General Edward Beale, Charles Lummis, George Sterling, Lincoln Steffens, Henry Canby, Van Wyck Brooks, Herbert Hoover, H. G. Wells, Daniel MacDougal, Ansel Adams, Albert Bender, and, finally, Frank Applegate. These were mutually unthreatening relationships, for the most part, because the men were either married or uninterested in a romantic liaison with Austin for various reasons. Her strong appeal to the minds of gifted men was undeniable, as was her need to cultivate these friendships despite the social prohibitions that sometimes gave rise to unpleasant and untrue stories about her.[59]

Although Austin was accepted most of the time with tolerance, and even love, by the spouses of the men with whom she had special friendships, she overstepped the limits on occasion. When Austin proposed that Frank Applegate's ashes be preserved until her own death, then mixed and scattered with hers, his wife summarily dismissed the suggestion as inappropriate.[60] Frank's sudden death of heart failure in 1931 prompted Austin to write to Adams that she was "overwhelmed with grief," adding: "Frank's death will make great changes in my plans."[61] Such midwestern connections remained a tender tie for the writer, a tie that was renewed and made stronger by research on her autobiography, *Earth Horizon*.

▲ ▲ ▲

EARTH HORIZON

I see now that it has been a mistake to try to write the story of my life as a woman distinct from my life as an artist. Yet I was moved to make the attempt because of the conviction arrived at through years of intimacy with most of the women who have made my generation notable, that the life of a gifted woman is, in respect to the things that are supposed to count most with women, always a squalid affair.

—*Manuscript fragment,* A Woman of Genius

Why the autobiography, Austin's final major work, should have caused her such considerable anxiety eludes easy explanation. The prospect of dealing with the examined life—her own—precipitated a self-consciousness that she had been able to avoid in other works, despite their extensive autobiographical content. "All this Mary business is a nuisance; having to stop and tell why she did things and what she thought about them," she complains half-way through *Earth Horizon* (p. 204).

The research for the book deluged the writer with the facts of her past from the many places where she had lived and worked. Her efforts to document her life suggest an attention to facticity that sets her apart from Edith Wharton, Willa Cather, Sherwood Anderson, Ellen Glasgow, and other literary autobiographers of her period. Beginning in 1929, Austin recorded her search for sources in detailed notes. From George Jordan of Carlinville she requested a photograph of "Mary Patchen as she was in about 1860," referring to her father's first sweetheart. From the Reverend D. J. McMillan of New York she asked for

Austin's autobiography, Earth Horizon, *was published in 1932, the year Will Connell took this photograph.*

background "about a colored boy picked by the 7th Illinois during the war." From Margaret Snell Casner, she solicited a doctoral thesis on "original research into medicinal and domestic use of plants by pioneer settlers of Illinois," and to a parish clerk in Yorkshire, England, she wrote seeking information about her father, who was born at Gilling in 1833. She cast nets among her writer friends. Austin requested from Edna Ferber the "names of Mississippi steam boats plying up and down the river in 1851," the year her father had emigrated to Illinois. She called upon Adolf Berle in New York to supply "unpublished photographs of women with whom I was associated in the feminist fight: Henrietta Rodman, Elizabeth Gurley Flynn, Rose Snyderman, and Emma Goldman."[1]

Even Stafford Wallace Austin, from whom the writer had been divorced some fifteen years earlier, did not escape her queries. She pressed him for a "short sketch of his family," for the exact name of the ranch where they had first met in 1890, and for "photographs of the country around Bakersfield and Inyo."[2] Wary of what she planned to do with the material, Wallace urged her to leave the task "to the regular biographers who will write you up anyhow after you are dead." Nonetheless, he supplied what she wanted.[3] Austin did not confine questions about such personal matters to her own family. She probed Eve (Lummis) DeKalb for details of where and when she had met her former husband, Charles Lummis, and requested a childhood photograph of Eve's son, Amado, with her own daughter, Ruth. She also asked if Eve could find the dates of Charlotte Perkins Gilman's divorce from Walter Stetson and of Stetson's remarriage to Grace Ellery Channing.[4] Some of her correspondents complied with her requests more readily than others. Eve, pained by Austin's query, asked her to refrain from using the details of her divorce from Lummis in *Earth Horizon*.

Attention to the minutiae of daily life—the births of children, the particulars of household routines, conversations overheard, details of illnesses and deaths—have caused more than one critic to differentiate the autobiographies of women writers from those of men. Suzanne Juhasz lists "significance, objectivity, distance" as "the major critical criteria for autobiography that dominate the writing of modern critics of the genre." These attributes are frequently absent from women's autobiographies. Because the shape of their lives is often unlike that of men, women's autobiographies possess a quite different form and content from men's. "In their form, women's lives tend to be like the stories they tell: they show less a pattern of linear development towards some clear goal than one of repetitive, cumulative, cyclical structure.

. . . Even if a woman is a professional and conducts her work life largely according to male patterns . . . it is generally not easy or usual for her to separate out neatly the powerful domestic and personal relationship-oriented strands in her life," writes Juhasz.[5]

Hence, not surprisingly, houses and their decoration surface as important considerations in both Austin's and Edith Wharton's autobiographies. Social gatherings occupy a significant place in Wharton's and Gertrude Atherton's accounts of their lives. In *A Backward Glance*, Wharton tells us it was her habit to write in bed in the mornings; Austin chronicles the daily rhythm in Lone Pine, describing "a Chinese plaza there, a resort of the Chinese cooks and house boys of the surrounding mines, where, as the Chinese year came round each season, there would be Geisha girls dancing and juggling" (*EH* 286). (It is curious that Austin would include the Japanese geisha in her description of the Chinese quarter.) "Dailiness matters to most women," Juhasz notes, "and dailiness is by definition never a conclusion, always a process."[6]

Austin's approach to autobiography suggests a pattern of discovery that reaches beyond "the sum total of incidents and observations," a definition proposed by one critic.[7] That Austin's representation of her life refused to cohere according to the pattern she had limned—the mandala inherent in her use of the term *earth horizon*—exemplifies the formal problems facing the woman autobiographer, for whom dailiness is as significant as distance and objectivity. "When first it was proposed to me that I write my autobiography, I anticipated great pleasure in the undertaking," Austin writes in her preface, "for I thought it meant the re-living of my important occasions, the setting of them in their significant order, and so bringing the events of my life into a pattern consistent with my acutest understanding of them." The process of writing confirmed what she had appreciated all along: "It has always been a profound realization of my life that there was a pattern under it, which, though not always realizable when it occurred, explained and extenuated, in the end saved me from irreparable disaster" (*EH* vii).

The first task Austin set herself was to define the nature of her vision. Before she had reached the age of twenty, she was in communion with her destiny. "I would write imaginatively, not only of people, but of the scene, the totality which is called Nature, and . . . I would give myself intransigently to the quality of experience called Folk, and to the frame of behavior known as Mystical." With this introductory statement in mind, the reader is prepared for a certain reluctance on the part of the autobiographer to indulge in reflection, uncertainty, or even exploration of her life. *Earth Horizon* would be an apologia for what she knew from the first about herself. Austin defined her task as defending the self-knowledge and "genius" that had shaped her destiny as a writer and prophet. She traced her mystical roots from childhood, when she experienced "Power" in "the presence of God under the walnut tree, the Friend in the woods, [and] I-Mary—with the wish and intention to write" (*EH* 74).

The frequent scathing indictments in her autobiography she reserved for those whose vision was insufficient to recognize "the pattern" within that she had discerned from youth. "And because it turned out that what was so clear to me was not at all clear to the others," she continues, "because I was repressed and misguessed in respect to my normal tendencies, because I suffered in the expression of them, it seemed to me the happiest of incidents that I should be able to release these early certainties, uncramp the scroll of my mind in autobiographical freedom" (*EH* vii). The work of uncramping was not always joyous, however. In 1930 and 1931, Austin often alluded to her difficulty with the autobiographical project. In a letter to Albert Bender, she admitted "Although I have already done the most laborious part, which is assembling the material . . . I had no idea how much work it would be or I shouldn't have undertaken it."[8]

In part, the autobiography presented unprecedented problems of organization. In a conversation with the Yugoslavian-born writer Louis Adamic, Austin remarked, "I had to cut out so much that I sort of got out of key and I am not at all sure that I have succeeded in any respect." Adamic thought that Austin's autobiography manifested the author's "confusion" about her subject. He enjoyed the early part of *Earth Horizon* immensely, perhaps because of its colorful evocation of America during the settlement of the midwestern frontier and the emergence of Carlinville as a typical small town of the period, but he criticized later parts as "very rigid and incomplete."[9]

Most reviewers discovered excellence in Austin's last major effort, however. William Allen White found it a book of "genuine distinction." Dorothy Van Doren, writing in the *Nation*, noted that "as a record of the frontier and what remained after the frontier was gone," it would "seem illuminating for some time to come." The reviewer in *Commonweal* found *Earth Horizon* a perplexing mixture of typical autobiographical anecdotes and engrossing narrative. "It is a rich, profound and deeply interesting tale . . . full of many irritations for the reader to whom . . . Mary Austin matters most; the reader who knows that her mystical quest finds its true materials in her poetry, her desert and mountain stories and essays, and who thinks that her contacts with mere literary people, mere scribes of this world are a waste of her time and talent, turning her aside from her quest." Perhaps the *Boston Transcript*'s reviewer best understood Austin's purpose in writing her autobiography when he summed up its importance as "primarily the account of one writer's progress."[10]

In *Earth Horizon*, Austin gives an absorbing account of how a woman of pioneer stock, stimulated by few of the cultural influences that might be expected in a literary life but having faith in her own imagination, leapt over seemingly insurmountable barriers of geography, gender, and class to write some thirty books, each important in its own way. As Constance Rourke, herself an important advocate of native American culture, commented in the *New Republic*, Austin's autobiography is "unique in its testimony as to those ancestries and perceptions and social coherences fundamental for the imaginative writer."[11]

With *Earth Horizon*, Austin reached a greater audience than ever before. During the summer of 1932, during an exhausting lecture tour of Montana, she learned that the book had been designated a Literary Guild selection. This, she informed Adams, "insures certain sales which I could not otherwise depend upon."[12] In November of that year she reported to Carey McWilliams, a young writer and biographer of Ambrose Bierce who had helped her with research in California, that "it has started out well and gives every indication of becoming a best seller." At the same time, she criticized McWilliams for misinterpreting several details of her book and for commenting in a review that he considered her attention to "subjective" and "mystical" experiences "limitations." She added: "The attitude of standing aloof and superior merely because you have had no such experiences yourself, does not seem to me quite justified nor in key with what I expect of you."[13] The previous year Austin had told McWilliams that work on *Earth Horizon* was going "very slowly." She had made the painful discovery "that when you come to say the last thing you expect to say about yourself, it is not an easy matter." In the midst of writing she asked McWilliams to read her manuscript, an unusual request for Austin to make. "Nothing I have written has been more difficult for me to judge," she told him.[14]

Before writing *Earth Horizon*, Austin had surveyed the autobiographies of several of her contemporaries and formed decided views about them. "Such a lot of unimportant obscenity in Dreiser's, and too much boot-licking in Hamlin Garland's," she told Adamic. She faulted Gertrude Atherton's *Adventures of a Novelist* for being "too revealing in unimportant matters and not revealing enough in the really significant phases." According to Austin, most autobiographies suffered from being written when their authors "were old . . . [and] no longer vitally connected with their times, and thus unable to imagine what in their generation remained significant for the present generation and what might be significant for future generations." What she deemed essential, she told Adamic, was "to reveal oneself sufficiently as one writes so that a reader a year, a decade, or a century hence will be able to see what sort of person the writer was when *he* wrote."[15]

Women Writers and Their Autobiographies

It is somewhat surprising that Austin could not empathize with Atherton's experience as the daughter of a divorced mother. In the 1860s, when Atherton's mother obtained her divorce, her "grandfather and grandmother had the sympathy of the community." Her father was dropped by society, while her mother "was ostracized as had she been a leper wandering the streets in a cowl, a warning bell in her hand." Atherton's account demonstrated that California changed very little in its attitudes toward divorce between the 1860s and the early twentieth century. Atherton had married into a wealthy society family, more like Wharton's than Austin's. However, each of these three writers dwells on the lack of recognition her writing earned in her family. For Atherton, "it was quite twelve years after I published my first novel before the painful subject that I wrote at all was mentioned by any of the family in my presence."[16] Wharton's experience differed only slightly. "None of my relations ever spoke to me of my books, either to praise or blame—they simply ignored them," she wrote, adding that "among the immense tribe of my New York cousins . . . the subject was avoided as if it were a kind of family disgrace, which might be condoned but could not be forgotten."[17]

Austin's story in *Earth Horizon* of the cold reception to her first literary effort varies only slightly from the accounts given by Wharton and Atherton. The first of her stories, "The Mother of Felipe," was published in the *Overland Monthly* in November 1892, after Austin had delivered her daughter in her mother's Bakersfield home.[18] Her mother read it to her while she was still in bed, "but she could never be got to express an interest in it. 'I think you could have made more of it,' Mary finally dragged out of her." She found her mother's total indifference appalling. "Where was now the triumph and encouragement that should go to one's first professional adventure!" (*EH* 240).

The reader of *Earth Horizon* is struck by Austin's preoccupation with the profession of writing, a concern shared by other women writers of her period who wrote autobiographies: Atherton, Ellen Glasgow, Wharton, Gertrude Stein and, to a certain extent, Willa Cather, whose one semiautobiographical work, *Not Under Forty*, disguises as much as it reveals. Comparing these works becomes increasingly interesting when one considers that each of the writers was single: Atherton was widowed at an early age from her difficult husband, Austin and Wharton were divorced, and Glasgow, Stein, and Cather never married.

Austin, quite naturally fascinated by her own life, states directly, "I don't see why it should be so much the literary mode just now to pretend that ideas are not intrinsically exciting and that one's own life isn't interesting to oneself" (*EH* 217). In that courageous stroke she rid herself of one of the major problems of the autobiographer: that of foregrounding the authentic self. Austin may not be any more successful than any other autobiographer in representing a liberated self (or selves). Yet *Earth Horizon* takes the autobiographical impulse to another level, revealing Austin's remarkable preoccupation with the self—from an initial recognition of "I-Mary" in childhood to the inherently self-conscious act of crafting her autobiography as a mature writer.

Austin was convinced of the importance of her work from the outset of her career, and never shrank from announcing it. This intrepidity set her apart from other writers. Wharton, for example, may have thought her own work every bit as important as that of any other writer of the day, but she preferred to strike a more modest pose when discussing it. In an article entitled "Confessions of a Novelist," she wrote, "I have hesitated for some time before beginning this article, since any attempt to analyze work of one's own doing seems to imply that one regards it as likely to be of lasting interest, and I wish at the outset to repudiate any such assumption."[19] The title of Austin's autobiography, an exercise in shedding self-consciousness, is also the title of an Indian song that speaks of the search of the "inquiring soul" for the authentic self. "In the song of Earth Horizon man wanders in search of the Sacred Middle from which all horizons are equidistant, and his soul happily at rest. Once the Middle is attained, all the skyey rings that encircle earth's six quarters dissolve into the true zone of reality, and his spirit, no longer deflected by the influences of false horizons, swings freely to its proper arc" (*EH* 274).

In her perceptive analysis of *Earth Horizon*, Rae Galbraith Ballard speculates that the mandala symbol chosen by the writer owes as much to Austin's reading of Emerson and Jung as to her contact with Indians. Ballard interprets Austin's life as conforming closely to the mandala, emphasizing Austin's perception of self intertwined with her identities of mystic, naturist, folklorist, and writer. A rejection of "false horizons" required Austin at twenty-six to move beyond her marital situation "out of the sacred quarter for which [women] were bred and brought up,"[20] beyond the "perpetual torment of a creative talent not yet accommodated to its proper medium . . . the harassment of the led horse, held too precious to be allowed to pull in harness, and not free to seek its proper pastures" (*EH* 275).

Discarding her midwestern inheritance, particularly orthodox Methodism—an event precipitated by her mother's death—was central to her search for "a new Middle where the inquiring soul could be at rest" (*EH* 274). More than Wharton, Cather, Glasgow, Stein, or Atherton, Austin represents in her autobiographical journey toward a fully individuated self the torment of a woman whose expectations of self collided radically with her acculturation to the traditional role of womanhood and with her family's expectations for her. "Nobody had wanted children more than Mary did; few intellectuals of her generation have clung more obstinately to the idea of a home, a house, a garden, the familiar use of hospitality," Austin writes in the third-person voice that she employed in *Earth Horizon* to achieve distance from her subject. This passage, remonstrative in tone, reads like a passionate defense of her femininity. "Few have sacrificed more to the fulfillment of the pattern of man and woman working together for a converging point on the Earth Horizon" (*EH* 274). Austin's conflicting interests in domesticity and a writing career bear out Patricia Spacks's observation that "happiness derives from relationship; unhappiness follows when obligations conflict or cannot be fulfilled."[21] Certainly Austin identified herself as "feminine" and "womanly" while choosing a life that directed her away from responsibilities traditionally assigned to women.

What distinguishes Austin's autobiography from those of her contemporaries is her way of inscribing the "feminine" on her writing. As Virginia Woolf succinctly put it, "A woman's writing is always feminine; it cannot help being feminine; at its best it is most feminine; the only difficulty lies in defining what we mean by feminine."[22] Austin's deep-seated conflict about her feminine identity, which caused her enormous anguish, is at the crux of what Adamic termed the "confusion" in *Earth Horizon*. In seeking to fulfill her expectations of self as a writer at the cost of abandoning her marriage and child, Austin set herself at odds with the consensual definitions of femininity current in her time. She perceived herself as a "maverick," both as a woman and as a writer. Dealing with the "distressful search for a new personal direction," which for Austin meant an authentic voice in her writing, she realized that "what her own generation must bear was the renunciation of just that power to please (to be loved and leaned upon) which still sicklies with its sticky sweetness the constructive purpose of America" (*EH* 278). In renouncing the "power to please," she set herself a most difficult course both in her personal life and in her literary career.

Austin's strategy for coming to terms with her disjunctive life surfaces in the autobiography as a spiritual quest for fulfillment. Her life among the Indians in Inyo while still a young woman provided the source "of illumination and reformation of [her] own way of thought" (*EH* 267). In Bishop, California, where she witnessed the violence of white men toward Indian women, she advanced in her "spiritual growth *away from* the orthodox Protestant expression of it," realizing that "life is essentially remediable, undefeatable; the thing was to discover the how of it" (*EH* 268). In this aspect of overcoming, her life story is akin to certain eighteenth-century women's spiritual autobiographies, which describe their struggles to discover salvation in orthodoxy in order to forge a unique spiritual relationship with God.[23] The essential difference in Austin's spiritual autobiography is that her search, as she represents it, is bereft of a sense of community with anyone except the Indians. As a wife, a mother, a sister, and a creative writer, she recalled, "the thing that Mary suffered from in the middle nineties was loneness; by which I mean to indicate a state of lacking human resort, rather than any emotional state which involved feeling sorry for herself" (*EH* 268).

In Search of a Mother

Perhaps the biggest lack in Austin's life was a rich and meaningful connection with her mother. Her account of this crucial relationship in *Earth Horizon* gives resonance to Adrienne Rich's contemporary analysis of the mother-daughter relationship fraught with possibilities "for the deepest mutuality and the most painful estrangement."[24] Austin repeatedly turns to her mother only to find the relationship empty of understanding; at every significant crisis when she seeks tenderness or advice, she meets criticism or rebuff. Cast aside by her mother in childhood after the deaths of her father and sister in 1878, Austin longed for a maternal closeness that was lavished on her brothers. Susanna

Hunter's reserve distanced her from her daughter's emotional needs, and it is painfully clear that Austin recognized her mother's incapacity for understanding her craving for encouragement and understanding.

"Then," she wrote, "there was that very real and heartrending anguish of the creative worker before the medium and method of individual expression has been mastered, which is, I suppose, always ludicrous to the onlooker not himself tormented by it. As it turned out, no help from the outside ever did arrive for that, although in the first onset of the struggle, after Mary had discovered that the teaching she had in painting was not only inadequate but an interference to direct expressiveness, and before the use of literary forms had become easily available, she had cried out once to her mother—who else?—and Susie had not understood it" (*EH* 269). Austin portrays her mother not as deliberately cruel but as oblivious to the inner torment of those around her. Mrs. Hunter appears to have fit the definition of the simple or "healthy soul" in William James's schema.[25]

The intensity of Austin's alienation from her mother suggests why she went to great lengths to get material about the mysterious Mary Patchen, her father's sweetheart before his engagement to Susanna Hunter. From sources in Carlinville she discovered that Patchen was "a young woman of about twenty years of age, not tall, but somewhat over medium height; of erect well developed figure, strong, plain regular features, high forehead, large mouth, light brown hair and blue gray eyes." Austin was particularly struck by the testimony of one of her father's friends that "the basis of intimacy between George Hunter and Mary Patchen was that of congenial intellectuality and a like interest in literature." The relationship between the couple had gone awry because of a misunderstanding. According to one source, Patchen "had high ideals and exceptional mentality, yet with all this an element of credulity which sometimes made her an easy mark for charlatans of divers kinds."[26] An enthusiastic student, she had been tricked into the bigamous marriage by an itinerant lecturer on astronomy. When the truth came out, "the community gathered itself into a posse" and "Miss Patchen went into the seclusion which the refined sensibility of the period demanded" (*EH* 37). Eventually she married another man and George Hunter married Susanna Graham.

Although Austin had six female relatives named Mary, she intimates in *Earth Horizon* that she was Mary Patchen's namesake. Her extreme interest in this woman, who she imagined might have been her mother under different circumstances, may imply that Patchen's qualities of mind were those she found deficient in her natural mother. In *Earth*

Horizon, Austin relates that she received a visit from Mary Patchen Snyder while she was lecturing in San Diego. During their conversation Austin complained that her mother cared little about her writing. The older woman recalled visiting the Hunters before Austin was born and said she "was grieved" when she realized that Susanna Hunter "didn't want" her (*EH* 316). Mary Patchen Snyder's love for George Hunter and for her was clear to Austin. Patchen "was touched by those things which seemed to derive directly from my father, especially the things of outdoors and the literary criticism. . . . She showed herself familiar with the most intimate of my writing." Most of all, Patchen "was moved by the passages which expressed the feeling I had for the West; she had thought they were the things he would have appreciated" (*EH* 317). In Mary Patchen, Austin recaptured the mother she had thought was lost to her.

Yet if Mrs. Hunter had been the compassionate and encouraging presence that her daughter wished for, would Austin have felt driven to discard the traditional role engendered by her midwestern upbringing and seek release in the creative impulse? A deep burr of resentment, caused specifically by her mother's negativism, fomented the "loneness" that Austin felt as she was growing up and entering young womanhood. The alienation that Atherton, Wharton, and Austin experienced produced a singular independence; rather than emulating their mothers, they sensed their individuality and dedicated themselves to writing.[27] Yet the death of her mother wrenched Austin with unexpected force. "It is only when the tree is green that the cut bough bleeds," she wrote (*EH* 273).

Austin on many occasions expressed her distrust of psychoanalysis, Freudian theory in particular. The paradigm of women's experience that psychoanalyst Karen Horney constructed in the 1920s describes Austin's relationship with her mother and brothers more accurately than Freudian theories. Women's jealousy of their brothers and tension with their mothers, according to Horney, derive from their devalued place in the family. Daughters struggle between dependency and ambition, and rage is the inevitable result. "Horney's emphasis on the cultural pattern of preference for sons suggests that parents are disappointed with daughters whether or not there is an actual son who is favored in contrast," writes Marcia Westkott. In the dissemination of cultural values through the structure of the family, "daughters experience pervasive devaluation and a sense of inferiority."[28]

Horney theorized that the perceptive daughter consciously or unconsciously understands the mother's role in perpetrating disempowering cultural values within the family constellation. The daughter either overtly displays hostility or develops other strategies to vent or repress her anger toward mother and family. Austin's excursion into autobiography attempts to represent a journey toward self-knowledge, a process that forced her to contend with bitter truths about her place in the Hunter clan. That her autobiographical undertaking awakened deep feelings of hostility repressed during her childhood is not to be wondered at. In important respects the power relations within middle-class family life, although painful to her, helped to shape her career as a writer.

Disharmony in the Pattern

The familial cankers exposed in *Earth Horizon*—Austin's allegations against her mother and her animus against Wallace Austin and her brother George—deserve a critical examination. From the evidence, Wallace's major fault was his inability to be the man Mary wanted him to be. He was utterly at a loss in the literary circles that Mary had begun to associate with when she moved to Carmel, and he refused to follow her. In addition, he was undeniably the father of their retarded child and was the logical target for her "tainted blood" theory. As for George, he reaped unkind treatment in his sister's autobiography for his part in refusing to grant her custody of young Mary Hunter, on the grounds that the girl had a stable life in Los Angeles with her stepmother under his capable guardianship.

According to those who most closely observed Hunter and Austin family politics, several passages about her immediate family in Austin's autobiography are factually inaccurate. Austin's venomous resentment of her younger brother jars the carefully balanced description of her literary career. She chooses to depict George as callous during her serious illness, refusing to attend her at her sickbed and stubbornly pursuing the old quarrel between them about young Mary Hunter's best interests. Due to George's neglect, Austin charged, her niece suffered mental stress.

> For myself, I could do nothing but suffer. I lay in bed in great pain for eight months, and in great anxiety about Mary [Hunter], about whom my brother would take no steps. He was frightened and fell back on the family attitude. He did not believe my physician; he would not even consent to a physical examination of

Mary; it was all my queerness. If Mary would abandon me and put herself absolutely in his hands, he might do something for her, but otherwise, not. In the end he sent me a few hundred dollars, and when my house was completed [in Santa Fe] so that I could leave it, I took Mary to a hospital, went myself to another, and had an operation from which I was a year in recovering. What I discovered was that not only had I been obliged to give up my commission, but the manuscript of the novel which I had half-completed was missing. In the confusion of my illness and moving, it had been lost. (*EH* 357) [29]

When the doctors examined Mary Hunter, however, their finding was an ailment that might be summarized as "too much Aunt Mary." The dispute between George Hunter, a respected Los Angeles neurologist, and his sister escalated into a bitter feud that was apparently unresolved when he was murdered by a deranged female patient while making a house call in 1933.

George's wife, Geraldine, had been an extreme irritant to Austin. She accused Geraldine of conspiring to steal family letters and photographs that she wanted to use in her autobiography. In a letter to George in 1927, her anger reached a feverish pitch. "Your wife stole the letters our father wrote to our mother, while Jim's [their brother's] furniture was stored in your house. Yes, Jim told me that Geraldine simply appropriated personal property merely because it has been temporarily forgotten. And when your wife jeeringly refused even to let me have those letters copied for my autobiography, and when a short time after that she went through my trunk while I was visiting you, without my permission and took the only picture of my father to have copied, and cracked it in the process, then I knew the theft had been deliberate." [30]

The real issue between George and Mary Austin, however, was the fight for the custody of Mary Hunter. Never able to rid herself of guilt over her handling of Ruth's illness and long-term care, Austin interpreted her exclusion from Mary's guardianship as a criticism of her maternal abilities. In anger and frustration, she displaced her guilt about her own unfortunate daughter onto George, accusing him of "neglect" with regard to Mary Hunter. "What I, as the head of the family am interested in, is my youngest niece," she wrote in 1927. "I shall do what I can to rescue Mary as she wants to be rescued. And when Geraldine's [George's daughter] time comes, I will do what I can to rescue her, being just as sure that she will eventually appeal to me as I was that Mary would. I am telling you these things, as I told you them about Mary so that you will have no excuse in ignorance. As the head of the family, if you fail with her as you did with Mary, I will not hold you guiltless."[31]

Many other factors figure in here: the premature death of Austin's father, her longstanding feelings of rejection, and her exclusion from the family, which she believed was based on her femaleness. Clearly, her mother valued the maleness of her brothers. Nevertheless, it is difficult to reconcile the George Hunter who wrote so many conciliatory letters to his sister with the George of Austin's autobiography, just as it is difficult to square the mild-mannered, compliant Wallace Austin who left her his insurance policy after his death in 1932 with the unflattering portrait she creates in *Earth Horizon*.[32] Writing to Austin in 1925, George attempted to mollify her: "We are neither of us as young as we used to be and some day one of us will be left with a great heartache. . . . I am humbly sorry for my fault in the matter [of the missing correspondence and photographs] and can only say that whatever I may have done . . . was an error of judgement and lack of wisdom rather than intent."[33]

Austin's propensity for taking umbrage was well known even among her closest friends. Daniel MacDougal receives only two brief mentions in *Earth Horizon*, the attentive Ansel and Virginia Adams not a single one. Austin's relationship with MacDougal ended abruptly soon after the publication of *The Land of Journeys' Ending* in 1924. She was ill intermittently for the next two years. MacDougal fell into disfavor because, she wrote, he "failed to realize my condition, and seemed vexed with me because I could not give him the same interest and attention that he had always had from me."[34] As early as 1922 Austin had written to MacDougal about "repression" and "inhibitions" preventing her from free "expression . . . in a personal way," perhaps alluding to expressions of intimacy that she was incapable of demonstrating.[35] Yet Austin insisted that their relationship had withered because of his lack of understanding.

Austin persistently believed that no one cared when she suffered, despite the attention lavished on her by many friends in Santa Fe. The pattern of harmony that she suggests is the underlying motif of her life is disturbed in *Earth Horizon*, largely because of her perception that people failed to pay attention to her as a person, as a writer, and as a prophet. Austin demanded and often received praise as a riveting speaker and an eloquent writer. But although she worked harder than many of her male contemporaries to compel the attention of her public, her autobiography reveals how perilously close her career sometimes came to oblivion, and how subject she was to the common misunderstanding and misuse of a talented woman's artistic gifts during this tumultous period in American cultural life.

The tragic elements that emerge in Austin's autobiography reflect the distortions that marked her life and often marred her work. Unquestionably, didacticism and resentment seeped into her writing. *Earth Horizon* accurately reflects her worldview, one of desperate longing for interdependence and community symbolized by the holistic "earth horizon"—a worldview that unfortunately was subverted by a host of fragmenting personal dissatisfactions. In the powerful last paragraph of her paradoxical autobiography, her prophetic vision of the cosmos blends with a tragic perception of her own life:

> I have not been entirely happy in my adjustments. I have suffered in my life, in my means, in my reciprocal relations; but I have this pride and congratulation, that I have not missed the significance of the spectacle I have been privileged to witness. I have not only had the pleasure of associating with those who have known what it means, but I have had glimpses of its meaning. . . . I have seen that the American achievement is made up of two splendors: the splendor of individual relationships of power to make and do rather than merely to possess, the aristocracy of creativeness; and that other splendor of realizing that in the deepest layers of ourselves we are incurably collective. At the core of our Amerindian life we are consummated in the dash and color of collectivity. It is not that we work upon the cosmos, but it works in us. I suffer because I achieve so little in this relation, and rejoice that I have felt so much. As much as I am able, I celebrate the Earth Horizon. (*EH* 368)

Mary Austin died in her sleep on August 13, 1934, as a result of a heart attack brought on by coronary disease.[36] Death, she had long proclaimed, held no fear for her. "If death is a gate, and not the dead end of a passage," she had written, "I shall get through by means of what I have learned as folklorist, as mystic, as artist."[37]

NOTES

INTRODUCTION

1 I owe this insight to Mary Hunter Wolf, Austin's niece.

2 Louis Adamic, *My America* (New York: Harper and Brothers, 1938), 480. See also Franklin Walker's excellent introduction to Austin in *The Mother of Felipe and Other Early Stories* (Los Angeles: Book Club of California, 1950), 12.

3 Carl Van Doren, Introduction to Austin, *The Land of Little Rain*, (Boston: Houghton Mifflin, 1950), xi. Adamic, *My America*, 480.

4 Virginia Woolf, "Women and Fiction," in *Granite and Rainbow* (New York: Harcourt Brace Jovanovich, 1958), 66. Jack London, *Martin Eden* (New York: Macmillan, 1909).

5 See "Production Record Summary," Jan. 31, 1905, to March 14, 1934, Houghton Mifflin Company Collection, Houghton Library, Harvard.

6 Letter, Austin to Houghton Mifflin, July 16, [1907], Mary Austin Collection, Henry E. Huntington Library (hereafter cited as HEH). See also her letters to Houghton Mifflin of Sept. 24, 1914; Jan. 8 and 28, 1918; Aug. 5, 1927; and Feb. 1, 1929, Houghton Mifflin Company Collection, Houghton Library, Harvard.

7 Austin, *The Young Woman Citizen* (New York: Woman's Press, 1918), 19.

8 The list of books and articles about women writers and canon making is long; the following have been particularly helpful in my work: Annette Kolodny, "Some Notes on Defining a 'Feminist Literary Criticism,'" *Critical Inquiry* 2 (Fall 1975): 75–92; Elaine Showalter, "Women's Time, Women's Space: Writing the History of Feminist Criticism," *Tulsa Studies in Women's Literature* 3 (Fall 1984): 29–43; Showalter, *The New Feminist Criticism* (New York: Pantheon, 1985); and Nina Baym, *Women's Fiction: A Guide to Novels by and about Women in America, 1820–1870* (Ithaca, N.Y.: Cornell University Press, 1978).

9 Kolodny, "Dancing through the Minefield," in Showalter, *The New Feminist Criticism*, 156.

10 Among the histories and anthologies that overlook Austin are Sandra Gilbert and Susan Gubar, eds., *The Norton Anthology of Literature by Women* (New York: W. W. Norton, 1985); Alfred Kazin, *On Native Grounds* (New York:

Harcourt Brace Jovanovich, 1942); William Rose Benet, *The Reader's Encyclo-pedia*, 2d ed. (New York: Crowell, 1965) [although the 1948 edition includes Austin]; Robert E. Spiller et al., *Literary History of the United States*, 3d ed. (New York: Macmillan, 1963); Frederick J. Hoffman, *The Twenties* (New York: Viking, 1955); Joseph Collins, *Taking the Literary Pulse* (New York: Doran, 1924); Cynthia Griffin Wolff, ed., *Classic American Women Writers* (New York: Harper and Row, 1980); and Henry Seidel Canby, *American Memoir* (Boston: Houghton Mifflin, 1947). Austin receives one brief mention in Emory Elliott, ed., *The Columbia Literary History of the United States* (New York: Columbia University Press, 1988). One Austin story appears in Marcia Muller and Bill Pronzini, eds., *She Won the West: An Anthology of Western and Frontier Stories by Women* (New York: Morrow, 1985).

11 See especially Augusta Fink, *I-Mary* (Tucson: University of Arizona Press, 1983); Helen MacKnight Doyle, *Mary Austin: A Woman of Genius* (New York: Gotham House, 1939); T. M. Pearce, *Mary Hunter Austin* (Boston: Twayne, 1965); Pearce, *The Beloved House* (Caldwell, Idaho: Caxton Printers, 1940); Thurman Wilkins, "Mary Austin," in Edward T. James, ed., *Notable American Women, 1607–1950* (Cambridge, Mass.: Harvard University Press, 1971), 67–69; and Lois Burns, "Mary Hunter Austin," in *American Woman Writers*, vol. 1 (New York: Ungar, 1979), 74–76.

12 As Fink establishes in her biography, *I-Mary*, this ego identity was key to Austin's development as a writer. Austin's version of how she discovered this second, inviolable aspect of herself is found in *Earth Horizon* 46–47, 56, 74, 85–86, 94, 231, 277, and 282.

13 David Bromwich, "The Uses of Biography," *The Yale Review* 73 (Winter 1984): 161–76. Ralph Barton Perry, *In the Spirit of William James* (New Haven: Yale University Press, 1938), 35–36.

CHAPTER I. BEGINNINGS

1 Lewis Atherton, *Main Street on the Middle Border* (Bloomington: Indiana University Press, 1984), 11.

2 Letter, E. R. Turnbull to Austin, Dec. 13, 1930, HEH.

3 Letter, Effie Curtis to Austin, Dec. 18, 1932, HEH.

4 Letter, Anna Burns to Austin, Jan. 10, 1931, HEH. Anna Peter Burns, Austin's cousin, kept track of Graham and Dugger family history; the Peter family relocated to Wichita, Kan., so Mary scarcely knew these first cousins. See "Family History Chart," HEH, and Fink, *I-Mary*, 8–11.

5 Austin, "How I Found the Thing Worth Waiting For," *Survey* 61 (Jan. 1, 1929): 434.

6 Obituary, "George Hunter," *The Carlinville Democrat*, Oct. 30, 1878. See also Fink, *I-Mary*, 13.

7 George Hunter, enlistment paper, July 25, 1861, HEH.

8 Letter, D. J. McMillan to Austin, April 10, 1929, HEH.

9 Hunter was promoted to captain on Aug. 30, 1863, according to the Springfield, Ill., Office of the Adjutant General (documented March 18, 1929, HEH).

10 Letter, McMillan to Austin, April 10, 1929; Fink, *I-Mary*, 8–9.

11 Ibid.

12 *The Carlinville Free Democrat*, March 11, 1862.

13 Typed, undated MS notes for Austin's autobiography titled "Addenda," p. 1, HEH. This set of notes, beginning in 1867–1868, the year of Austin's birth, contains notations on family news, Carlinville news, and national news as it pertains to Carlinville. Mary Hunter Wolf remembers researching newspaper files in Carlinville for her aunt; both visited Carlinville in 1929. The notes seem to have been augmented and shaped into final form by Austin.

14 Ibid., p. 3. Obituary, *The Carlinville Democrat*, Oct. 30, 1878.

15 Addenda, 1868–1872, pp. 2–8. Hunter's paper appeared in the *Carlinville Democrat*, Dec. 6, 1872.

16 *St. Nicholas* (1873–1940) was a much-respected children's magazine edited during Mary's childhood by Mary Mapes Dodge, who attracted writers of quality fiction and poetry to its pages—Louisa May Alcott, Rebecca Harding Davis, and many more. Mrs. Hunter later canceled the subscription, undoubtedly because she was forced to cut back on such luxuries after her husband's death.

17 For further information about widowhood during this period, see Joyce D. Goodfriend, "Denver Widows, 1880–1910," in Arlene Scadron, *Widowhood and the American Southwest, 1848–1939*, Working Paper no. 17 (Tucson: Southwestern Institute for Research on Women, 1983). Mrs. Hunter's experiences are borne out in this research even though she was from the Midwest.

18 Richard Lingeman, *Small Town America: A Narrative History, 1620 to the Present* (Boston: Houghton Mifflin, 1980), 271–72. See also Nancy A. Hewitt, *Women's Activism and Social Change: Rochester, New York, 1822–1872* (Ithaca, N.Y.: Cornell University Press, 1984) for a useful discussion of the myriad organizations through which women exerted social and political influence despite their disenfranchisement in mid- to late nineteenth-century America.

19 Addenda, 1880–1881, p. 16.

20 Addenda, pp. 18–19; *EH* 142–50; program, Ninth Annual Meeting, Illinois WCTU, Carlinville, Sept. 20–22, [1882], HEH. See also Frances Willard, *Woman and Temperance* (1883; reprint, New York: Arno, 1972); Willard, *Glimpses of Fifty Years: An Autobiography of an American Woman* (1889; reprint, New York: Source Book Press, 1970); and Edward James, ed., *Notable American Woman* (Cambridge, Mass.: Harvard University Press, 1971), 1:321–22. An excellent theoretical analysis of the temperance movement is Ruth Bordin, *Woman and Temperance: The Quest for Power and Liberty, 1873–1900* (Philadelphia: Temple University Press, 1981). Ellen DuBois, "The Radicalism of the Woman Suffrage Movement: Notes toward the Reconstruction of Nineteenth Century Feminism," *Feminist Studies* 3 (Fall 1975):63–71, explores aspects of the WCTU that constituted a radical strategy for social reform.

21 Addenda, 1882, p. 17.

22 Program, Ninth Annual Meeting, Illinois WCTU, Sept. 20–22, [1882], HEH.

23 Addenda, 1882, p. 18. Austin, "The Thing World Waiting For," 434.

24 Lingeman, *Small Town America*, 305–06. See also Gertrude Atherton, *Main Street* (Bloomington: Indiana University Press, 1984), 139–42.

25 See Lingeman, *Small Town America*, 273.

26 Austin, "The Town that Doesn't Want a Chautauqua," *The New Republic* 47 (July 7, 1926); *EH* 56–57.

27 Mary Hunter's certificate of church membership, Sept. 9, 1883, HEH.

28 See Lingeman, *Small Town America*, 130–31.

29 See Elizabeth K. Nottingham, *Methodism and the Frontier* (New York: Columbia University Press, 1941), esp. 131–32.

30 Austin, *Experiences Facing Death* (Indianapolis: Bobbs-Merrill, 1931), 25–26.

31 Photograph, "Mary's family when she was twelve," Box 55, HEH.

32 Austin, "Woman Alone," reprinted in Elaine Showalter, ed., *These Modern Women* (Old Westbury, N.Y.: Feminist Press, 1978), 81.

33 Letter, Austin to George Hunter, Jan. 15, 1927; see also Austin to Hunter, April 15, 1927, HEH.

34 Lester Ward, "Genius and Woman's Intuition," *Forum* 9 (June 1890):408. Ward continued, "It would seem to be the better part of valor to make a virtue of necessity, and, accepting the inevitable, to endeavor to tame them into harmlessness, and if possible to win them back to the fold, by offering them a few grains of sense and crumbs of knowledge." See Rosalind Rosenberg's fine analysis of Ward in *Beyond Separate Spheres* (New Haven: Yale University Press, 1982), 36–43.

35 Austin, "Woman Alone," 82.

36 See, for example, Austin's accusatory letter to George Hunter dated Jan. 15, 1927 (HEH), in which she accuses her brother of stealing family papers to thwart her autobiographical efforts.

37 Quoted by Charles Rosenberg and Carroll Smith-Rosenberg in *No Other Gods* (Baltimore: Johns Hopkins University Press, 1976), 61; see also 55–56. The entire chapter, "The Female Animal: Medical and Biological Views of Women," helps to isolate and define those prescriptive elements of women's gender role that are formally and informally controlled in society.

38 Jean Strouse, *Alice James: A Biography* (Boston: Houghton Mifflin, 1980), 159. See Barbara Sicherman's well-researched article "The Uses of a Diagnosis: Doctors, Patients, and Neurasthenia," in Judith Walzer Leavitt and Ronald L. Numbers, *Sickness and Health in America: Readings in the History of Medicine and Public Health* (Madison: University of Wisconsin Press, 1978), 25–38.

39 Rosenberg, *Beyond Separate Spheres*, xiv.

40 Kazin, *On Native Grounds*, 128.

41 See Austin, "Sex Emancipation through War," *The Forum*, May 1918:609–20; "Greatness in Women," *The North American Review* 217 (Jan.–June 1923):197–

203; and "Woman and Her War Loot," *Sunset* 42 (Feb. 1919): 13–15. Rosenberg gives a useful discussion of biological determinism in *Beyond Separate Spheres*, 5–12.

42 Austin, "Science for the Unscientific," *The Bookman* 55, no. 6 (Aug. 1922): 565.

43 Austin, "Woman Alone," 82.

44 Rosenberg, *Beyond Separate Spheres*, 148.

45 Atchison, Topeka, and Santa Fe brochure, ca. 1884, Western Americana Collection, Beinecke Rare Book and Manuscript Library, Yale University.

46 Charles Dudley Warner, "Our Italy," *Harper's Magazine*, Nov. 1890–Feb. 1891: 271; reprinted in *Washington Irving and Our Italy* (Hartford, Conn.: American, 1904). See also Kevin Starr, *Americans and the California Dream, 1850–1915* (New York: Oxford University Press, 1983), particularly the chapter "An American Mediterranean," which traces the identification of California with Italy and Greece in the American mind.

47 Charles Nordhoff, *California for Health, Pleasure, and Residence* (New York: Harper and Brothers, 1875), 130.

48 Ibid., 131, 121, and 132.

49 "Voters of the City," *Los Angeles Tribune Annual* (1889), 22.

50 *Los Angeles Tribune Annual* (1889), quoted in Austin, "Woman Alone," 82.

51 Austin, "Woman Alone," 82. Austin quoted in Franklin Walker, *A Literary History of Southern California* (Berkeley: University of California Press, 1950), 191–92. *Los Angeles Tribune Annual* (1889), 29.

52 Fink, *I-Mary*, 23–24.

53 Austin, "Los Angeles 1888," typescript, HEH.

54 Austin, "Art Influence in the West," *The Century Magazine*, April 1915: 829.

55 "One Hundred Miles on Horseback" was reissued in 1963 in a limited edition by Dawson's Book Shop in Los Angeles. Subsequent references are to this edition.

56 F. O. Matthiessen, *Sarah Orne Jewett* (Boston: Houghton Mifflin, 1929), 99.

57 Walker, *Literary History*, 190. Donald Ringler, Introduction to *One Hundred Miles on Horseback*, x.

58 "Kern County," *Los Angeles Tribune Annual* (1889), 59.

59 Kolodny, *The Land Before Her*, xiii.

60 Ringler, Introduction, xiii.

61 Walker, *Literary History*, 192.

62 Austin, "Kit Carson and Beale" (transcription of Beale's personal narrative, 1889), MS 1, HEH.

63 Richard Bailey, *Heritage of Kern* (Bakersfield: Kern County Historical Society, 1956), 15–17. I am indebted to Prof. Howard Lamar for sharing with me his interpretation of Beale.

64 Austin, typescript attached to handwritten 1904 notes, July 24, 1917, HEH.

65 Hilde Bruch gives a readable analysis of how the family figures in this disturbing illness in *The Golden Cage: The Enigma of Anorexia Nervosa* (Cambridge, Mass.:

Harvard University Press, 1978). See also Marlene Boskind-Lodahl, "Cinderella's Stepsisters: A Feminist Perspective on Anorexia Nervosa and Bulimia," *Signs* 4 (Winter 1976): 342–56.

66 Austin, "Art Influence in the West," 831.

CHAPTER 2. THE EARLY CALIFORNIA YEARS

1 Letter, Cleveland Diaz to Austin, Jan. 10, 1898, HEH.

2 Austin, *The Children Sing in the Far West* (Boston: Houghton Mifflin, 1928), vii.

3 See Starr, *Americans*, 197–200. Starr credits Norris as coming "the closest in his generation's attempt to put the ranch era into significant fiction."

4 A good portrait of Beale appears in Bailey, *Heritage of Kern*, 14–19.

5 Starr gives a detailed account of Beale's extraordinary career in *Inventing the Dream: California through the Progressive Era* (New York: Oxford University Press, 1985), 22–29. He writes, "It is no exaggeration to say that . . . Edward Fitzgerald Beale *was* the Tejon, and the Tejon was Edward Fitzgerald Beale for the remaining decades of the nineteenth century" (22).

6 See Fink, *I-Mary*, 42–49.

7 Van Wyck Brooks and Otto L. Bettmann, *Our Literary Heritage* (New York: Dutton, 1956), 218.

8 Starr, *Inventing the Dream*, 124.

9 Elaine Showalter, "Feminist Criticism in the Wilderness," in Showalter, ed. *The New Feminist Criticism*, 262–63. "For some feminist critics," she writes, "the wild zone, or 'female space,' must be the address of a genuinely women-centered criticism, theory, and art, whose shared project is to bring into being the symbolic weight of female consciousness, to make the invisible visible, to make the silent speak."

10 See Judith Thurman, *Isak Dinesen: The Life of a Storyteller* (New York: St. Martin's, 1982).

11 Gertrude Atherton, *California: An Intimate History* (New York: Harper and Brothers, 1914), 34.

12 Richard Drinnon, *Facing West: The Metaphysics of Indian-Hating and Empire-Building* (Minneapolis: University of Minnesota Press, 1980), 211. However, Drinnon asserted that throughout her life Austin "shared with contemporaries certain social Darwinian notions about 'primitives' and 'Dawn Man'" (210). This is discussed further in chapter 6.

13 Letter, Austin to Henry Seidel Canby, April 1, 1930, HEH.

14 Virginia Woolf, *A Room of One's Own* (New York: Harcourt, Brace and World, 1957), 36.

15 See Vera Norwood, "The Photographer and the Naturalist: Laura Gilpin and Mary Hunter Austin in the Southwest," *Journal of American Culture* 5 (Summer 1982): 1–28.

16 Letter, Mary Hunter Wolf to author, April 22, 1986.

17 See William Harland Boyd, *A California Middle Border: The Kern River Country*, (Richardson, Tex.: Havilah Press, 1972).

18 See *EH* 190–91; Nordhoff, *California*, 128; and David Lavender, *California: Land of New Beginnings* (Lincoln: University of Nebraska Press, 1987), 314–16.

19 *EH* 221. Fink terms the relationship "a marriage of convenience" (*I-Mary*, 51–64).

20 Letter, Stafford Wallace Austin to Mary Austin, July 19, [1929?], HEH.

21 See R. W. B. Lewis, *Edith Wharton: A Biography* (New York: Harper and Row, 1975), 53.

22 See Nancy Chodorow, *The Reproduction of Mothering* (Berkeley: University of California Press, 1978). Chodorow has speculated that "in Western society, the separation of domestic and public spheres—of domestic reproduction on the one hand and social production and the state on the other—has been sharpened through the course of industrial capitalist development, producing a family form reduced to its fundamentals, to women's mothering and maternal qualities and heterosexual marriage, and continuing to produce male dominance" (10). Chodorow further suggests that during the Oedipal and post-Oedipal periods, a girl recognizes the similarity of her own and her mother's bodies. When she learns to identify the gender-related disempowerment that accompanies sameness with the mother and difference from the father, she may rebel against the mother as the primary cause of her inability to seize power in a world of male hegemony. Whether it is useful to apply contemporary social theory to a world shaped by radically different social forces is debatable. Showalter, "Feminist Criticism in the Wilderness," 258, discusses the strength of bonds between mothers and daughters. See also Mary Ryan, *Cradle of the Middle Class* (New York: Cambridge University Press, 1981), 192–202.

23 Gertrude Atherton complained of being similarly mismatched. Describing her wealthy husband, scion of one of California's old Hispanic families, she wrote: "If a woman's place is in the home, a man's place is anywhere else between the hours of nine and six, and it seemed to me the worst trial I had been yet called upon to endure was having a husband continually on my hands. I couldn't talk to him . . . he was jealous of the very books I read" (*Adventures of a Novelist* [New York: Liveright, 1932], 82).

24 Austin, "Woman Alone," 83. Compare the case of Emily Chubbuck [Judson] (1817–1854), described in Ryan, *Cradle of the Middle Class*, 221–22. A very popular writer, Chubbuck married late and unhappily, sacrificing her career for domesticity.

25 See Carolyn Johnston, *Jack London: An American Radical?* (Westport, Conn.: Greenwood Press, 1984), 181–82, for a discussion of the contradictory theorists London invoked in developing his unique interpretation of socialism.

26 Austin, "The Thing Worth Waiting For," 435. Drinnon scoffs at Austin's understanding of Marxism in *Facing West*, 199–211.

27 Johnston, *Jack London*, 44.

28 Fink, *I-Mary*, 92, 224. See Austin, "Making the Most of Your Genius," part 1, *The Bookman* 58 (Nov. 1923):246–51; part 2, ibid. (Jan. 1924):528–34; and part 3, ibid. (Feb. 1924):626–31.

29 Letter, Austin to Henry James Forman, Sept. 17, 1918, Dept. of Special Collections, University Research Library, UCLA.

30 Austin, "The Mysticism of Genius: The Study of a Mystic Who Was a Genius," *The Century Magazine*, Dec. 1924:216.

31 Austin, "The Religious Consciousness," undated manuscript in file titled "The Nature of Religious Consciousness," HEH.

32 Nordhoff, *California*, 228.

33 Austin, "The Mother of Felipe," *The Overland Monthly*, Nov. 1892; reprinted in *The Mother of Felipe and Other Early Stories*, (San Francisco: Book Club of California, 1950), 17–26. "The Conversion of Ah Lew Sing" (1896); reprinted in *One Smoke Stories* (Boston: Houghton Mifflin, 1934), 96–109.

34 Van Wyck Brooks, *The Confident Years* (New York: Dutton, 1955), 212–13.

35 Nina Baym, "Melodramas of Beset Manhood: How Theories of American Fiction Exclude Women Authors," *American Quarterly* 33 (1981); repr. in Showalter, *The New Feminist Criticism*, 71.

36 Starr, *Americans*, 199–200.

37 Letter, Austin to Jack London, April 10, [n.d.], HEH.

38 Letter, Austin to Jack London, Dec. 18, 1915, HEH. Annette Kolodny, in a major essay on the task of feminist literary criticism titled "Dancing through the Minefield," states persuasively that "males ignorant of women's 'values' or conceptions of the world will, necessarily, be poor readers of works that in any sense recapitulate their codes" (Showalter, *The New Feminist Criticism*, 156). It follows that such men will be equally poor writers of works that envision women's world and language.

39 Franklin Walker, *San Francisco's Literary Frontier*, 269. For biographical accounts of Ina Coolbrith, see Walker, "Ina Donna Coolbrith," in James, *Notable American Women*, vol. 1:379–80; Starr, *Americans*, 385–90; and Shelley Armitage, "Ina Donna Coolbrith," in Lina Mainiero, ed., *American Women Writers* (New York: Ungar, 1979), vol. 1:399–401. By the time Austin placed her work in the *Overland Monthly*, the periodical's golden period was past; Bret Harte, Ambrose Bierce, John Muir, and Charles Warren Stoddard belonged to the preceding generation. (The magazine ceased publication in 1875 and was revived in 1883.) For a discussion of San Francisco's literary periodicals, see Starr, *Americans*, 133, and John Brazil, "Literature, Self, and Society: The Growth of a Political Aesthetic in Early San Francisco" (Ph.D. diss., Yale University, 1975).

40 Letter, Coolbrith to Austin, June 23, 1904, HEH. See also Fink, *I-Mary*, 63; and *EH* 229–32.

41 MS, 1905, HEH; also published in Austin, *The American Rhythm* (New York: Harcourt, Brace, 1923), 111–22.

42 Donald Ringler, "Kern County Days, 1888–1892," *Southern California Quarterly* 45 (March 1963):61, 53.

43 In a letter to the author of April 22, 1986, Mary Hunter Wolf writes: "I think my aunt always believed that the fact that there was a retarded aunt who was kept quite secret and apart as well as an alcoholic relative or two on Wallace's side—I have no confirmation of it but this was always her intimation—was the reason for her own daughter's retardation."

44 Austin, "Woman Alone," 83–84.

45 Letter, Austin to Charles Lummis, Dec. 28, 1918, HEH. Fink, *I-Mary*, 83, discusses the possibility that Ruth's birth defect derived from Mary.

46 Austin, "Woman Alone," 84; *EH* 256–57.

47 "Sabina," a poem by Savilla Graham, unpublished MS, HEH.

48 Austin, "The Truscott Luck," in *The Mother of Felipe and Other Stories*, 92.

49 Carl Van Doren, Introduction, xi.

50 Austin, "Woman Alone," 84.

51 Letter, Mary Hunter Wolf to author, April 22, 1986.

52 Fink, *I-Mary*, 80–81.

53 Helen MacKnight Doyle, *Mary Austin: Woman of Genius* (New York: Gotham House, 1939), 179; letters, Doyle to Austin, Sept. 18, 1932, and Oct. 16, 1933, HEH.

54 Fink (*I-Mary*, 120) states that Ruth was in a private institution, as does Austin. Other sources state that Santa Clara was a state institution. Mary Hunter Wolf presumed that Ruth was in a state asylum (conversation with author, Dec. 13, 1984). According to the *Santa Clara News* (March 1, 1901), Osborne Hall was a private sanitarium for the "feeble minded." It was opened by Dr. Antrim Osborne in 1901 after the California State Institution for the Feeble Minded and Epileptic moved to Eldridge. I am grateful to Bea Lichtenstein for sharing her research on the two sanitariums with me.

55 See Removal Permit, Dept. of Health, San Mateo, Calif. (Aug. 7, 1922) for Ruth's ashes to be removed to Carmel; and Permit for Removal of Cremated . . . Human Remains, Dept. of Public Health, Monterey, Calif. (July 17, 1929) for Ruth's "forgotten" ashes, stored for many years in an unpaid-for vault in Monterey, to be removed to Santa Fe, HEH. See also response of lawyer Samuel E. Vermilyea to Austin about California law regarding custody in the matter of Mary Hunter's custody, Feb. 28, 1919, HEH.

56 Letter, Austin to Charles Lummis, Dec. 28, 1918, HEH.

57 Robert Griswold, *Family and Divorce in California, 1850–1890* (Albany: State University of New York Press, 1982), 28.

58 Austin, *The Ford* (Boston: Houghton Mifflin, 1917), 171.

59 Ellen Key, *Love and Marriage* (New York: Huebsch, 1910).

60 Ellen Key, *Love and Ethics* (New York: Huebsch, 1912), 11.

61 Carl N. Degler, *At Odds* (New York: Oxford University Press, 1980), 26–51. Griswold, *Family and Divorce*, 175.

62 Bordin, *Woman and Temperance*, 114–15.

63 I am indebted to Nancy Cott's careful analysis of the difference between Key and Gilman in *The Grounding of Modern Feminism* (New Haven: Yale University Press, 1987), 47–49.

64 Griswold, *Family and Divorce*, 174.

65 Austin, "Frustrate," *The Century Magazine*, Jan. 1912:470.

66 Ibid., 467.

CHAPTER 3. A WRITER'S DEBUT

1 Letter, Wallace to Mary Austin, [July 2, 1929], HEH; Carroll Smith-Rosenberg, *Disorderly Conduct* (New York: Oxford University Press, 1985), 208. In Smith-Rosenberg's analysis of late nineteenth-century hysteria, the "suffering" woman achieved dominance "when suffering from dramatic and ever-visible symptoms. . . . Consciously or unconsciously, [women] had thus opted out of their traditional role."

2 Doyle, *Mary Austin*, 193.

3 Ibid., 194.

4 Ringler, "Kern County Days," 59.

5 See James McKeen Cattell, "The School and Family," *Popular Science Monthly* 74 (Jan. 1909):91–92.

6 Doyle, *Mary Austin*, 193.

7 Carl G. Jung, *Man and His Symbols* (New York: Dutton, 1964), 213, 215.

8 See Mary A. Hill, *Charlotte Perkins Gilman: The Making of a Radical Feminist* (Philadelphia: Temple University Press, 1980), 144–46; also 131–35.

9 Letter, Austin to Eve Lummis, July 19, 1929, HEH.

10 "An Unnatural Mother," *Impress* 2 (Nov. 17, 1894):4–5; repr. in Ann J. Lane, ed., *The Charlotte Perkins Gilman Reader* (New York: Pantheon, 1980), 57–65.

11 Charles F. Lummis, *Out West: Los Angeles and Her Makers* (Los Angeles: Out West Magazine Co., April 1909), 366. See also Lawrence Clark Powell, "Charles F. Lummis: The Land of Poco Tiempo," in *Southwest Classics* (Tucson: University of Arizona Press, 1974), 43–55. Starr describes the characteristics of "Arroyo Culture" in *Inventing the Dream*, 107–09.

12 Ben Field, "Charles Fletcher Lummis," *Overland Monthly*, July 1929:197–223. See also Dudley Gordon, *Charles F. Lummis: Crusader in Corduroy* (Los Angeles: Cultural Assets, 1972) and Starr, *Americans*, 397–401.

13 Field, "Charles Fletcher Lummis," 203.

14 Letter, Lummis to Austin, Nov. 24, 1904, HEH. See also T. M. Pearce, *Literary America, 1903–34* (Westport, Conn.: Greenwood Press, 1979), 17–21.

15 Letter, Lummis to Austin, Nov. 14, 1904, HEH. See also Pearce, *Literary America*, 18.

16 Starr, *California*, 398.

17 Letter, Austin to Frances [Eve Lummis] DeKalb, Aug. 14, 1929, HEH. Lummis called Eve "Eva"; later she preferred to be called Frances.

18 Starr, *California*, 398.

19 Letter, Austin to Eve Lummis, [1904?], HEH. Austin's remark about the margins probably referred to the copious marginal illustrations by the noted artist E. Boyd Smith. Austin remained a stickler about illustrations throughout her career. "The illustrations must be equal in authority to the text. No man can stick a feather in the hair of a studio model and call it an Indian for my book," she wrote to Ferris Greenslet on Jan. 8, 1918 (Houghton Mifflin Company Collection, Houghton Library, Harvard).

20 Letter, Austin to Eve Lummis, [1904?], HEH. See also Fink, *I-Mary*, 119.

21 A photograph in the Austin Collection (HEH) is labeled "Moody Castle where the final chapters of The Land of Little Rain were written—Harriet Baldwin's house at San Diego, 1902." Baldwin was a member of the Arroyo Seco group.

22 Letter, Ina Coolbrith to Austin, June 23, 1904, HEH.

23 Fink, *I-Mary*, 99. See also Powell, *Southwest Classics*, 52. Powell refers to Eve Lummis as "Eva."

24 See letter, Austin to Eve [Lummis] DeKalb, July 19, 1929, HEH.

25 Letters, Austin to Frances [Eve Lummis] DeKalb, Aug. 14, 1929; Austin to Lummis, Dec. 28, 1918, HEH.

26 Letter, [*The Atlantic Monthly*] Editors to Austin, Feb. 25, 1902, HEH.

27 Letter, Austin to Eve Lummis, [1904], HEH.

28 Review quoted in Doyle, *Mary Austin*, 198.

29 Letter, Austin to Eve Lummis, [1904], HEH.

30 Ibid.

31 See Doyle, *Mary Austin*, 195, 206.

32 See letter, Wallace to Mary Austin, July 2, 1929 (postmark), HEH; and Fink, *I-Mary*, 120.

33 Letter, Austin to Charles Moody, June 27, [1904?], Charles A. Moody Collection 100, Box 53, Dept. of Special Collections, University Research Library, UCLA.

34 Letter, Moody to Austin, Nov. 3, 1904, quoted in Pearce, *Literary America*, 10–11.

35 Ibid., 11.

36 Doyle, *Mary Austin*, 206: A photograph in the Austin Collection (HEH) of a Paiute Indian woman is labeled "An Ancient Mahala, My Servant at Independence," suggesting that Austin had domestic assistance.

37 Carolyn Merchant, *The Death of Nature* (New York: Harper and Row, 1983), 102.

38 Henry Chester Tracy, *The American Naturists* (New York: Dutton, 1930), 245, 295.

39 Doyle, *Mary Austin*, 207–08. See also letter, Wallace to Mary Austin, July 2, 1929 (postmark), HEH.

40 Letter, Wallace Austin to A. R. Orr, Feb. 4, 1904, HEH.

41 Letter, George Hunter to Austin, [n.d.], HEH.

42 Letter, Wallace Austin to A. R. Orr, Feb. 4, 1904, HEH.

43 Mary Austin, "How I Learned to Read and Write," in *My First Publication*, ed. James D. Hart (San Francisco: Book Club of California, 1961), 63.

44 Letters, Wallace to Mary Austin, Sept. 22, 1929, and May 13, 1930, HEH. With regard to Wallace's insurance policy, see letter, George Hunter to Mary Austin, March 28, 1932, HEH.

45 Austin, "How I Learned to Read and Write," 64.

46 Ibid.

47 Other writers have discussed the angel at their writing tables, notably New Zealand novelist Janet Frame in her autobiography *An Angel at My Table* (New York: Braziller, 1984). Frame invokes Rilke's poem "Vergers": "Reste tranquille, si soudain / L'Ange à ta table se décide; / Efface doucement les quelques rides / Que fait la nappe sous ton pain."

48 T. M. Pearce, Introduction to *The Land of Little Rain* (Albuquerque: University of New Mexico Press, 1974), vii.

49 Louise Maunsell Field, "Mary Austin, American," *The Bookman* 75 (Dec. 1932): 820. See also Rockwell D. Hunt, "California's Stately Hall of Fame: Mary Hunter Austin," *Los Angeles Times*, Jan. 19, 1941.

50 Mary Hunter Wolf, conversation with author, Dec. 1984.

51 Cynthia Ozick, "Truman Capote Reconsidered," in *Art and Ardor* (New York: Dutton, 1984), 82.

52 Jackson Lears, *No Place of Grace* (New York: Pantheon, 1981), 6.

53 James Rupert, "Mary Austin's Landscape Line in Native American Literature," *Southwest Review*, Autumn 1983:389.

54 Lears, *No Place of Grace*, 138.

55 Austin, *The Basket Woman* (Boston: Houghton Mifflin, 1904), vii.

56 Lawrence Clark Powell, "California Classics Reread," *Westways* 50 (April 1968):2.

57 Austin, "How I Learned to Read and Write," 65.

CHAPTER 4. AMONG THE CARMELITES

1 Letter, Austin to Carey McWilliams, June 14, 1929, Dept. of Special Collections, University Research Library, UCLA. McWilliams, a sociologist, attorney, and writer, was editor of the *Nation* from 1955 to 1979.

2 Fink, *I-Mary*, 122.

3 Letter, Austin to Miss Williams, Oct. 27, [1905?], Dept. of Special Collections, University Research Library, UCLA, Austin Collection 100, Box 53.

4 See Doyle, *Mary Austin*, 218.

5 Letter, Austin to Miss Williams, Oct. 27, [1905?].

6 Austin, "The Tremblor," in David Starr Jordan, ed., *The California Earthquake of 1906* (San Francisco: A. M. Robertson, 1907), 341–43.

7 Austin, "George Sterling at Carmel," *The American Mercury* 11 (May 1927):66.

8 David Starr Jordan, "Report to U.S. Census Bureau," 1880, quoted in Austin's

notes "La Ensenadita de Carmelo," [n.d.], HEH.

9 Austin, "Notes at Seven Pines—beginning July 12, '04," MS, [pp. 1–2], HEH. Perhaps too much has been made of these instances of Austin's mysticism, especially in light of the revelations of other writers. Thornton Wilder wrote in his journal of viewing in a dream the creation of *The Skin of Our Teeth*: "Had I not all my writing life been convinced of the fact that the subconscious writes our work for us, digests during the night or in *its* night the demands we make upon it, ceaselessly groping about for the subject's outlets, tapping at all the possibilities, finding relationship between all the parts to the whole and to one another—had I not long been convinced of this I would have been the other night" (Donald Gallup, ed., *The Journals of Thornton Wilder, 1939–1961* [New Haven: Yale University Press, 1985], 23.

10 Letter, Austin to Sonia Levien, Oct. 11, 1918, HEH. See also her letter to Levien of Sept. 1, 1917.

11 See Austin, "Notes on Prince Sittings," typescript, Feb. 14, 1920, HEH.

12 Austin, "Notes at Seven Pines," [p. 1].

13 Austin, "George Sterling at Carmel," 65. See also Fink, *I-Mary*, 113–22; "George Sterling" in James Hart, ed., *The Oxford Companion to American Literature* (New York: Oxford University Press, 1983); and the *Overland Monthly* 85 (Nov. 1927), an entire issue devoted to Sterling.

14 Henry F. May, *The End of American Innocence* (New York: Oxford University Press, 1979), 88.

15 Austin, "George Sterling," 65.

16 Ibid. Austin tells essentially the same story about her first meeting with Sterling in *EH* 297.

17 *EH* 297. Austin gives a slightly different account of the afternoon in "George Sterling," 65.

18 Stuart Benedict, ed., *The Literary Guide to the United States* (New York: Facts on File, 1981), 211.

19 Ella Winter, *And Not to Yield* (New York: Harcourt, Brace and World, 1963), 128, 129. In 1903 the Carmel Development Company offered waterfront lots at $50, cottages at $500, and cottage rentals at $6 per month, according to a Carmel publication *Game and Gossip* (Dec. 1977), 10.

20 Carey McWilliams, "A Letter From Carmel," *The Carmelite*, Jan. 15, 1930:4.

21 Augusta Fink, *Monterey* (San Francisco: Chronicle Books, 1972), 241.

22 Austin, "George Sterling," 66, 72. See also Austin, "A Poet in Outland," *Overland Monthly and Out West Magazine* 85 (Nov. 1927):331.

23 Austin, "George Sterling," 72.

24 Letter, Sterling to Austin, Sept. 1, 1910, HEH.

25 Austin, "George Sterling," 72.

26 David Starr Jordan, *California and the Californians* (San Francisco: A.M. Robertson, 1907), 46.

27 *EH* 302. For evidence of their friendship, see Carrie Sterling's letter to Austin, Dec. 16, 1914, HEH.

28 Letter, Austin to Charmian London, July 4, 1927, HEH.

29 Austin, "George Sterling," 67–68; essentially the same story appears in *EH* 299.

30 See letter to Sterling dated Oct. 20, 1910, in *The Letters of Ambrose Bierce*, Bertha Clark Pope, ed. (San Francisco: Book Club of California, 1922), 163.

31 See Franklin Walker, *Ambrose Bierce: The Wickedest Man in San Francisco* (San Francisco: Colt Press, 1941), 18. See also Wilson Follett, "Ambrose Bierce," *The Bookman* 68 (Nov. 1928):284–90.

32 Letter to Sterling, March 12, 1906, in Pope, *The Letters of Ambrose Bierce*, 114.

33 Ibid., 116.

34 May, *American Innocence*, 88.

35 Austin, "George Sterling," 69; see also *EH* 299.

36 Austin, "George Sterling," 69.

37 From Austin, "Three at Carmel," *The Saturday Review of Literature* 5 (Sept. 29, 1928):165.

38 Doyle, *Mary Austin*, 239.

39 Austin, "The Tremblor," 359.

40 Letters to Sterling, Aug. 11, 1906, and May 24, 1910, in Pope, *The Letters of Ambrose Bierce*, 121, 154.

41 Fink, *Monterey*, 243.

42 Austin, "George Sterling," 66. For a description of Carmel's metamorphosis between 1927 and 1936, see Winter, *And Not to Yield*, 127–35.

43 Letter, Sterling to Austin, Sept. 1, 1910, HEH.

44 Fink, *Monterey*, 241.

45 Letter, Austin to Houghton Mifflin, July 16, 1907, HEH.

46 Letters, Austin to Houghton Mifflin, Sept. 30, 1907 (with note affixed signed "W.S.B."); W. S. Booth [Houghton Mifflin] to Austin, Sept. 10, 1907, HEH.

47 Fink, *Monterey*, 223.

48 Austin, "The Garden Book, Carmel-By-the-Sea," MS, May 1, 1913, [p. 1], HEH.

49 Austin, "The Garden Book," [p. 2]. Austin bought property sold very cheaply by the Carmel Development Company. For $250 down and an additional $1,612.50, she bought lots 9, 11, 12, 13, 14, 15, 16, 17, 18, 19, 20, and 32, according to documents in Box 24a, HEH. The usual terms were $250 down and monthly payments of $5 for additional lots.

50 Kevin Starr, "Mary Austin: Mystic, Writer, Conservationist," *Sierra Bulletin*, Nov.–Dec. 1976:34.

51 Doyle, *Mary Austin*, 219–20.

52 Austin, "George Sterling," 69. French, whose poetry Sterling greatly admired, committed suicide at his home after Austin went abroad in 1907.

53 Ibid., 70.

54 Letter, Austin to Jack London, April 10, [n.d.], HEH.

55 Austin, *Outland*, published in England under the pseudonym Gordon Stairs (London: John Murray, 1910). For background on the creation of the novel,

see Austin, "A Poet in Outland," *Overland Monthly and Out West Magazine* 85 (Nov. 1927):331.

56 Van Wyck Brooks, *The Confident Years*, 278.

57 Letter, Austin to Miss Williams, Oct. 27, [n.d.], HEH.

58 For a later fictional critique of marriage, see Austin, "American Marriage," *The American Mercury* 6 (Sept. 1925):1–6.

59 "Summons to Appear before the Superior Court of California," County of San Bernadino, Oct. 21, 1914, HEH.

60 Fink, *I-Mary*, 120.

61 Kate Chopin, *The Awakening* (1899; repr., New York: W. W. Norton, 1976), 113.

62 Lewis, *Edith Wharton*, 154.

63 David Brion Davis, *Homicide in American Fiction, 1798–1860* (Ithaca, N.Y.: Cornell University Press, 1958), 209.

64 See Davis, *Homicide*, 179–209.

65 See George Levine, "Realism Reconsidered," in John Halperin, ed., *The Theory of the Novel: New Essays* (New York: Oxford University Press, 1974), 238.

66 Letter, Austin to London, April 10, [n.d.], HEH.

67 *The Sturdy Oak: A Composite Novel of American Politics* (New York: Henry Holt, 1917).

68 Carl Van Doren, *Three Worlds* (New York: Harper and Brothers, 1936), 191, 190, 189, 194.

69 Ibid., 193.

70 *The New York Times*, May 16, 1908:280; *Outlook* 89 (June 6, 1908):314.

71 Doyle, *Mary Austin*, 220.

72 Austin, "A Poet in Outland," 331. *Santa Lucia* is dedicated to Charlotte Hoffman, in whose Carmel home Austin apparently stayed when she was completing the novel. The dedication reads: "To C.H. / To the kindly rooftree / The hospitable board / And the beauty of friendliness."

73 Pearce, *Mary Hunter Austin*, 14.

74 Fink, *I-Mary*, 148.

75 Doyle, *Mary Austin*, 228, 229.

76 Zora Neale Hurston, *Their Eyes Were Watching God* (1937; repr., New York: Negro Universities Press, 1969), 9.

77 Patricia Meyer Spacks, *Gossip* (New York: Alfred A. Knopf, 1985), 7.

78 Marjorie Pryse, Introduction to Austin, *Stories from the Country of Lost Borders* (New Brunswick, N.J.: Rutgers University Press, 1987), xxxiii.

79 Spacks, *Gossip*, 5.

80 Ibid., 3, 7.

81 Ibid., 13.

82 Despite her initial disillusionment with the theater, Austin wrote several other plays on Indian subjects. One of them, *Fire*, was successfully produced at the Forest Theater in 1914.

83 "Four New American Plays," *The New York Times*, June 4, 1911: sec. 6, 347.

84 Adolph Klauber, "Making a Pale Face of the Noble Red-Man," *The New York Times*, March 5, 1911: sec. 7, 2.

85 Letter, Edward Curtis to Austin, [1911], HEH.

86 Program, *The Arrow Maker*, HEH. Austin's appreciation of authentic American Indian dance drama was refined with later study and experience. See Austin, "American Indian Dance Drama," *The Yale Review* 19 (June 1930):732–45.

87 Elmire Zolla, *The Writer and the Shaman*, trans. Raymond Rosenthal (New York: Harcourt Brace Jovanovich, 1973), 190.

88 Austin, *The Arrow Maker* (New York: Duffield, 1911), x, 11.

89 Van Wyck Brooks, "Reviewer's Note-Book," *The Freeman*, June 9, 1920:311.

90 Austin, *The Arrow Maker*, xi–xii.

91 John Collier, "Back of Our Footlights: The Half-Forgotten Social Functions of the Drama," *Survey*, June 5, 1915:213.

92 Zolla, *The Writer and the Shaman*, 189–90.

93 Austin, *The Arrow Maker*, 125, 126.

94 Ibid., xii.

CHAPTER 5. LITERARY NEW YORK

1 I am most grateful to Karen Langlois of Claremont College, who is writing a dissertation on the New York years of Mary Austin, for providing me with the following chronology: 1912 in New York; 1913 in California; 1914, January–June in New York, June–October in California, October–December in New York; 1915 in New York, with a brief visit to California; 1916 in New York; 1917 in New York, with a brief stay in California; 1918, January–May in New York, May–October in California, November in Santa Fe; 1919 in Santa Fe; 1920 in New York; 1921, January–April in New York, April–October in England, October–December in New York; 1922–25 in New York, with trips to Santa Fe until she relocated there permanently in 1925. Austin was sensitive about her royalties from books; hence, she kept better records of her earnings from journalism and lecturing—earnings that paid her bills. The Austin file of the Houghton Mifflin Company Collection, held by the Houghton Library at Harvard, indicates that for most of her career Austin could not support herself on her book royalties.

2 Letter, Austin to W. S. Booth [Houghton Mifflin], June 11, 1907, HEH.

3 Letter, Austin to Messrs. Houghton, Mifflin & Co., Sept. 10, 1907, HEH. See Karen Langlois, "Mary Austin and Houghton Mifflin Company: A Case Study in the Marketing of a Western Writer," *Western American Literature* 23 (Summer 1988):31–42.

4 Letter, Austin to Daniel MacDougal, May 10, [1922], HEH. During 1922 her meager earnings were supplemented by her friends. *No. 26 Jayne Street* (1920) had been a financial failure for her.

5 Mary Austin, "New York Notebook," 1911, HEH, Box 24c.

6 Clipping from *New York World*, Aug. 13, 1913, in "New York Notebook," 1913.

7 Letter, Austin to MacDougal, March 8, [1922], HEH.

8 "New York Notebook," 1911.

9 Letter, Austin to MacDougal, Jan. 28, [1922], HEH (italics added).

10 Mary Austin, "New York: Dictator of American Criticism," *The Nation* 111 (July 31, 1920):129.

11 Ibid. Curiously, Austin includes Gertrude Stein in her list of literary "gentlemen."

12 Ibid., 130.

13 See, for example, Paul Lauter, "Race and Gender in the Shaping of the American Literary Canon: A Case History from the Twenties," *Feminist Studies* 9 (Fall 1983):435–63.

14 Austin quoted in Pearce, *Beloved House*, 56.

15 Letter, Ernestine Evans to Austin, [n.d.], HEH.

16 The National Arts Club Constitution and Membership List (1928), 4, HEH, Box 54; Mary Hunter Wolf, interview with author, Dec. 1984; Austin quoted in Pearce, *Beloved House*, 56.

17 William Webster Ellsworth, "Speech at Dinner for Mary Austin," National Arts Club, Jan. 8, 1922, typescript, HEH. See Joseph Hergesheimer, "The Feminine Nuisance in American Literature," *The Yale Review* 10 (July 1921):716–25.

18 Letter, Austin to MacDougal, Jan. 9, 1922, in Pearce, *Literary America*, 154–55. In the sixty-two surviving letters that Austin wrote to MacDougal, she addressed him as "dear friend." See also Fink, *I-Mary*, 203–04, for an account of this dinner.

19 See Lawrence Clark Powell, "A Prophetic Passage," *Westways* (Feb. 1973):61–62. Powell writes: "What Mary Austin lacked in beauty she made up in a commanding presence. Though *oversupplied with male hormones,* she did not emulate Willa Cather and take a woman companion" (my emphasis).

20 Letter, Austin to MacDougal, Jan. 9, 1922, quoted in Pearce, *Literary America*, 155.

21 Ibid.

22 Ibid., 156.

23 Letter, Austin to MacDougal, May 10, [1922], HEH.

24 Letter, Carl Van Doren to Austin, Jan. 9, 1922, HEH.

25 Letter, Austin to MacDougal, Dec. 31, 1921, HEH.

26 Letter, Austin to MacDougal, Jan. 9, 1922, quoted in Pearce, *Literary America*, 156.

27 Letter, Austin to MacDougal, Jan. 2, [1922], HEH.

28 See David Seldeman, *The New Republic: A Voice of Modern Liberalism* (New York: Praeger, 1986) for a carefully researched, revisionist historical analysis of the magazine.

29 Letter, Herbert Croly to Mabel Sterne, Aug. 1, 1919, HEH.

30 Letter, Austin to MacDougal, Jan. 28, 1922, HEH. Austin incorrectly identifies Hallowell as "Halliday" in her autobiography.

31 Letter, Croly to Austin, Nov. 3, 1924, HEH.

32 Henry Seidel Canby, *American Memoir* (Boston: Houghton Mifflin, 1947), 303.

33 Letter, Canby to Austin, July 30, 1920, Canby Collection, Beinecke Rare Book and Manuscript Library, Yale University.

34 Letter, Austin to MacDougal, Dec. 31, 1921, HEH.

35 Letter, Austin to MacDougal, Jan. 2, [1922], HEH.

36 Canby, *American Memoir*, 303, 304, 332, 305–06.

37 Elizabeth Shepley Sergeant, *Willa Cather: A Memoir* (Lincoln: University of Nebraska Press, 1953), 226. In an interview, Mary Hunter Wolf remembered seeing Cather writing letters in her aunt's study. A photograph sent to "Lady" Canby, now in the Canby Collection at Yale, was labeled by Austin, "The corner of my library where Cather wrote the first chapters of Death Comes for the Archbishop in the Summer of 1926." See also Pearce, *Beloved House*, 176–77, and Phyllis Robinson, *Willa: The Life of Willa Cather* (New York: Holt, Rinehart, and Winston, 1984), 254.

38 See Robinson, *Willa*, 246.

39 Letter, Austin to Ferris Greenslet, Dec. 6, 1930, HEH.

40 Mary Hunter Wolf, interview with author, Dec. 13, 1984.

41 Mary Austin, "On the American Scene," *The Saturday Review of Literature*, Aug. 11, 1928:34.

42 Letter, Austin to MacDougal, Dec. 31, 1921, HEH.

43 Letter, Willa Cather to E. K. Brown, Oct. 7, 1946, Cather Collection, Beinecke Rare Book and Manuscript Library, Yale University.

44 This is a central argument in Sharon O'Brien's analysis of Cather in *Willa Cather: The Emerging Voice* (New York: Oxford University Press, 1986).

45 Lois P. Rudnick, "Mabel Dodge Luhan and the Myth of Southwestern Particularity," Southwest Institute for Research on Women, Working Paper no. 7 (1982), 4; Rudnick, *Mabel Dodge Luhan* (Albuquerque: University of New Mexico Press, 1984), x.

46 Letter, Austin to Mabel Dodge Luhan, Oct. 15, [1924], Luhan Collection, Beinecke Rare Book and Manuscript Library, Yale University (hereafter cited as Beinecke/Luhan).

47 Lincoln Steffens, *The Autobiography of Lincoln Steffens* (New York: Harcourt Brace, 1931), 654.

48 Steffens, *Autobiography*, 655; also see letter, Steffens to Jack Reed, Nov. 19, 1914, in *The Letters of Lincoln Steffens*, vol. 1, 1889–1919 (New York: Harcourt Brace, 1938); Steffens quoted in Justin Kaplan, *Lincoln Steffens* (New York: Simon and Schuster, 1974), 201; Karen Langlois, "Mary Austin and Lincoln Steffens," *Huntington Library Quarterly* 49 (Autumn 1986):31–42; Glaspell quoted in Kaplan, *Steffens*, 201.

49 Elizabeth Shepley Sergeant, "Mary Austin: A Portrait," *Saturday Review of Literature*, Sept. 8, 1934:96.

50 Austin, "American Women and the Intellectual Life," *The Bookman* 53 (Aug. 1921):481, 483; see also Rosenberg, *Beyond Separate Spheres*.

51 Austin, "American Women," 484. See Peter Conn's analysis of Gilman's thought and *Women and Economics* in *The Divided Mind* (Cambridge: Cambridge University Press, 1983), 158.

52 Austin, "American Women," 483, 485.

53 Letter, Austin to Mabel Dodge Luhan, [1925], Beinecke/Luhan.

54 See Ina Sizer Cassidy, "I-Mary and Me," *New Mexico Quarterly* 9 (Nov. 1939): 203–11.

55 Fink, *I-Mary*, 207; see pp. 204–19 for a fine account of the particulars of the Austin/MacDougal relationship described in the correspondence; Powell, "A Prophetic Passage," 62–63.

56 Austin, Introduction and section titled "Terminology," *Everyman's Genius* (Indianapolis: Bobbs-Merrill, 1925).

57 Austin, Introduction to *Everyman's Genius*.

58 "Bequest of Brain to Cornell University, Ithaca, N. Y.," Dec. 15, 1927. Mary Hunter Wolf, a witness, does not remember this bequest being carried out. The form read: "Recognizing the need of studying the brains of educated persons in order to determine their weight, form, and fissural pattern, the correlation with bodily and mental powers of various kinds and degrees and the influence of sex, age, and inheritance, the undersigned bequeaths her brain to be preserved in the Burt G. Wilder Brain Collection."

59 "Memorandum in Respect to a Bequest of a Brain to Cornell University for the Preservation for Study in the Burt G. Wilder Brain Collection." See also William Leach, *True Love and Perfect Union* (New York: Basic Books, 1980), 44–50, for an excellent discussion of Wilder's place in the American scientific imagination of the nineteenth century. Wilder, a feminist, was a generation older than Austin. His writings on sexual relations were in line with hers.

60 Dashiell Hammett, "Review of *Everyman's Genius*," *Forum*, Aug. 1925:317. I am grateful to Dorothy Mandel for calling this to my attention.

61 Nancy Porter, "Afterword," in Austin, *A Woman of Genius* (Old Westbury: Feminist Press, 1985), 296–97.

62 "Note on Biography and Autobiography," *Everyman's Genius*, 358. Compare Austin in Showalter, *These Modern Women*, 78–86.

63 See Porter, "Afterword," 213; labor organizer Helen Gurley Flynn recalled that Austin was a sister member. Austin, not much of a "joiner," must have attended infrequently, as she does not appear in Judith Schwarz's carefully documented *Radical Feminists of Heterodoxy: Greenwich Village, 1912–1940* (Lebanon, N.H.: New Victoria, 1982). Cott, *The Grounding of Modern Feminism*, 38, writes that "heterodoxy epitomized the Feminism of the time." Cott reminds us that the term *feminism* first surfaced in the 1910s.

64 Letter, Jack London to Austin, Nov. 5, 1915, in Pearce, *Literary America*, 73–74.

65 Ibid.

66 William Allen White, "A Woman of Genius" (review of *Earth Horizon*), *The Saturday Review of Literature* 11 (Nov. 12, 1932):235.

67 See Porter, "Afterword," *WOG*, 300; see also Pearce, *Mary Hunter Austin*, 40. At the Fabian Summer School, Inez Haynes Irwin introduced Austin to H. G. Wells, a great admirer of her work; also present were California feminist Anne Martin, who was a friend of the Hoovers until Herbert Hoover had to bail her out of jail after a feminist demonstration in London, and Marie Stopes, the feminist author of *Married Love*, an important book for Austin.

68 Willa Cather, Preface (1932) to *Song of the Lark* (Boston: Houghton Mifflin, 1983).

69 Theodore Dreiser, *The Genius* (Cleveland: World Publishing, 1915).

70 See Porter, "Afterword," *WOG*, 304.

71 Cather, *The Song of the Lark*, 552.

72 Mary Austin received 15 percent royalties on *No. 26 Jayne Street*, which was published on May 14, 1920. Houghton Mifflin estimated that sales of 3,172 copies would cover their costs. Even if this many copies had been sold, Austin's royalties would have amounted to only $951.60 minus the $750 paid as an advance to her in May 1920. Houghton Mifflin tried to get fifteen publishers (including several in England) to take the novel; all declined it; "Production Record Summary," Jan. 31, 1905, to March 14, 1934, Houghton Mifflin Company Collection, Houghton Library, Harvard. Austin wrote: "The financial failure of '26 Jayne Street' led to my temporary abandonment of the novel form, and a reversion to books of an earlier type. I republished in America a book written for A. and C. Black, of London, 'Land of the Sun,' in which I had recorded the final impact of the California scene, the California which I had known and felt before it succumbed to the tourist assault. I began the work of revamping 'The American Rhythm,' adding to it a more extended survey of aboriginal poetry and copious notes. Also I began to prepare a new volume on the Southwest, 'The Land of Journeys' Ending'" (*EH* 337).

73 *The Dial* 69 (Oct. 1920): 432; Ludwig Lewisohn in *The Nation* 110 (June 19, 1920): 827; *The New York Times* (May 23, 1920), 271; Henrietta Malkiel in *The New York Call* (July 25, 1920), 11. For a fuller account of the production, see Karen Langlois, "Mary Austin and the New Theatre: The 1911 Production of *The Arrow Maker*," *Theatre History Studies* 8 (1988):71–87.

74 This ethos is the subject of William Leach's *True Love and Perfect Union*.

75 Leach, *True Love*, 11.

76 Letter, Austin to Herbert Hoover, June 4, 1918, quoted in Pearce, *Literary America*, 94.

77 Ibid. Mary Hunter Wolf shared with me her impression of Austin's friendship with Hoover.

78 Austin anticipates recent feminist analysis of material circumstances. See, for example, Dolores Hayden, *The Grand Domestic Revolution* (Cambridge, Mass.: MIT Press, 1981).

79 Van Wyck Brooks, "Reviewer's Note-Book," *The Freeman*, June 9, 1920:311.

In *Love and the Soul-Maker* (New York: D. Appleton, 1914), Austin created a dialogue about true love and the possibilities inherent in marriage to use love for creative projects and personal transcendence.

80 Brooks, "Note-Book," 311.

81 Ibid.

82 Letter, Brooks to Austin, Tuesday morning [n.d., 1920], HEH.

83 Letter, Brooks to Gray, Thursday morning [n.d., 1920], HEH.

84 Letter, Brooks to Austin, June 24, 1920, HEH.

85 Pearce, *Literary America*, 125.

86 Brooks, "Note-Book," 311.

87 Carl Van Doren, *Contemporary Novelists* (New York: Macmillan, 1922), 142.

88 Letter, Austin to Carl Van Doren, [July, 1923], in Van Doren, *Three Worlds*, 191. In this letter Austin puts Ruth's age at 11 when she was committed to an institution; the girl was probably nearer to age 13.

89 Letter, Austin to MacDougal, Oct. 28, [1922], HEH.

90 Nina Auerbach, "Magi and Maidens," *Critical Inquiry*, Winter 1981:286, 284.

91 Letter, Austin to MacDougal, Jan. 2, [1922], HEH.

92 Alicia Ostriker, *Writing Like A Woman* (Ann Arbor: The University of Michigan Press, 1986), 146.

CHAPTER 6. THE SOUTHWEST BECKONS

1 Lois Rudnick: *Mabel Dodge Luhan* (Albuquerque: University of New Mexico Press, 1984), x, xi, 303.

2 Arrell Morgan Gibson, *The Santa Fe and Taos Colonies* (Norman: University of Oklahoma Press, 1983), 219.

3 Rudnick, "Re-Naming The Land: Anglo Expatriate Women in the Southwest," in Norwood and Monk, *The Desert Is No Lady*, 15.

4 Lawrence Clark Powell, "A Prophetic Passage," 62; letter, Austin to Luhan, April 29, [1923], Beinecke/Luhan.

5 Austin, "Why I Live in Santa Fe," *The Golden Book Magazine* 16 (Oct. 1932): 306, 307. The estimated cost of Austin's house was $9,975; the outside dimensions were 35 by 78 feet; see "Permit to Erect Residence in Santa Fe," Sept. 30, 1925, HEH. The home is now occupied by the Gerald Peters Gallery, additions and many improvements having been made. Photographs of the house appear in the Austin Collection photographs at the Huntington Library and in Pearce's *Beloved House*. Mary Hunter Wolf has shared her recollections of the house with me.

6 Dudley Wynn, "Mary Austin, Woman Alone," *The Virginia Quarterly Review*, Spring 1937:250, 247.

7 Pearce, *Beloved House*, 42.

8 Letter, Austin to Sinclair Lewis, Dec. 12, 1920, Beinecke/Lewis Collection.

9 Austin quoted in Pearce, *Beloved House*, 78.

10 Austin to Franklin K. Lane, Jan. 16, 1919, HEH.

11 Rudnick, *Luhan*, 178, 179.

12 Letters, Austin to Luhan, July 26, 1922, and Feb. 1 [1923], Beinecke/Luhan. Austin often used the singular when referring to "the Indian," as if Indians were a uniform category.

13 Letter, Austin to Luhan, April 4, 1923, Beinecke/Luhan.

14 Richard Drinnon, *Facing West: The Metaphysics of Indian-Hating and Empire-Building* (Minneapolis: University of Minnesota Press, 1980), 205.

15 Rudnick, *Luhan*, 176. For an illuminating discussion of Mabel and Tony's marriage, see pp. 238–41.

16 Rudnick, "The Myth," 4.

17 Letter, Luhan to Austin, Nov. 2, [1923?], HEH.

18 Letter, Luhan to Austin, Taos, Thursday, [1923], HEH.

19 Letter, Austin to Daniel MacDougal, Aug. 15, 1923, HEH.

20 Rudnick, *Luhan*, 139. See Mabel Dodge Luhan, *Intimate Memories: Background* (New York: Harcourt Brace, 1933) and *Lorenzo in Taos* (New York: Alfred A. Knopf, 1932), Luhan's only published book-length work before Austin's death.

21 Mabel Dodge Luhan, *Winter in Taos* (New York: Harcourt Brace, 1935), 93.

22 Ibid., 131.

23 Letter, Austin to Luhan, [1925], Beinecke/Luhan.

24 Austin, *Isidro* (Boston: Houghton Mifflin, 1905), 267.

25 Sandra M. Gilbert, "Costumes of the Mind: Transvestism in Modern Literature," *Critical Inquiry* 7 (Winter 1980):394, 397.

26 See Gilbert in Showalter, *The New Feminist Criticism*, 391–417.

27 See Margaret Homans, "'Her Very Own Howl,'" *Signs* 9 (Winter 1983):186–205; Rachel Blau DuPlessis, "For the Etruscans," in Showalter, *The New Feminist Criticism*, 271–91. Both these feminist critics use the term *oppressive male authority*.

28 Pearce, *Mary Hunter Austin*, 97.

29 Ibid., 95, 96. Pearce praises the novel for "the pictorial enrichment which nature brings to the eye, the spiritual presence felt in the outer world, the fundamental truths in folkways, the need for communal sharing, the education of men to women's new role in the world, the analysis of individual as well as social values in patterns, and the true relation of sex to human motivation."

30 See Thorstein Veblen, "The Barbarian Status of Women," *American Journal of Sociology* 4 (Jan. 1899):503–14. In all her writings on sexual relations, Austin demonstrates a familiarity with Veblen's views on patriarchy and the subservient status of women in modern society, especially in marriage.

31 Austin, "Sex in American Literature," *The Bookman* 57 (June 1923):389.

32 Mabel Dodge Luhan, "Mary Austin: A Woman," in *Mary Austin: A Memorial* (Santa Fe: Laboratory of Anthropology, 1944), 19–20.

33 Ibid., 22.

34 Letter, Austin to Luhan, [1925], Beinecke/Luhan.

35 Ibid.

36 Letter, Austin to Luhan, Dec. 5, 1922, Beinecke/Luhan.

37 Mary Hunter Wolf, interview with the author.

38 Letter, Austin to Luhan, April 30, [early 1920s], Beinecke/Luhan.

39 Letter, Austin to Luhan, May 10, [n.d.], Beinecke/Luhan.

40 Letter, Austin to Luhan, March 5, 1920, Beinecke/Luhan.

41 Letter, Austin to Luhan, May 22, [1922], Beinecke/Luhan.

42 Letter, Austin to Luhan, Dec. 5, 1922, Beinecke/Luhan. Some of Austin's magazine essays from this period include "Science for the Unscientific," *The Bookman* 55 (Aug. 1922):561–66; "The Need for a New Social Concept," *The New Republic* 26 (Aug. 9, 1922):298–301; "Religion in the United States," *The Century Magazine* 104 (Aug. 1922):527–38; "Greatness in Women," *The North American Review* 217 (Jan.–June 1923):197–203; "Do We Need a New Religion?" *The Century Magazine* 106 (Sept. 1923):756–64; "Sex in American Literature," *The Bookman* 57 (June 1923):385–93; "Women as Audience," *The Bookman* 55 (March 1922); and many reviews.

43 Letter, Austin to Luhan, Oct. 8, [1924], Beinecke/Luhan.

44 Letter, Austin to Luhan, Sept. 28, [1920], Beinecke/Luhan.

45 Ibid.

46 Anon., "The Literary Spotlight, XXII: Mary Austin," *The Bookman* 58 (Sept. 1923):47, 51.

47 Sinclair Lewis quoted in Pearce, *Beloved House*, 49.

48 Letter, Austin to Lewis, Dec. 12, 1920, HEH.

49 Letter, Austin to Lewis, Feb. 28, 1931, Beinecke/Lewis Collection.

50 See letter, Lewis to Austin, May 27, [n.d.], HEH.

51 Letter, Luhan to Austin, [n.d.], HEH.

52 Letter, Austin to Luhan, Nov. 12, [n.d.], Beinecke/Luhan.

53 Letter, Austin to Luhan, March 5, [1920], Beinecke/Luhan.

54 Letter, Austin to Luhan, Aug. 26, 1929, Beinecke/Luhan.

55 Mary Hunter Wolf, conversation with author; letter, Austin to Luhan, Aug. 26, 1929, Beinecke/Luhan.

56 Austin, "Sex in American Literature," 393.

57 Letter, Austin to Luhan, Sept. 25, [1925], Beinecke/Luhan; Austin, "Sex in American Literature," 387; Austin, *Everyman's Genius*.

58 Letter, Austin to Luhan, Sept. 25, [1925].

59 See Carroll Smith-Rosenberg, "The Female World of Love and Ritual: Relations between Women in Nineteenth-Century America," *Signs* 1 (Autumn 1975):29. Smith-Rosenberg's analytical framework to describe female relationships posits a spectrum defined by "committed heterosexuality" at one end and "uncompromising homosexuality" at the other, with "a wide latitude of emotions and sexual feelings" lying between. Her continuum is useful for recognizing the very wide range of female friendship patterns that existed among nineteenth-century women, as well as women whose formative years occurred in the early twentieth century.

60 Letter, Austin to Luhan, [1925], Beinecke/Luhan.

61 Letter, Austin to Luhan, June 23, [n.d.], Beinecke/Luhan.

62 Letter, Austin to Luhan, May 14, [1922], Beinecke/Luhan. See Austin, *Everyman's Genius*.

63 See Howard Lamar, ed., *The Reader's Encyclopedia of the American West* (New York: Crowell, 1977), 237–39, for biographical material on Collier's reformist career. See also letter, Austin to Luhan, Feb. 21, [1923], May 16, [1923?], and May 25, [1923], Beinecke/Luhan.

64 See Austin's extensive correspondence with Densmore, HEH. The twelve volumes documenting Densmore's work among the Indians of almost every American tribe, held by the Smithsonian Institution's Bureau of American Ethnology, has received extravagant praise from modern translators Yvor Winters and Kenneth Rexroth. For a good biographical introduction, see Thomas Vennum, "Frances Densmore," in Barbara Sicherman and Carol Hurd Green, eds., *Notable American Women: The Modern Period* (Cambridge, Mass.: Harvard University Press, 1980), 185–86.

65 Letter, Austin to Luhan, Nov. 9, [1920], Beinecke/Luhan.

66 Austin in *The Yale Review* 19 (June 1930):732–45. See also Austin's response to Alice Corbin Henderson's criticism of her use of the word *Amerind*, letter to the Chicago *Daily News*, June 8, 1922.

67 Letter, Witter Bynner to Austin, May 26, 1930, HEH. See also Pearce, *Literary America*, 227–42, for other letters and biographical information on Bynner, a colorful Santa Fe figure.

68 Letter, Austin to Arthur Davison Ficke, March 27, 1930, HEH.

69 Letters, Austin to Luhan, Nov. 9, [1920], and Dec. 12, 1920, Beinecke/Luhan. An article by D. H. Lawrence about the West and Walter Lippmann's response in *The New Republic* (Dec. 15, 1920) prompted Austin's indignation.

70 Letter, Austin to Luhan, Jan. 1, [1922], Beinecke/Luhan.

71 See letters, Austin to Luhan, Jan. 12 and 27, [1923], Beinecke/Luhan. See Lamar, *Reader's Encyclopedia*, 238a for information about Collier's affiliation with women's clubs.

72 Burke and Austin quoted in Gibson, *The Santa Fe and Taos Colonies*, 215; Austin, "Social and Economic Constitution of the New Mexico Pueblo" (furnished to Senator Bratton for congressional report), Santa Fe, n.d., HEH.

73 Gibson, *Colonies*, 224, 242.

74 Lawrence C. Kelly, *The Assault of Assimilation: John Collier and the Origins of Indian Policy Reform* (Albuquerque: University of New Mexico Press, 1983), xxv.

75 Letter, Austin to Luhan, Feb. 1, [1923]. Letters, Austin to Collier, April 22 and May 6, 1930, Sterling Memorial Library, Yale University (hereafter cited as SML).

76 Letters, Collier to Austin, April 18, 1930, and Austin to Collier, April 22, 1930, SML; see also Austin's letter to Collier, April 11, 1930, SML. The Leavitt Bill, containing many provisions for Indian arts and crafts, was passed in 1932. It was not until a year after Austin's death that a federal act was passed to appoint

an arts and crafts board to protect the Indian crafts market and to "promote economic welfare" of "Indian tribes and the Indian wards of the government" (U.S. Code Annotated Title 25, 305a, Aug. 27, 1935, Ch. 748, Stat. 891).

77 Letter, Austin to Collier, May 6, 1930, SML.

78 Letter, Austin to Luhan, May 25, [1923], Beinecke/Luhan.

79 Austin, "Why Americanize the Indian?" *The Forum* 82 (Sept. 1929):167. Statistics taken from the *Annual Report of the Commissioner of Indian Affairs* for the fiscal year ending June 30, 1925 (HEH) reveal that almost 10,000 Indian youngsters were in government reservation boarding schools, 8,500 in nonreservation boarding schools, and 6,000 were in mission boarding schools. Of the 65,000 Indian youths in school, 34,452 were in public schools; 12,190 youths were eligible but not in school. The Indian population in the U.S., exclusive of Alaska, totaled 175,539 males and 174,056 females. Austin's close friend and neighbor Frank Applegate served on the board of the El Rito School in New Mexico.

80 Austin, "The Return of Sally Jack," *The Brown Book of Boston*, Nov. 1900:134–35.

81 Austin, "Why Americanize the Indian?" 169; letter, Austin to Luhan, May 25, [1923], Beinecke/Luhan. See Kate Peck Kent, *Navajo Weaving* (Santa Fe: School of American Research Press, 1985) for important background on the first phase of the "rug period" (1895–1940) and the influence of the trading posts on the styles and patterns of weaving.

82 Letter, Austin to Collier, May 16, 1930, SML.

83 Letter, Austin to Secretary Ray Lyman Wilbur, March 4, 1931, HEH.

84 Wynn, "Mary Austin," 249.

85 Drinnon, *Facing West*, 210.

86 Letter, Austin to Collier, May 26, 1930, SML.

87 See Drinnon, *Facing West*, 210–11.

CHAPTER 7. THE PHOTOGRAPHIC IMAGINATION

1 Powell, *Southwest Classics*, 95.

2 Ina Sizer Cassidy, "I-Mary and Me: The Chronicle of a Friendship," *The New Mexico Quarterly* 9 (Nov. 1939):210.

3 Ibid., 205.

4 Letter, E. Bickner Kirk (art editor of *The Century*) to Austin, Oct. 4, 1923, HEH. Instead the book was illustrated by John Edwin Jackson, selected by the magazine.

5 Letter, Howard Lamar to author, Feb. 23, 1987.

6 Ralph F. Bogardus, "The Photographer's Eye: Henry James and the American Scene," *History of Photography* 8 (July–Sept. 1984):179, 186.

7 Stieglitz quoted in F. Richard Thomas, *Literary Admirers of Alfred Stieglitz* (Carbondale: University of Southern Illinois Press, 1983), 9.

8 Ibid., 7.

9 See Robert Doty, *Photo-Secession: Stieglitz and the Fine-Art Movement in Photography* (New York: Dover, 1978).

10 See Alfred Stieglitz, *Camera Work: A Pictorial Guide*, ed. Marianne Fulton Margolis (New York: Dover, 1978), ix–xi; and Doty, *Photo-Secession*, 28. Others who exhibited as Photo-Secessionists included Edward Steichen, Joseph Keiley, George Seeley, Clarence White, Gertrude Käsebier, Frank Eugene, Heinrich Kühn, Adolf DeMeyer, and Paul Strand.

11 Bogardus, "The Photographer's Eye," 194.

12 Vera Norwood, "The Photographer and the Naturalist: Laura Gilpin and Mary Austin in the Southwest," *Journal of American Culture* 5 (Summer 1982):1.

13 Martha A. Sandweiss, "Laura Gilpin and the Tradition of American Landscape Photography," in Norwood and Monk, *The Desert Is No Lady*, 63.

14 Norwood, "The Photographer and the Naturalist," 24.

15 See Laura Gilpin, *The Enduring Navajo* (Austin: University of Texas Press, 1968). The first major study of Gilpin's life and career is Martha A. Sandweiss, *Laura Gilpin: An Enduring Grace* (Austin: University of Texas Press/Amon Carter, 1986).

16 Ansel Adams, *Ansel Adams: An Autobiography* (Boston: Little, Brown, 1985), 87.

17 Virginia Adams, conversation with author, Jan. 6, 1987.

18 *Ansel Adams*, 87.

19 Letter, Bender to Austin, March 23, 1929, HEH.

20 *Ansel Adams*, 89.

21 Mary Hunter Wolf, conversation with author, Jan. 30, 1987.

22 *Ansel Adams*, 92, 93–94.

23 Letter, Adams to Austin, Jan. 31, 1929 (postmark), HEH.

24 Letter, Austin to Adams, Feb. 23, 1929, HEH.

25 Ibid.

26 Austin, typescript notes, "Lectures," 1922–1931, HEH. Austin signed a contract with Houghton Mifflin on Feb. 8, 1929, to publish both *Earth Horizon* and *Starry Adventure*. The publisher agreed to pay her an advance of $2,500 for *EH* in five installments between Feb. 8, 1929, and April 1930. A separate record for *SA* indicates payment of a $1,250 advance on Feb. 8, 1929. *SA* was published on May 27, 1931, *EH* on Aug. 26, 1932. "Production Record Summary," Jan. 31, 1905 to March 14, 1934, Houghton Mifflin Company Collection, Houghton Library, Harvard.

27 Letter, Adams to Austin, Jan. 31, 1929 (postmark), HEH. See also *EH* 35–38.

28 See letters, Charlotte Sander, Adult Education Council of Chicago, to Austin, Oct. 15, 1932, and May 14, 1930; Margaret Huston, Stanford University, to Austin, Jan. 26, 1928; and Ethel Strohmeier, University of California, Berkeley, to Austin, Feb. 21, 1928, HEH.

29 Letter, Austin to MacDougal, May 4, [1923], HEH.

30 Austin, "Women as Audience," *The Bookman* 55 (March 1922):3.

31 Ibid.

32 Austin, typescript, [1925?], 6, HEH.

33 *Ansel Adams*, 89.

34 Letter, Adams to Austin, Jan. 29, 1929 (postmark), HEH.

35 Ibid.

36 *Ansel Adams*, 91.

37 Ibid., 90.

38 Letter, Adams to Bender, Jan. 15, 1931, quoted in Nancy Newhall, *Ansel Adams: The Eloquent Light* (San Francisco: Sierra Club, 1963), 65.

39 The portrait of Tony Lujan is beautifully reproduced in *Ansel Adams*, 93. Austin had strongly urged Adams that *Taos Pueblo* should bear a dedication to the Indians. It read: "Dedicated to Our Friends at the Taos Pueblo to Whose Interested and Intelligent Cooperation Is Owed the Historic and Human Authenticity of This Book."

40 Letter, Austin to Adams, Aug. 30, 1929, HEH.

41 Ibid.

42 Letter, Austin to Adams, Sept. 1929, HEH.

43 Letter, Austin to Adams, April 9, 1930, HEH. The number of copies that Adams quotes for the edition is 75; the Huntington Library copy is identified as 84 in a limited edition of 108.

44 Letters, Austin to Adams, Jan. 2, 1931, HEH.

45 Letter, Adams to Austin, May 21, 1930, HEH. Ansel Adams and Mary Austin, *Taos Pueblo* (San Francisco: The Grabhorn Press, 1930; facs. repr., Boston: New York Graphic Society, 1977). The original edition of *Taos Pueblo* is rare and priced at $2,500 and above, making it the most valuable edition of any Austin work.

46 Quoted in Newhall, *Ansel Adams*, 65.

47 Letter, Austin to Adams, May 21, 1931, HEH.

48 Letter, Austin to Adams, Aug. 25, 1931, HEH.

49 Austin, *The Land of Little Rain*, with photographs by Ansel Adams (Boston: Houghton Mifflin, 1950). The dustjacket of the Adams edition emphasized the relationship of the work of the photographer to that of the writer: "Only a great photographer like Ansel Adams could match with pictures the splendor and intimacy of her words."

50 Ansel Adams, "Notes on Mary Austin," pamphlet (Independence, Calif., 1968), 7.

51 Letter, Austin to Bender, Oct. 9, 1929, Bender Collection, Mills College, Oakland, Calif. (hereafter cited as Mills College/Bender).

52 Ibid. This, of course, contradicts what we know of Mabel Dodge Luhan's financial aid to Austin during the 1920s.

53 Mary Hunter Wolf has generously shared with me her insights about her aunt's illnesses and her discussions with her aunt's physician. Even when Austin was informed that she was not critically ill, she continued to "agitate for treatment," in Mrs. Wolf's words.

54 Letter, Austin to Bender, [n.d.], Mills College/Bender.

55 Letter, Austin to Bender, March 9, 1928, Mills College/Bender.

56 In an undated letter to Austin (HEH), George Hunter tells her that their brother Jim's insurance money of $6,500, together with another $500, had been placed in trust for Mary Hunter's education.

57 Letter, Effie Curtis to Austin, Dec. 31, 1929, HEH.

58 Pearce, *Mary Hunter Austin*, 55.

59 I am indebted to Mary Hunter Wolf for offering me this insight.

60 Virginia Adams, conversation with author, Jan. 6, 1987.

61 Letter, Austin to Adams, Feb. 14, [1931], HEH.

CHAPTER 8. *EARTH HORIZON*

1 "Requests for Autobiographical Material" (mailing list), Box 24b, HEH.

2 Ibid.

3 Letter, Wallace to Mary Austin, July 2, 1929 (postmark), HEH.

4 Letters, Austin to Eve [Eva Lummis] DeKalb, July 19, 1929, and to [Eve] Frances [Lummis] DeKalb, Aug. 14, 1929, HEH.

5 Suzanne Juhasz, "Towards a Theory of Form in Feminist Autobiography," in Estelle C. Jelinek, ed., *Women's Autobiography: Essays in Criticism* (Bloomington: Indiana University Press, 1980), 222, 224.

6 Juhasz, "Feminist Autobiography," 224.

7 Wayne Shumaker quoted by Juhasz, ibid., 223.

8 Letter, Austin to Albert Bender, Oct. 14, 1930, Mills College/Bender.

9 Adamic, *My America*, 479.

10 William Allen White, *The Saturday Review of Literature* 9 (Nov. 12, 1932):235; Dorothy Van Doren, *The Nation* 135 (Dec. 7, 1932):567; Michael Williams, *Commonweal* 17 (Jan. 25, 1933):362; W. E. Harris, *The Boston Transcript*, Nov. 5, 1932:1.

11 Constance Rourke, *The New Republic* 73 (Dec. 21, 1932):166.

12 Letter, Austin to Ansel Adams, Aug. 9, 1932, HEH.

13 Letter, Austin to Carey McWilliams, Nov. 26, 1932, Dept. of Special Collections, University Research Library, UCLA. In 1933, Austin received royalties of $2,418 from a single title out of total royalties of $4,135.12. *Earth Horizon*, its sales boosted by the Literary Guild, must have been responsible for the one large royalty figure that year; see "Income" [1933], HEH.

14 Letter, Austin to McWilliams, Sept. 1, 1931, Dept. of Special Collections, University Research Library, UCLA.

15 Adamic, *My America*, 477, 478.

16 Atherton, *Adventures of a Novelist*, 8–9, 61.

17 Wharton, *A Backward Glance* (New York: D. Appleton-Century, 1934), 144.

18 Austin, "The Mother of Felipe," *Overland Monthly*, Nov. 1892.

19 Edith Wharton, "Confessions of a Novelist," *The Atlantic Monthly* 151 (April 1933):385.

20 Rae Galbraith Ballard, "Mary Austin's *Earth Horizon*: The Imperfect Circle" (Ph.D. diss., Claremont Graduate School, 1977), i–ii.

21 Patricia Spacks, "Selves in Hiding," in Jelinek, *Women's Autobiography*, 123.

22 Virginia Woolf quoted in Showalter, "Feminist Criticism in the Wilderness," 247.

23 See Carol Edkins, "Quest for Community: Spiritual Autobiographies of Eighteenth-Century Quaker and Puritan Women in America," in Jelinek, *Women's Autobiographies*, 39–52.

24 Adrienne Rich, *Of Woman Born* (New York: Bantam, 1981), 226.

25 See William James, *The Varieties of Religious Experience* (New York: New American Library, 1985), especially "The Religion of Healthy-Mindedness," 76–108. James writes: "I speak not only of those who are animally happy. I mean those who, when unhappiness is offered or proposed to them, positively refuse to feel it, as if it were something mean and wrong" (p. 77).

26 Letter, C. L. Stoddard to George F. Jordan, [n.d.], HEH. See also *EH* 35–38.

27 I am indebted to John Cody, whose analysis of Emily Dickinson's relationship with her mother in *After Great Pain: The Inner Life of Emily Dickinson* (Cambridge, Mass.: Harvard University Press, 1971) sparked this train of thought about Austin and her contemporaries.

28 Marcia Westkott, *The Feminist Legacy of Karen Horney* (New Haven: Yale University Press, 1986), 84. In a letter written after her older brother's death and before her younger brother's induction into the Army, Austin refers to herself as "the only man of the family" (Austin to Ferris Greenslet, Jan. 8, 1918, Houghton Mifflin Company Collection, Houghton Library, Harvard).

29 This tangled story has been unraveled for me somewhat by Mary Hunter Wolf. In a conversation on Dec. 13, 1984, Mrs. Wolf said that she believed her aunt suffered a severe writing block prior to 1927. The condition was so debilitating that Austin claimed the manuscript of her half-completed novel had been stolen by her niece. Mrs. Wolf suggested the possibility that no such manuscript existed.

30 Letter, Austin to George Hunter, April 15, 1927, HEH. Mary Hunter Wolf believes that Geraldine Hunter may well have tried to thwart Austin, but that the writer's response was irrational, as indeed it seems to have been.

31 Ibid. Also see references to George Hunter in *Earth Horizon*, 55, 84, 92, 95, 132–33, and 192–93.

32 In a letter dated March 28, 1932 (HEH), George Hunter advised Mary that the matter of Wallace's insurance money had been straightened out and that she would receive some $2,000. George often advised her on business affairs, even after her insulting letters to him.

33 Letter, George Hunter to Austin, Nov. 1925, HEH.

34 Letter, Austin to Frances [Eve Lummis] Rhoades, Aug. 14, 1929, HEH.

35 Letter, Austin to MacDougal, Jan. 27, [1922], HEH.

36 Letter, Dr. Cadis Phipps to Dr. John Ames, Nov. 5, 1932, HEH.

37 Austin, *Experiences Facing Death*, 279.

BIBLIOGRAPHY

A Note on Manuscript Sources

The most complete collection of Mary Austin's correspondence, family papers, files, and unpublished manuscripts is held by the Huntington Library in San Marino, California. Other primary sources on which I have relied are in the Mabel Dodge Luhan and Western Americana collections, Beinecke Rare Book and Manuscript Library, Yale University; the Collier Papers, Sterling Memorial Library Manuscripts, Yale; and the Houghton Mifflin Company Collection, Houghton Library, Harvard University. Additional relevant material is housed in the Special Collections of the University Research Library, University of California, Los Angeles; the Bender Collection, Mills College, Oakland, California; and the State Records Center and Archives in Santa Fe (especially the Spanish Colonial Arts Society Shop Collection, the Seligman Collection, and the Boaz Long Papers).

Published Works by Mary Austin

BOOKS

Listed here are the books by Mary Austin that were published during her lifetime, as well as several posthumous collections of her stories. A number of reprint editions are noted; others are listed in the bibliographies compiled by Augusta Fink in *I-Mary* (Tucson: University of Arizona Press, 1983) and by T. M. Pearce in *Mary Hunter Austin* (New York: Twayne, 1965). Unless otherwise noted, all references in the text are to the original editions.

The American Rhythm. New York: Harcourt, Brace, 1923. Reprints. Boston: Houghton Mifflin, 1930; New York: AMS Press, 1970.

The Arrow Maker. New York: Duffield, 1911. Rev. ed. Boston: Houghton Mifflin, 1915.

The Basket Woman. Boston: Houghton Mifflin, 1904. Reprint. New York: AMS Press, 1969.

Cactus Thorn. Reno: University of Nevada Press, 1988.

California: Land of the Sun. London: A. and C. Black, 1914; New York:
    Macmillan, 1914. Rev. ed. *Lands of the Sun*. Boston: Houghton Mifflin, 1927.
Can Prayer Be Answered? New York: Farrar and Rinehart, 1934.
The Children Sing in the Far West. Boston: Houghton Mifflin, 1928.
Christ in Italy. New York: Duffield, 1912.
Earth Horizon: An Autobiography. Boston: Houghton Mifflin, 1932.
Everyman's Genius. Indianapolis: Bobbs-Merrill, 1925.
Experiences Facing Death. Indianapolis: Bobbs-Merrill, 1931.
The Flock. Boston: Houghton Mifflin, 1906.
The Ford. Boston: Houghton Mifflin, 1917.
The Green Bough. New York: Doubleday, Page, 1913.
Indian Pottery of the Rio Grande. Pasadena, Calif.: Esto, 1934.
Isidro. Boston: Houghton Mifflin, 1905. Reprint. New York: Gordon Press,
    1973.
The Land of Journeys' Ending. New York and London: The Century Company,
    1924. Reprint. Tucson: University of Arizona Press, 1983.
The Land of Little Rain. Boston: Houghton Mifflin, 1903. Reprints.
    Albuquerque: University of New Mexico Press/Zia, 1974; New York:
    Penguin, 1988. Abridged version, with photographs by Ansel Adams. Boston:
    Houghton Mifflin, 1950.
Love and the Soul Maker. New York: Appleton, 1914.
Lost Borders. New York and London: Harper and Brothers, 1909.
The Lovely Lady. New York: Doubleday, Page, 1913.
The Man Jesus. New York and London: Harper and Brothers, 1915. Rev. ed. *A
    Small Town Man*. New York and London: Harper and Brothers, 1925.
The Mother of Felipe and Other Early Stories. Ed. Franklin Walker. Los Angeles:
    Book Club of California, 1950.
No. 26 Jayne Street. Boston: Houghton Mifflin, 1920.
One Hundred Miles on Horseback (1889). Los Angeles: Dawson's Book Shop,
    1963.
One Smoke Stories. Boston: Houghton Mifflin, 1934.
Outland (Gordon Stairs, pseud.). London: John Murray, 1910. New York: Boni
    and Liveright, 1919.
Santa Lucia. New York and London: Harper and Brothers, 1908.
Starry Adventure. Boston: Houghton Mifflin, 1931.
Stories from the Country of Lost Borders. Ed. Marjorie Pryse. New Brunswick, N.J.:
    Rutgers University Press, 1987.
Taos Pueblo. Photographs by Ansel Adams. San Francisco: Grabhorn Press, 1930.
    Facsimile reprint. New York: New York Graphic Society, 1977.
The Trail Book. Boston: Houghton Mifflin, 1918.
Western Trails: A Collection of Short Stories. Ed. Melody Graulich. Reno:
    University of Nevada Press, 1987.
A Woman of Genius. New York: Doubleday, Page, 1912; Boston: Houghton

Mifflin, 1917. Reprints. New York: Arno Press, 1977; Old Westbury, N.Y.: Feminist Press, 1985.

The Young Woman Citizen. New York: Woman's Press, 1918.

JOURNALISM, SHORT STORIES, ESSAYS, AND POETRY IN PERIODICALS

Because Austin wrote prolifically for magazines and journals—she contributed some two hundred pieces to more than sixty-five periodicals—I list only the material that I have consulted. The most comprehensive listing of Austin's publications in magazines remains *Mary Austin: Bibliography and Biographical Data*, California Library Research *Digest*, Monograph no. 2 (Berkeley, 1934). However, even this source is incomplete.

"Aboriginal Fiction." *The Saturday Review of Literature* 6 (Dec. 28, 1929).

"The American Form of the Novel." *The New Republic* 30 (April 12, 1922).

"American Indian Dance Drama." *The Yale Review* 19 (June 1930).

"American Marriage." *The American Mercury* 6 (Sept. 1925).

"American Women and the Intellectual Life." *The Bookman* 53 (Aug. 1921).

"Art Influence in the West." *The Century Magazine* 89 (April 1915).

"The Divorcing of Sina." *Sunset: The Pacific Monthly* 40 (June 1918).

"Do We Need a New Religion?" *The Century Magazine* 100 (Sept. 1923).

"The Fabian Summer." *The Bookman* 54 (Dec. 1921).

"The Finding of the Chuckwalla." *The Youth's Companion* 100 (Dec. 9, 1926).

"Folk Literature." *The Saturday Review of Literature* 5 (Aug. 11, 1928).

"The Forward Turn." *The Nation* 125 (July 20, 1927).

"Frustrate." *The Century Illustrated Monthly Magazine* 83 (Jan. 1912).

"George Sterling at Carmel." *The American Mercury* 11 (May 1927).

"Greatness in Women." *The North American Review* 217 (Jan.–June 1923).

"How I Found the Thing Worth Waiting For." *Survey* 61 (Jan. 1, 1929).

"How I Learned to Read and Write." Reprinted in *My First Publication*. Ed. James D. Hart. (San Francisco: Book Club of California, 1961).

"Hunt of Arizona." *The Nation* 127 (Nov. 28, 1928).

"In Papagueria." *The Nation* 127 (July 18, 1928).

"The Little Coyote." *The Atlantic Monthly* 89 (Feb. 1902).

"The Lone Woman Goes to War." *The Los Angeles Times*, April 28, 1918.

"Love Coming Late." *The Nation* 127 (July 11, 1928).

"Making the Most of Your Genius, I: What Is Genius?" *The Bookman* 58 (Nov. 1923).

"Making the Most of Your Genius, II: Training Your Talent." *The Bookman* 58 (Jan. 1924).

"Making the Most of Your Genius, III: The Education of the Writer." *The Bookman* 58 (Feb. 1924).

"Mary Austin on Marrying Successfully." *The Los Angeles Times World Magazine,*
     Dec. 15, 1912.
"The Mysticism of Jesus." *The Century Magazine* 109 (Dec. 1924).
"The Need for a New Social Concept." *The New Republic* 26 (Aug. 9, 1922).
"New York: Dictator of American Criticism." *The Nation* 111 (July 31, 1920).
"On the American Scene." *The Saturday Review of Literature* 5 (Aug. 11, 1928).
"One-Smoke Stories." *The Yale Review* 22 (Spring 1933).
"A Poet in Outland." *The Overland Monthly and Out West Magazine* 85 (Nov.
     1927).
"The Pot of Gold." *Munsey's Magazine* 25 (April–Sept. 1901).
"Power and Johnson: West is West." *The Nation* 110 (May 15, 1920).
"The Protected Sex." *Harper's Weekly,* May 8, 1915.
"Regional Culture in the Southwest." *Southwest Review* 14 (July 1929).
"Regionalism in American Fiction." *English Journal* 21 (Feb. 1932).
"Religion in the United States." *The Century Magazine* 104 (Aug. 1922).
"Rural Education in New Mexico." *The University of New Mexico Bulletin* 2 (Dec.
     1, 1931).
"Science for the Unscientific." *The Bookman* 55 (Aug. 1922).
"The Search for Jean Baptiste." *St. Nicholas* 31 (Sept. 1903).
"The Sense of Humor in Women." *The New Republic* 41 (Nov. 26, 1924).
"Sex Emancipation through War." *The Forum* 59 (May 1918).
"Sex in American Literature." *The Bookman* 57 (June 1923).
"A Shepherd of the Sierras." *The Atlantic Monthly* 87 (July 1900).
"Supernaturals in Fiction." *The Unpartizan Review* 13 (March 1920).
"Three at Carmel." *The Saturday Review of Literature* 5 (Sept. 29, 1928).
"Three Tales of Love." *The American Mercury* 7 (March 1926).
"The Town That Doesn't Want a Chautauqua." *The New Republic* 47 (July 7,
     1926).
"Wanted: A New Method in Mexico." *The Nation* 110 (Feb. 21, 1920).
"Why Americanize the Indian?" *The Forum* 82 (Sept. 1929).
"Woman Alone." *The Nation* 124 (March 2, 1927).
"Woman and Her War Loot." *Sunset: The Pacific Monthly* 42 (Feb. 1919).
"Woman Looks at the World." *Pictorial Review* 26 (Nov. 1924).
"Women as Audience." *The Bookman* 55 (March 1922).

CONTRIBUTIONS TO BOOK-LENGTH WORKS

"Aboriginal American Literature." In John Macy, ed. *American Writers on
     American Literature.* New York: Liveright, 1931.
"The Temblor." In David Starr Jordan, ed. *The California Earthquake.* San
     Francisco: A. M. Robertson, 1907.
The Sturdy Oak: A Composite Novel of American Politics. New York: Henry Holt,
     1917.

Additional Sources

Adamic, Louis. *My America, 1928–1938*. New York: Harper and Brothers, 1938.

Adams, Ansel. *Ansel Adams: An Autobiography*. Boston: Little, Brown, 1985.

Atherton, Gertrude. *Adventures Of a Novelist*. New York: Liveright, 1932.

Atherton, Lewis. *Main Street on the Middle Border*. Bloomington: Indiana University Press, 1984.

Auerbach, Nina. "Magi and Maidens." *Critical Inquiry* 8 (Winter 1981):281–300.

Ballard, Rae Galbraith. "Mary Austin's *Earth Horizon*: The Imperfect Circle." Ph.D. diss., Claremont Graduate School, 1977.

Bashford, Herbert. "The Literary Development of the Pacific Coast." *The Atlantic Monthly* 92 (July 1903):1–8.

Baym, Nina. "Melodramas of Beset Manhood: How Theories of American Fiction Exclude Women Authors." *American Quarterly* 33 (Summer 1981): 123–39.

Bogardus, Ralph F. "The Photographer's Eye: Henry James and the American Scene." *History of Photography* 8 (July–Sept. 1984):179–96.

Bordin, Ruth. *Woman and Temperance: The Quest for Power and Liberty, 1873–1900*. Philadelphia: Temple University Press, 1981.

Brazil, John. "Literature, Self, and Society: The Growth of a Political Aesthetic in Early San Francisco." Ph.D. diss., Yale University, 1975.

Brooks, Van Wyck. *The Confident Years: 1885–1915*. New York: Dutton, 1955.

———. "Reviewer's Note-Book." *The Freeman*, June 9, 1920:311.

Brooks, Van Wyck, and Otto L. Bettman. *Our Literary Heritage*. New York: Dutton, 1956.

Canby, Henry Seidel. *American Memoir*. New York: Houghton Mifflin, 1947.

Cassidy, Ina Sizer. "I-Mary and Me: The Chronicle of a Friendship." *New Mexico Quarterly* 9 (Nov. 1939):203–11.

Cather, Willa. *Death Comes for the Archbishop*. New York: Alfred A. Knopf, 1925.

———. *The Professor's House*. New York: Alfred A. Knopf, 1925.

———. *Not Under Forty*. New York: Alfred A. Knopf, 1936.

———. *The Song of the Lark*. Boston: Houghton Mifflin, 1915.

Chodorow, Nancy. *The Reproduction of Mothering: Psychoanalysis and the Sociology of Gender*. Berkeley: University of California Press, 1978.

Collins, Joseph. *Taking the Literary Pulse*. New York: George H. Doran, 1924.

Conn, Peter. *The Divided Mind*. Cambridge: Cambridge University Press, 1983.

Cott, Nancy. *The Grounding of Modern Feminism*. New Haven: Yale University Press, 1987.

Davis, David Brion. *Homicide in American Fiction, 1798–1860*. Ithaca, N.Y.: Cornell University Press, 1958.

Degler, Carl. *At Odds: Women and the Family in America from the Revolution to the Present*. New York: Oxford University Press, 1980.

Doyle, Helen MacKnight. *Mary Austin: Woman of Genius*. New York: Gotham House, 1939.

Drinnon, Richard. *Facing West: The Metaphysics of Indian-Hating and Empire-Building*. Minneapolis: University of Minnesota Press, 1980.

Dubois, Ellen Carol. *Feminism and Suffrage: The Emergence of the Independent Women's Movement in America, 1848–1869*. Ithaca, N.Y.: Cornell University Press, 1978.

Faragher, John Mack. *Women and Men on the Overland Trail*. New Haven: Yale University Press, 1979.

Field, Louise Maunsell. "Mary Austin, American." *The Bookman* 75 (Dec. 1932): 819–21.

Fink, Augusta. *I-Mary: A Biography of Mary Austin*. Tucson: University of Arizona Press, 1983.

———. *Monterey*. San Francisco: Chronicle Books, 1972.

———. "Gertrude Atherton and the New Woman." *California Historical Quarterly* 55 (Fall 1976): 194–209.

Frank, Waldo. *Our America*. New York: Boni and Liveright, 1919.

Fryer, Judith. *Felicitous Space: The Imaginative Structures of Edith Wharton and Willa Cather*. Chapel Hill: University of North Carolina Press, 1986.

Gibson, Arrell Morgan, *The Santa Fe and Taos Colonies: Ages of the Muses, 1900–1942*. Norman: University of Oklahoma Press, 1983.

Gilbert, Sandra. "Costumes of the Mind: Transvestism as Metaphor in Modern Literature." *Critical Inquiry* 7 (Winter 1980): 392–417.

Gilman, Charlotte Perkins Stetson. *Women and Economics: A Study of the Economic Relation Between Men and Woman As a Factor in Social Evolution*. Boston: Small, Maynard, 1898. Reprint. New York: Harper and Row, 1966.

Gilpin, Laura. *The Enduring Navajo*. Austin: University of Texas Press, 1968.

Glasgow, Ellen. *The Woman Within: An Autobiography*. New York: Harcourt Brace Jovanovich, 1954. Reprint, New York: Hill and Wang, 1980.

Gordon, Dudley. *Charles F. Lummis: Crusader in Corduroy*. Los Angeles: Cultural Assets, 1972.

Griswold, Robert L. *Family and Divorce in California, 1850–1890*. Albany: State University of New York Press, 1982.

Hammett, Dashiell. Review of *Everyman's Genius. The Forum*, Aug. 1925: 317.

Hergesheimer, Joseph. "The Feminine Nuisance in American Literature." *The Yale Review* 10 (July 1921): 716–25.

Hewitt, Nancy A. *Women's Activism and Social Change: New York, 1822–1872*. Ithaca, N.Y.: Cornell University Press, 1984.

Hill, Mary A. *Charlotte Perkins Gilman: The Making of a Radical Feminist, 1860–1896*. Philadelphia: Temple University Press, 1980.

Homans, Margaret. "'Her Very Own Howl.'" *Signs* 9 (Winter 1983): 186–205.

Houghland, Willard, ed. *Mary Austin: A Memorial*. Santa Fe: Laboratory of Anthropology, 1944.

Hurston, Zora Neale. *Their Eyes Were Watching God*. Philadelphia: Lippincott, 1937. Reprint. New York: Negro Universities Press, 1969.

James, Edward T., ed. *Notable American Women, 1607–1950*. 3 vols. Cambridge, Mass.: Harvard University Press, 1971.

Jelinek, Estelle C., ed. *Women's Autobiography: Essays in Criticism*. Bloomington: Indiana University Press, 1980.

Johnston, Carolyn. *Jack London: An American Radical?* Westport, Conn.: Greenwood Press, 1984.

Jordan, David Starr, ed. *The California Earthquake*. San Francisco: A. M. Robertson, 1907.

Jung, Carl G. *Man and His Symbols*. New York: Dutton, 1964.

Kaplan, Justin. *Lincoln Steffens: A Biography*. New York: Simon and Schuster, 1974.

Kazin, Alfred. *On Native Grounds*. New York: Harcourt, Brace and World, 1942.

Kelly, Lawrence C. *The Assault of Assimilation: John Collier and the Origins of Indian Policy Reform*. Albuquerque: University of New Mexico Press, 1983.

Kent, Kate Peck. *Navajo Weaving*. Santa Fe: Schools of American Research Press, 1985.

Kolodny, Annette. "Some Notes on Defining a 'Feminist Criticism.'" *Critical Inquiry* 2 (Fall 1975):75–92.

———. *The Land Before Her: Fantasy and Experience of the American Frontiers, 1630–1860*. Chapel Hill: University of North Carolina Press, 1984.

Kunitz, Stanley J. *Living Authors*. New York: H. W. Wilson, 1931.

Lamar, Howard R. *The Far Southwest, 1846–1912: A Territorial History*. New York: W. W. Norton, 1970.

———, ed. *The Reader's Encyclopedia of the American West*. New York: Crowell, 1977.

Lane, Ann J., ed. *The Charlotte Perkins Gilman Reader*. New York: Pantheon, 1980.

Langlois, Karen S. "Mary Austin and the Houghton Mifflin Company: A Case Study in the Marketing of a Western Writer." *Western American Literature* 23 (Summer 1988):31–42.

———. "Mary Austin and Lincoln Steffens." *Huntington Library Quarterly* 49 (Autumn 1986):357–82.

———. "Mary Austin and the New Theatre: The 1911 Production of *The Arrow Maker*." *Theatre History Studies* 8 (1988):71–87.

Lavender, David. *California: Land of New Beginnings*. Lincoln: University of Nebraska Press, 1987.

Leach, William. *True Love and Perfect Union: The Feminist Reform of Sex and Society*. New York: Basic Books, 1980.

Lears, Jackson. *No Place of Grace*. New York: Pantheon, 1981.

Lewis, R. W. B. *Edith Wharton: A Biography*. New York: Harper and Row, 1975.

Lingeman, Richard. *Small Town America*. Boston: Houghton Mifflin, 1980.

Lisle, Laurie. *Portrait of an Artist: A Biography of Georgia O'Keeffe*. New York: Washington Square Press, 1980.

"The Literary Spotlight: Mary Austin." *The Bookman* 58 (Sept. 1923):47–52.

London, Jack. *Martin Eden*. New York: Macmillan, 1909.

Luhan, Mabel Dodge. *Intimate Memories: Background*. New York: Harcourt Brace, 1933.

———. *Lorenzo in Taos*. New York: Alfred A. Knopf, 1932.

———. *Winter in Taos*. New York: Harcourt Brace, 1935.

MacWilliams, Carey. *Ambrose Bierce: A Biography*. 2d ed. New York: Archon Books, 1967.

MacWilliams, Carey, ed. *The California Revolution*. New York: Grossman, 1968.

Martin, Anne. "A Tribute to Mary Austin." *The Nation* 139 (Oct. 10, 1934):409.

Matthiessen, F. O. *Sarah Orne Jewett*. Boston: Houghton Mifflin, 1929.

May, Henry. *The End of American Innocence*. New York: Oxford University Press, 1979.

Merchant, Carolyn. *The Death of Nature*. New York: Harper and Row, 1983.

Newhall, Nancy. *Ansel Adams: The Eloquent Light*. San Francisco: Sierra Club, 1963.

Nordhoff, Charles. *California for Health, Pleasure, and Residence*, New York: Harper and Brothers, 1875.

Norwood, Vera. "The Photographer and the Naturalist: Laura Gilpin and Mary Austin in the Southwest." *Journal of American Culture* 5 (Summer 1982):1–28.

Norwood, Vera, and Janice Monk. *The Desert Is No Lady*. New Haven: Yale University Press, 1987.

Nottingham, Elizabeth K. *Methodism and the Frontier*. New York: Columbia University Press, 1941.

O'Brien, Sharon. *Willa Cather: The Emerging Voice*. New York: Oxford University Press, 1986.

Olney, James. *Metaphors of Self: The Meaning of Autobiography*. Princeton: Princeton University Press, 1972.

O'Neill, William. *Divorce in the Progressive Era*. New Haven: Yale University Press, 1967.

Ostriker, Alicia. *Writing Like a Woman*. Ann Arbor: University of Michigan Press, 1983.

Overton, Grant M. *The Women Who Make Our Novels*. New York: Dodd, Mead, 1928.

Ozick, Cynthia. *Art and Ardor*. New York: Dutton, 1984.

Pattee, Fred L. *The New American Literature, 1890–1930*. New York: Century, 1930.

Pearce, T. M. *The Beloved House*. Caldwell, Idaho: Caxton Printers, 1940.

———. *Mary Hunter Austin*. New York: Twayne, 1956.

Pearce, T. M., ed. *Literary America, 1903–1934: The Mary Austin Letters*. Westport, Conn.: Greenwood Press, 1979.

Perry, Ralph Barton. *In the Spirit of William James*. New Haven: Yale University Press, 1938.

Person, Leland S. "The American Eve: Miscegenation and Feminist Frontier Fiction." *American Quarterly* 37 (Winter 1985):668–85.

Porter, Nancy. Afterword to Austin, *A Woman of Genius*. Old Westbury, N.Y.: Feminist Press, 1985.

Powell, Lawrence Clark. "California Classics Reread." *Westways* 60 (April 1968): 2–4.

———. "Mary Hunter Austin: 1868–1934." *Arizona and the West* 10 (Spring 1968):1–4.

———. "A Prophetic Passage." *Westways* 65 (Feb. 1973):61–65.

———. *Southwest Classics*. Tucson: University of Arizona Press, 1974.

Rich, Adrienne. *Of Woman Born*. New York: Bantam, 1981.

Ringler, Donald. "Kern County Days, 1888–1892." *Southern California Quarterly* 45 (March 1963):25–63.

Robinson, Phyllis C. *Willa: The Life of Willa Cather*. New York: Holt, Rinehart and Winston/Owl, 1983.

Rosenberg, Charles. *No Other Gods: On Science and American Social Thought*. Baltimore: Johns Hopkins University Press, 1976.

Rosenberg, Rosalind. *Beyond Separate Spheres*. New Haven: Yale University Press, 1982.

Rothman, Ellen K. *Hands and Hearts: A History of Courtship in America*. New York: Basic Books, 1984.

Rudnick, Lois Palken. *Mabel Dodge Luhan*. Albuquerque: University of New Mexico Press, 1984.

Rupert, James. "Mary Austin's Landscape Line in Native American Literature." *Southwest Review* 68 (Autumn 1983):376–90.

Sandweiss, Martha A. *Laura Gilpin: An Enduring Grace*. Austin: University of Texas Press, 1986.

Scadron, Arlene. *Widowhood and the American Southwest, 1848–1939*. Working Paper no. 17. Tucson: Southwestern Institute for Research on Women, 1983.

Schlissel, Lillian. *Women's Diaries of the Westward Journey*. New York: Schocken, 1982.

Schwarz, Judith. *Radical Feminists of Heterodoxy: Greenwich Village, 1912–1940*. Lebanon, N.H.: New Victoria, 1982.

Sergeant, Elizabeth Shepley. "Mary Austin: A Portrait." *The Saturday Review of Literature* 8 (Sept. 1934):96.

———. *Willa Cather: A Memoir*. Lincoln: University of Nebraska Press, 1953.

Showalter, Elaine. "Feminist Criticism in the Wilderness." *Critical Inquiry* 8 (Winter 1981):179–205.

Showalter, Elaine, ed. *The New Feminist Criticism: Essays on Women, Literature and Theory*. New York: Pantheon, 1985.

———. *These Modern Women: Autobiographical Essays from the Twenties*. Old Westbury, N.Y.: Feminist Press, 1978.

Sicherman, Barbara, and Carol Hurd Green, eds. *Notable American Women: The Modern Period*. Cambridge, Mass.: Harvard University Press, 1980.

Smith, Henry. "The Feel of Purposeful Earth: Mary Austin's Prophecy." *New Mexico Quarterly* 1 (Feb. 1931):17–33.

Smith-Rosenberg, Carroll. *Disorderly Conduct: Visions of Gender in Victorian America.* Oxford: Oxford University Press, 1985.

———. "The Female World of Love and Ritual." *Signs* 1 (Autumn 1975):1–29.

Smith-Rosenberg, Carroll, and Charles Rosenberg. "The Female Animal: Medical and Biological Views of Women." In Charles Rosenberg. *No Other Gods.* Baltimore: Johns Hopkins University Press, 1976.

Spacks, Patricia Meyer. *Gossip.* New York: Alfred A. Knopf, 1985.

Starr, Kevin. *Americans and the California Dream, 1850–1915.* New York: Oxford University Press, 1973.

———. *Inventing the Dream: California through the Progressive Era.* New York: Oxford University Press, 1985.

———. "Mary Austin: Mystic, Writer, Conservationist." *Sierra Bulletin* 61 (Nov.–Dec. 1976):34.

Steffens, Lincoln. *The Autobiography of Lincoln Steffens.* New York: Harcourt Brace, 1931.

Sterling, George. *Thirty Five Sonnets.* San Francisco: Book Club of California, 1917.

Strouse, Jean. *Alice James: A Biography.* Boston: Houghton Mifflin, 1980.

Thomas, F. Richard. *Literary Admirers of Alfred Stieglitz.* Carbondale: University of Southern Illinois Press, 1983.

Tracy, Henry Chester. *The American Naturists.* New York: Dutton, 1930.

Trilling, Diana. "The House of Mirth Revisited." In Irving Howe, ed. *Edith Wharton: A Collection of Critical Essays.* Englewood Cliffs, N.J.: Prentice-Hall, 1965.

Van Doren, Carl. *Three Worlds.* New York: Harper and Brothers, 1936.

———. *Contemporary American Novelists.* New York: Macmillan, 1922.

Veblen, Thorstein. "The Barbarian Status of Women." *American Journal of Sociology* 4 (Jan. 1899):503–14.

———. *The Theory of the Leisure Class.* New York: Macmillan, 1899. Reprint. New York: New American Library, 1953.

Walker, Franklin. *Ambrose Bierce: The Wickedest Man in San Francisco.* San Francisco: Colt Press, 1941.

———. *A Literary History of Southern California.* Berkeley: University of California Press, 1950.

———. *A Literary History of the Southwest.* Berkeley: University of California Press, 1950.

———. *San Francisco's Literary Frontier.* New York: Alfred A. Knopf, 1939.

Ward, Lester. "Genius and Woman's Intuition." *Forum* 9 (June 1890):401–08.

Warner, Charles Dudley. "Our Italy." In *Washington Irving and Our Italy.* Hartford, Conn.: American, 1904.

Weigle, Marta, and Kyle Fiore. *Santa Fe and Taos: The Writers' Era, 1916–1941.* Santa Fe: Ancient City Press, 1982.

Wharton, Edith. *A Backward Glance*. New York: Appleton, 1934.

———. "Permanent Values in Fiction." *The Saturday Review of Literature* 10 (April 7, 1934):603–04.

White, William Allen. "A Woman of Genius." *The Saturday Review of Literature* 9 (Nov. 12, 1932):235–36.

Willard, Frances. *Glimpses of Fifty Years: An Autobiography of an American Woman*. 1899. Reprint. New York: Source Book Press, 1970.

Wolff, Cynthia Griffin, ed. *Classic American Writers*. New York: Harper and Row, 1980.

Woolf, Virginia. *Granite and Rainbow*. New York: Harcourt Brace Jovanovich, 1958.

Wyatt, David. "Mary Austin: Nature and Nurturance." In *The Fall into Eden: Landscape and Imagination in California*. New York: Cambridge University Press, 1986.

Wynn, Dudley. *A Critical Study of the Writings of Mary Hunter Austin, 1868–1934*. New York: Graduate School of Arts and Sciences, New York University, 1941.

———. "Mary Austin: Woman Alone." *Virginia Quarterly Review* 13 (April 1937):243–56.

INDEX

ABOUT THE AUTHOR

Esther F. Lanigan has taught American literature and feminist studies at the University of Colorado, Colorado College, Yale University, and most recently in the Department of English at the College of William and Mary. She earned her doctorate in American Studies from Yale University. She is the editor of *A Mary Austin Reader* (University of Arizona Press, 1996), and her biography *Mary Austin: Song of a Maverick* is considered the definitive study of the writer. She makes her permanent home in Colorado with her husband, Charles, and considers the West the locus of her literary interests. Lanigan is presently at work on a book about couples whose artistic lives flourished in the West during the first third of the century.

	DATE DUE	
MAY 1 0 1997		
APR 0 4 2003		